DEFENDING LUTHER'S REFORMATION

Defending Luther's Reformation

Its Ongoing Significance in the Face of Contemporary Challenges

Edited by

JOHN A. MAXFIELD

CONCORDIA PUBLISHING HOUSE · SAINT LOUIS

3558 S. Jefferson Ave., St. Louis, MO 63118-3968
1-800-325-3040 • www.cph.org

Manufactured in the United States of America

1 2 3 4 5 6 7 8 9 10 26 25 24 23 22 21 20 19 18 17

Contents

ABBREVIATIONS

AE	*Luther's Works: American Edition.* Volumes 1–30: Edited by Jaroslav Pelikan. St. Louis: Concordia, 1955–76. Volumes 31–55: Edited by Helmut Lehmann. Philadelphia/Minneapolis: Muhlenberg/ Fortress, 1957–86. Volumes 56–82: Edited by Christopher Boyd Brown and Benjamin T. G. Mayes. St. Louis: Concordia: 2009–.
BSLK	*Die Bekenntnisschriften der evangelisch-lutherischen Kirche.* 12th edition. Göttingen: Vandenhoeck & Ruprecht, 1998.
CCSL	*Corpus Christianorum: Series Latina.* Turnhout: Brepols, 1953–.
DWB	Jacob Grimm and Wilhelm Grimm. *Deutsches Wörterbuch.* 16 volumes in 32. Leipzig: S. Hirzel, 1854–1960.
ESV	English Standard Version of the Bible.
FC SD	Solid Declaration of the Formula of Concord.
Kolb-Wengert	Robert Kolb and Timothy J. Wengert, eds. *The Book of Concord: The Confessions of the Evangelical Lutheran Church.* Minneapolis: Fortress, 2000.
LC	Large Catechism.
LSB	The Commission on Worship of The Lutheran Church—Missouri Synod. *Lutheran Service Book.* St. Louis: Concordia, 2006.
NPNF[1]	*A Select Library of the Christian Church: Nicene and Post-Nicene Fathers: First Series.* Edited by Philip Schaff. 14 vols. New York, 1886–89. Reprint, Peabody, MA: Hendrickson, 1994.

SA	Smalcald Articles.
SC	Small Catechism.
SD	Solid Declaration of the Formula of Concord.
Tanner	*Decrees of the Ecumenical Councils.* Edited by Norman P. Tanner. 2 vols. London: Sheed & Ward; Washington, DC: Georgetown University Press, 1990.
Vg	Vulgate translation of the Bible.
WA	*D. Martin Luthers Werke: Kritische Gesamtausgabe.* 73 vols. in 85. Weimar: H. Böhlau, 1883–.
WA Br	*D. Martin Luthers Werke: Briefwechsel.* 18 vols. Weimar: H. Böhlau, 1930–.
WA DB	*D. Martin Luthers Werke: Deutsche Bibel.* 12 vols. in 15. Weimar: H. Böhlau, 1906–.
WA TR	*D. Martin Luthers Werke: Tischreden.* 6 vols. Weimar: H. Böhlau, 1912–21.

Introduction

John A. Maxfield

GOOGLE "REFORMATION 500" AND THERE APPEARS A HOST OF links to various websites detailing local and international events celebrating the five-hundredth anniversary of the beginning of the Protestant Reformation. The Lutheran World Federation, an international federation and communion of many nominal Lutheran church bodies, announced its "Luther Decade—500 Years of Reformation" some ten years ago, with a website, annual themes, and numerous events leading up to the official beginning of the Reformation year with an ecumenical service on October 31, 2016, in Lund, Sweden; the service featured the participation of Pope Francis alongside Lutheran World Federation president Munib A. Younan, as well as various other Catholic and Lutheran dignitaries. In Berlin, the Evangelische Kirche in Deutschland (EKD) kicked off its anniversary year with an ecumenical festival featuring political dignitaries and Catholic and Protestant church leaders, and for the first time the Martin Luther Medal of the EKD was awarded to a Roman Catholic, the former bishop of Mainz, Karl Cardinal Lehmann. Clearly, ecumenism is a central theme and value for the celebration of the five-hundredth anniversary of the Reformation in 2017, at least in Europe.[1]

1 Some reflections on the celebrations in Germany prior to the anniversary year are offered in Hartmut Lehmann, "The Quincentenary of the Protestant Reformation in Germany," *Lutheran Quarterly* 30, no. 3 (2016): 329–35. For insightful commentary on the service in the Lund cathedral and related ecumenical discussions, see Theodor Dieter, "Commemoration of the Reformation in Germany and Lund," *Lutheran Quarterly* 31, no. 1 (2017): 22–49.

Celebrating the Reformation on October 31 apparently goes back to 1617, the centennial of Luther's posting of the *Ninety-Five Theses*, or *Disputation on the Power and Efficacy of Indulgences*, on the door of the Castle Church in Wittenberg. Prior to the centennial year, the Reformation was commonly celebrated in various German localities on the anniversary of the introduction of the Reformation in that particular jurisdiction, or on the anniversary of the formal implementation of a Lutheran constitution or church order.[2] But for the centennial year the focus was on Martin Luther. In Saxony a coin was minted with the inscription: "To God alone the glory. First jubilee of the reform of popedom through Dr. Luther." Other coin inscriptions compared Luther to Moses and the prophets: "As Moses led Israel out from the harsh Egyptian bondage, so has Martin Luther led us out of the pope's darkness"; and "Martin Luther: Elijah of the Last Days."[3]

Fifty years ago at the 450th anniversary of the posting of the *Theses*, the scholarly world, especially in Germany, was in the midst of a debate about whether Luther had in fact posted the *Theses* on the door of the Castle Church in Wittenberg or whether this posting was a legend. Some years previous, Hans Volz had in various publications offered evidence that Luther posted his theses not on October 31, the eve of All Saints' Day, but on November 1. Kurt Aland responded in favor of the traditional date, and also to arguments of Catholic scholar Erwin Iserloh that Luther had not posted the *Theses* at all but had only mailed ("posted" in quite a different sense) them on October 31 to the archbishop of Mainz, Albert of Brandenburg.[4] On the basis of the documentary evidence, this debate can now be seen as irresolvable—there is strong evidence on

2 Robert Kolb, *Martin Luther as Prophet, Teacher, and Hero: Images of the Reformer, 1520–1620* (Grand Rapids: Baker Books, 1999), 126–27.

3 Ernst Walter Zeeden, *Martin Luther und die Reformation im Urteil des deutschen Luthertums: Studien zum Selbstverständnis des lutherischen Protestantismus von Luthers Tode bis zum Beginn der Goethezeit* (Freiburg: Herder, 1950), 2:69. Similar coins from the Reformation centennial are portrayed in the volume by Daniel Nathan Harmelink, *The Reformation Coin and Medal Collection of Concordia Historical Institute* (St. Louis: Concordia Historical Institute, 2016).

4 English translations appeared within a few years: Kurt Aland, ed., *Martin Luther's 95 Theses with the Pertinent Documents from the History of the Reformation* (St. Louis: Concordia, 1967, 2004 [German original 1965]); and Erwin Iserloh, *The Theses Were Not Posted: Luther between Reform and Reformation*, trans. Jared Wicks, introduction by Martin E. Marty (Boston: Beacon Press, 1968 [German original 1966]). A recent discussion of the relevant sources is offered in Volker Leppin and Timothy J. Wengert, "Sources for and against the Posting of the 'Ninety-Five Theses,'" *Lutheran Quarterly* 29, no. 4 (2015): 373–98.

both sides, namely, that Luther posted his *Theses* as was customary for a university theologian wanting to initiate a debate among scholars, or that Luther only sent his debate propositions to various church officials, humanist scholars, and friends. Circumstantial evidence is, however, quite strong that Luther did indeed post the *Theses*. What is most significant both for historians and for Christians generally is that it is now regarded as a legend, whether presented in nineteenth-century illustration or painting of the Romantic era or in modern feature film, when Luther is portrayed as an irate friar, hammer in hand, nailing his *Theses* protesting indulgences to the church door as a crowd swarms and perhaps makes off with the posted placard in order to broadcast them more broadly. But just as significant is the historical fact—and this cannot be doubted—that Luther wrote to Archbishop Albert on October 31 and enclosed his debating points on indulgences, and that the archbishop soon sent them to Rome, raising the question of whether they constituted heresy. Also a matter of fact is that Luther's opponents focused their charges on certain questions Luther had raised about the power of the pope and that Luther's concerns about the sacrament of penance in connection with the practice of selling indulgences faded into the background as the "Luther affair" now shook Christendom. Luther brought his pastoral concerns to the public in a *Sermon on Indulgence and Grace* written in simple and clear German and printed by March of the following year. This "sermon," twenty brief paragraphs, printed in an inexpensive eight-page pamphlet and easily read aloud in about ten minutes, soon became a publishing sensation as it went through at least thirteen printings in 1518 and nine more during the next two years.[5] By that time, as Luther penned his Latin treatise *On the Babylonian Captivity of the Church* in October 1520, he could point to the strenuous opposition of those who charged him with heresy as driving him far beyond his initial, partial acceptance of indulgences and the papacy to his vigorous opposition to both. In short, as the final chapter of Iserloh's book acknowledges, even if there were no posting of the *Theses* on Wittenberg church doors, October 31, 1517, still marked the beginning of the Protestant Reformation.

The character and shape of the Reformation was determined during the course of the next decade. As Luther noted again and again, in the years between 1518 and 1521 the sharp opposition he encountered from the papal church

5 Andrew Pettegree, *Brand Luther: 1517, Printing, and the Making of the Reformation* (New York: Penguin Press, 2015), 80–81 and 351 n. 64. In addition to the twelve or thirteen editions in 1518 mentioned by Pettegree, the *Sermon* was also published that year by Hans Dorn in a Low German (*Plattdeutsch*) translation in the North German trading town (*Hansestadt*) of Brunswick.

slowly forced him to increasingly radical convictions that he refused to retract but instead defended on the basis of Holy Scripture. During these early years, before the evangelical reform movement that emerged from Luther's preaching, contacts, and writings actually began to make changes in the teaching and religious practice of the Church, Luther published his convictions before the world in Latin treatises for scholars and in German publications for the broader public. He quickly became the most popular author of the century.[6] Several sermons in German, printed in 1519 and early 1520, communicated in clear and simple terms Luther's evangelical theology and new understanding of the sacraments as the promise of God made concrete, of Christian salvation received not by doing good works but solely through faith. But it was especially through five major treatises published in 1520—three in German, one in Latin, and the final one in both languages—that the Wittenberg friar announced his new theology and proposals for reform, transforming him into Luther the reformer.

Early in 1520 Luther was asked to clarify his position on good works, since the substance of his reform was to place faith in Christ, and not the performance of good works as prescribed by the Church, at the center of Christian teaching and piety. After some delay, what began as a short sermon became a major treatise with the simple title *On Good Works*. The reformer opens the treatise—an exposition of the Ten Commandments—by noting that the only good works are those commanded by God and, citing the words of Jesus recorded in John 6:28–29, establishing as a first principle that "the first, highest, and most precious of all good works is faith in Christ."[7]

Next Luther turned to address the question of what the Church is, through a reply to a theologian from the town of Leipzig who had attacked Luther for his denial that the pope is divinely appointed as the head of the universal Church. Augustine Alveld published his attack on Luther first in a Latin treatise (which Luther didn't think worthy of a response) and then in a German treatise aimed toward the people. In his German treatise *Against the Papacy at Rome*, Luther defined the Church not as the hierarchical body with the pope as its head (the Roman Church) but rather as a community of all who believe in Christ: "This community or assembly means all those who live in true faith, hope, and love. Thus the essence, life, and nature of Christendom is not a physical assembly, but an assembly of hearts in one faith."[8]

---

6 In addition to Pettegree, *Brand Luther*, see especially Mark U. Edwards Jr., *Printing, Propaganda, and Martin Luther* (Berkeley: University of California Press, 1994).

7 AE 44:23.

8 AE 39:65.

This emphasis on faith also pervades the other more frequently mentioned treatises of 1520. The *Appeal to the Christian Nobility of the German Nation for the Improvement of Christendom* is Luther's lengthy treatise calling for concrete steps to reform Christendom, that is, both the Church and the society that was shaped by the Church. In it Luther appeals to Christian rulers, with the newly elected Emperor Charles V at their head, to bring about reform in the Church "since the clergy, to whom this task more properly belongs, have grown quite indifferent."[9] The basis of this appeal is again grounded in Luther's doctrine of faith and the Church as a community of faith. For Luther denies that the clergy hold a spiritual status higher than the laity that gives them alone the right and responsibility to lead the Church. Luther tears down this "first wall" that had been barring reform by denying to lay rulers any jurisdiction in Church matters, not by removing from the clergy the status of "religious" but rather extending that status to all the baptized: "All Christians are truly of the spiritual estate, and there is no difference among them except that of office. . . . This is because we all have one baptism, one gospel, one faith, and are all Christians alike; for baptism, gospel, and faith alone make us spiritual and a Christian people."[10] Therefore: "Since those who exercise secular authority have been baptized with the same baptism, and have the same faith and the same gospel as the rest of us, we must admit that they are priests and bishops and we must regard their office as one which has a proper and useful place in the Christian community."[11] This is the doctrine of the priesthood of all believers, and Luther utilized it to appeal to the civil rulers of his day to use their office to promote reform in Christendom since the clergy, in particular the higher clergy of pope and bishops, were blocking reform.

Turning to the doctrine and administration of the sacraments in his Latin treatise *On the Babylonian Captivity of the Church*, Luther calls for a redefinition of the sacraments of the Church in terms of faith and their use as aids to (means of) faith. By this time (October), Luther knew that the papal bull threatening his excommunication was being published throughout the empire. At the opening of the treatise he recounts his own journey from being "entangled in the superstitions of Rome" when first raising questions and writing about indulgences to being forced by his opponents' arguments into rejecting the papacy as "the kingdom of Babylon and the power of Nimrod, the mighty hunter."[12] The treatise exposes the manifold ways the papal church was using the sacraments

9 AE 44:123.

10 AE 44:127.

11 AE 44:129.

12 AE 36:12.

to enslave consciences rather than freeing them. In the process Luther redefined the sacraments and reduced their number from seven to three (Baptism, penance, and the Lord's Supper), finally ending the treatise with two sacraments by subsuming penance (redefined as confession and absolution) under Baptism and stating that it is "nothing but a way and a return to baptism."[13]

Finally, in November 1520 Luther published his treatise on justification by faith, entitled *On Christian Liberty* in its Latin version (prefaced by an open letter addressed to the pope) and *The Freedom of a Christian* in its German version. Here again the reformer turns to define the Christian faith and on this basis to describe the nature of Christian life in the world. He begins by discounting the traditional scholastic definition of faith as one of the virtues, that is, a product of human striving for the good. "They do this because they have not experienced it and have never tasted the great strength there is in faith. It is impossible to write well about it or to understand what has been written about it unless one has at one time or another experienced the courage which faith gives a man when trials oppress him."[14] In other words, faith is not a human striving or virtue but is a gift of God that brings with it the power of a new life. Luther structures the treatise as an analysis of two propositions about that life, apparently contradictory but in fact both coming from St. Paul (1 Cor. 9:19; Rom. 13:8): "A Christian is a perfectly free lord of all, subject to none. A Christian is a perfectly dutiful servant of all, subject to all." The first proposition concerns Christian freedom and has to do with man's inner, spiritual nature (that is, the soul); Luther concludes that "no external thing has any influence in producing Christian righteousness or freedom, or in producing unrighteousness or servitude." "One thing, and only one thing, is necessary for Christian life, righteousness, and freedom. That one thing is the most holy Word of God."[15] The apostle Paul teaches us that this Word of God "is the gospel of God concerning his Son, who was made flesh, suffered, rose from the dead, and was glorified through the Spirit who sanctifies. To preach Christ means to feed the soul, make it righteous, set it free, and save it, provided it believes the preaching."[16] Thus just as Luther in his treatise *On Good Works* had described faith as the one good work that is the fount of all other good works, so here Luther again cites Jesus' statement "This is the work of God, that you believe in Him whom He has sent" (John 6:29), and describes Christian freedom and Christian life as flowing from faith alone: "It ought to be the first

13 AE 36:124.

14 AE 31:343.

15 AE 31:344–45.

16 AE 31:346.

concern of every Christian to lay aside all confidence in works and increasingly to strengthen faith alone and through faith to grow in the knowledge, not of works, but of Christ Jesus."[17]

After further describing the "incomparable benefits of faith," Luther goes on to explicate the second part of human life, which corresponds to his thesis: "A Christian is a perfectly dutiful servant of all, subject to all." This is life in the world according to the "outer man" or external conduct, relationships with others, and responsibilities in this life. The reformer describes various good works that God has commanded of every person according to his station in life, noting that such works do not make a Christian but are the means through which Christians show their faith and serve their neighbor. Before ending his treatise with a response to various misunderstandings that might lead to the abuse of Christian freedom, Luther characterizes the Christian as one who "lives not in himself, but in Christ and in his neighbor. Otherwise he is not a Christian. He lives in Christ through faith, in his neighbor through love."[18]

By the end of 1520 and before his excommunication in January 1521, Luther had become a reformer. But the reformation movement he and his writings inspired would begin in his absence. Luther's prince, Elector Frederick the Wise of Saxony, managed to secure the agreement of the newly elected emperor, the twenty-one-year-old Habsburg monarch Charles from Spain (but raised in the French-speaking Habsburg court in the Low Countries), that before any punishment for the heretic was applied by the state, Luther (who had been condemned by the Church) would be offered yet another opportunity to recant his views before the imperial diet as it met in Worms in the spring of 1521. On the way to Worms, Luther preached to enthusiastic crowds in Erfurt, one of the largest cities in Germany, where he had attended the university and had entered the Augustinian cloister more than fifteen years before. At Worms, too, there was clear evidence of popular support for the condemned heretic, and Worms had of late been a scene of revolts by the peasants and townspeople. Luther appeared before the Diet of the Empire on April 16 and again on April 17, but he was not offered an opportunity to defend his views. He must recant or be condemned, now by the civil authority of the emperor and the estates of the Holy Roman Empire of the German Nation. The final lines of his address have been celebrated as a defense of individual freedom of conscience and defiance of authority, but in fact his words speak of a conscience held captive to a different authority than either the Roman Church or the civil power:

17 AE 31:347.

18 AE 31:371.

> Since then your serene majesty and your lordships seek a simple answer, I will give it in this manner, neither horned nor toothed: unless I am convinced by the testimony of the Scriptures or by clear reason (for I do not trust either in the pope or in councils alone, since it is well known that they have often erred and contradicted themselves), I am bound by the Scriptures I have quoted and my conscience is captive to the Word of God. I cannot and I will not retract anything, since it is neither safe nor right to go against conscience. . . . May God help me, Amen.[19]

Not in the official minutes but appearing in the first published description of Luther's response before the emperor are the words "Here I stand, I cannot do otherwise."[20] Perhaps Luther did not include the phrase in his speech, but the narrative describes what in fact the reformer did: he stood his ground and refused to recant his views before the power of the empire just as he had before the power of the Church.

Luther stood alone at Worms, but Luther's Reformation involved many followers and soon some who chose to stake out other paths of reform. After his departure from the diet, Luther was condemned as an outlaw by an edict dated May 8 but actually approved on May 25 by the remaining estates after the diet had been formally closed and several of the estates had left, including Luther's prince, the elector of Saxony. By then Luther was safely ensconced in the Wartburg, a fortress castle within the realms of the elector of Saxony, outside the city of Eisenach, where Luther had gone to grammar school some twenty years previously. Luther lived in the Wartburg as an exile, busy at work writing letters to his supporters, postils (sermon studies), treatises, and most importantly his translation of the New Testament from the original Greek into German, using the reconstructed Greek text and new Latin translation published in 1519 by the Dutch humanist Erasmus.[21] During his absence the reform movement took shape in Wittenberg, led by, among others, Luther's university colleagues Andreas Karlstadt (1486–1541) and Philip Melanchthon (1497–1560) and including the fiery preacher Gabriel Zwilling (ca. 1487–1558), Luther's brother Augustinian. By the end of 1521, at the university and in the

---

19 AE 32:112–13.

20 See AE 32:113 n. 8.

21 Luther used the second (1519) edition with the title *Novum Testamentum omne*, which included the Greek text and Erasmus's own Latin translation, replacing the earlier *Novum Instrumentum omne* (1516), an edition that had included the traditional Latin Vulgate text alongside the Greek.

Augustinian cloister, the parish church St. Mary's, and All Saints' Chapel (Castle Church) of Wittenberg, these leaders began to implement the basic concrete changes that would be repeated again and again as Luther's Reformation took hold in various localities in Germany during the decade of the 1520s: private Masses (offered for the sins of the living and the dead) were discontinued; the Lord's Supper was consecrated by speaking the Words of Institution in German and was offered in both kinds (the bread and the wine) to all who communed; preaching and teaching of the Bible was offered more frequently and in German; monks and friars began to leave the cloisters; and several priests and then some monks got married, thus violating the law of celibacy and (for the monks) breaking their vows and as a result coming under the threat of ecclesiastical and even civil prosecution. In correspondence from the Wartburg, Luther voiced his support of the changes, although he disputed some of the arguments being made for these changes, especially by Andreas Karlstadt.[22]

In early December, his hair and beard grown out, dressed no longer in a friar's cowl but disguised as "Junker Jörg" (Knight George), Luther visited Wittenberg to see for himself how his Reformation was taking shape in his hometown. Generally he was delighted by the progress, but the day before his arrival, on December 3, some university students and townspeople became rowdy and harassed some of the priests of the parish church and friars of the Franciscan house in Wittenberg. While still in Wittenberg Luther wrote to his friend George Spalatin, who was court chaplain and secretary to Elector Frederick: "I was disturbed on the way [to Wittenberg] by various rumors concerning the improper conduct of some of our people, and [therefore] I have decided to issue a public exhortation on that subject as soon as I have returned to my wilderness."[23] From the Wartburg (his "wilderness") Luther later sent back to Wittenberg his response to the violence that threatened to turn his Reformation into a seditious and violent revolution: *A Sincere Admonition by Martin Luther to All Christians to Guard against Insurrection and Rebellion*, which appeared in print sometime early in 1522. In it Luther expressed doubt that things would go so far, but nevertheless he made his position quite clear: "I am opposed to those who rise in insurrection, no matter how just their cause, because there can be no insurrection without hurting the innocent and shedding their blood."[24] Reforms should be enacted in good order through the authorities that are responsible for

22 See, e.g., Luther's letters to Melanchthon dated August 1 and August 3, 1521 (AE 48:277–89).

23 AE 48:351–52.

24 AE 45:63.

the churches in any given area—if the bishops will not act, then through local preachers with the support of local or territorial civil governments. If the latter also are unwilling, those Christians seeking reform should first acknowledge their own sins because God is justly punishing them with such an anti-Christian regime; then they should pray; finally, supporters of reform should "let your mouth become such a mouth of the Spirit of Christ as St. Paul speaks . . . , 'Our Lord Jesus will slay him with the mouth of his Spirit' " (2 Thess. 2:8).[25] The only "uproar" that Luther would countenance is that waged by the Word of God: "Let us be wise, thank God for his holy word, and be bold with our mouths in the service of this blessed insurrection."[26]

This belief of Luther's that the Word of God alone will bring about the "blessed insurrection" needed to effect a true reformation, and that no kind of human uproar or show of force will accomplish it, has been misconstrued, attacked, and maligned ever since the early Reformation. Already during the controversy that developed after he had posted his *Ninety-Five Theses* on indulgences, Luther was charged with inciting discord and unrest within the Church and society. The papal bull threatening the Wittenberg friar with excommunication is known by its first words, *Exsurge Domine*, the Latin text of its opening:

> *Arise, O Lord*, judge thy cause; remember how fools scoff at thee all day. Incline thy ear to our prayer. For foxes have come to spoil the vineyard, whose wine press thou alone hast trodden. And when thou didst desire to ascend into heaven to the Father thou didst commit the care, government, and administration of this vineyard to Peter as the head and thy vicar and to his successors as the church triumphant. Now a wild boar from the forest threatens to ravage the vineyard, indeed, a wild animal threatens to pluck its fruit.[27]

But Luther's vision of reform through the Word alone was also attacked by some of his early followers. Andreas Karlstadt soon attacked Luther for proceeding too slowly for the sake of weak consciences, publishing belatedly in 1524 his pamphlet entitled *Whether We Should Go Slowly and Avoid Offending the Weak in Matters Pertaining to God's Will* in response to Luther's return to leadership of

---

25 AE 45:67.

26 AE 45:69.

27 Quoted from Carter Lindberg, ed., *The European Reformations Sourcebook* (Malden, MA: Blackwell, 2000), 36.

the Wittenberg movement in March 1522.[28] Thomas Müntzer (ca. 1489–1525), a zealous preacher who had studied at Wittenberg in the early years of Luther's reform movement, would later charge the reformer with complicity in the societal evils of Christendom by his opposition to violent revolution in the name of God. Müntzer published in the fall of 1524 his *Schutzrede* or defense (*apologia*) in response to Luther's second broadside against violence undertaken for the sake of reformation, his *Letter to the Princes of Saxony concerning the Rebellious Spirit* of July 1524.[29] Müntzer's defense opens with these words: "A highly provoked Vindication [*Schutzrede*] and a Refutation of the unspiritual soft-living Flesh in Wittenberg, whose robbery and distortion of Scripture has so grievously polluted our wretched Christendom [*Christenheit*]."[30]

Such criticisms of Luther's Reformation have persisted since his day and color also the commemoration of the Reformation in its quincentenary year. In our ecumenical age Luther is often characterized most essentially as a divisive figure, the Reformation viewed as a tragic division of the Church more than a much-needed and long-awaited reform of a burdensome Christianity and corrupt ecclesiastical hierarchy, or a renewal of pure doctrine and evangelical preaching and pastoral care. Luther's Reformation has been judged a failure, a religious movement that in fact had the unintended consequence of paving the way toward a secular age in which religion is maligned as evil or dismissed as irrelevant. Luther's central role in the Reformation has been disputed, as has the traditional conviction among historians that the Reformation itself was a significant epoch in the history of Christianity and of Western civilization. Among the reformers of the sixteenth century, Luther in particular has been judged intolerant, bigoted, anti-Semitic, Islamophobic, and an ideologue whose political thought contributed to the creation of oppressive European regimes of princely absolutism.

Defending Luther's Reformation is not intended as a response to all these sorts of criticisms of Luther and the Reformation he started and had a pivotal role in leading. It is published rather as a means of celebrating the five-hundredth anniversary of the beginning of the Reformation by presenting several essays, written by scholars who abide in the Lutheran confession of the Gospel, responding to

28 An English translation is available in *The Essential Carlstadt: Fifteen Tracts by Andreas Bodenstein (Carlstadt) from Karlstadt*, trans. and ed. E. J. Furcha (Scottsdale, PA: Herald Press, 1995), 247–68.

29 AE 40:49–59.

30 Translation (slightly modified) from *The Collected Works of Thomas Müntzer*, ed. and trans. Peter Matheson (Edinburgh: T&T Clark, 1988), 327.

some of the more significant criticisms of Luther and the Reformation shaped by his vision. Interpretation of the reformer's life and character is left to his capable biographers.[31] The essays that follow seek to unveil the significance of Luther and Luther's Reformation. Timothy Dost explores how Luther became a reformer of Christendom whose central place in the Reformation emerged already from the questions he posed in, and the controversy that developed over, his *Ninety-Five Theses* on indulgences. Jonathan Mumme grapples with the central message of Luther's Reformation—justification by faith—in conversation with the interpretive questions raised by N. T. Wright and the so-called New Perspective on Paul, wherein it is held that Luther and Protestantism since his time have misconstrued the Pauline message of the New Testament as a response to Jewish legalism and works-righteousness. Cameron MacKenzie addresses the question of authority and the Scripture principle (*sola scriptura*) in Luther's Reformation, focusing his critique on one articulation of the rather common view today that, for Luther, it is not God's authorship (and from this, the inerrancy, clarity, and sufficiency of Scripture) but rather the Gospel that is the source of Scripture's authority. John Maxfield unveils Luther's Old Testament exposition, responding to the prevailing view that Luther's interpretation is outmoded at best, surpassed by modern critical scholarship, and at worst a means of perpetuating medieval anti-Judaism or even the anti-Semitic hatred of a bigoted age. Jason Lane explores Luther's role as a Bible teacher through his biblical prefaces and shorter works devoted to explaining how the Bible is to be read and interpreted. Benjamin Mayes investigates Luther's understanding and reform of marriage and sexuality, one of the few areas where most evangelical reformers of the sixteenth century were in complete agreement, but where modern interpretations of Luther's views sometimes distort the evidence and display quite different agendas for a Christian ethics of sexuality and married life. Roland Ziegler's chapter brings our volume to a close by questioning a criticism of Luther, expressed repeatedly since the 1520s, that the reformer caused

---

31 Biographies of this most fascinating of men appear with regularity, often focused on interpreting a specific aspect of Luther's character and development as a reformer, e.g., Heiko A. Oberman, *Luther: Man between God and the Devil*, trans. Eileen Walliser-Schwarzbart (New York: Image Books/Doubleday, 1992); Robert Kolb, *Martin Luther: Confessor of the Faith* (Oxford: Oxford University Press, 2009); and Pettegree, *Brand Luther* (see above, p. 3 n. 5). A recent biography that admirably views Luther as an imperfect but compelling and engaging personality, a man who embodied the "simultaneously saint and sinner" reality of his own understanding of the human being in relation to God and neighbor, is Scott H. Hendrix, *Martin Luther: Visionary Reformer* (New Haven: Yale University Press, 2015).

a needless division among evangelicals and fractured the Reformation by his rejection of the Sacramentarians, that is, those evangelical reformers who criticized Luther's clear teaching and confession of the real presence of Christ's body and blood in the sacrament of the Lord's Supper, given to us Christians to eat and to drink.

The end of 2017 meets the conclusion of the "Luther Decade" and the culmination of celebrating the five-hundredth anniversary of the *Ninety-Five Theses*. But five hundred years ago, Luther's Reformation was in its infancy—nay, rather, was only taking on form in the womb of Luther's active mind and was soon to be nurtured in the cradle of the Reformation, the town of Wittenberg and its university. It was the decade of the 1520s when the Reformation took Europe by storm through a "blessed insurrection" of the Word of God that forever changed the Church. As the Christian Church lives in the world as a community of believers, of saints who yet remain sinners, Luther's Reformation could never live up to the idealism of its visionary protagonist. Luther knew and expected that; here was no utopian dreamer. But Luther's Reformation did result in a changed Christianity, one that endures today, shaping the faith and piety of Christian communities that continue to proclaim the Reformation Gospel, and having a salutary influence also in other Christian communions, Catholic and Protestant, where the Word of God is proclaimed among the gathered saints and where Christ's command is heeded, to make disciples of all nations by baptizing and teaching them to observe all that He has commanded (Matt. 28:19–20).

Martin Luther, Reformer of Christendom

Timothy P. Dost

As it stands, the title of this chapter certainly represents a bold and broad claim about the work of a single person. Martin Luther's reach, at least in the sixteenth century, was quite local in person even while he became the most popular author and probably the most famous person throughout Europe in his age. So the idea of "Luther, the Reformer of Christendom" must be qualified to focus on the Western (Latin) Church, or European Christendom, and it can be acknowledged that there were many regions and traditions of Christianity in his time where Luther's Reformation had little if any impact.

But as time passed Luther's influence on the Church, and on society in general, became more widespread. This is particularly the case if one takes into account the influences of both direct and indirect followers of his Reformation. For example, who could conceive of an effective John Calvin and the entire Reformed tradition without Calvin's self-acknowledged debt to Luther? Without the influence of Luther, how would King Henry VIII, who generally despised Luther and his reform, have proceeded in his "great matter" of seeking a divorce from his first wife in order to produce a male heir, in the process taking the Church of England out from under the umbrella of Rome? How would the Anabaptists and other radicals, who generally thought that Luther did not go far enough in his reform, have made their complaints so cogently known, or even have had the theological ammunition to express their individualism and personal belief in both the Gospel and the community of saints, without an effective source and counterpoise in Luther? The Swiss reformer Huldrych Zwingli's position was (he claimed) largely his own, but even he had to meet with Luther to attempt to hammer out a truce in order to effectively resist the efforts of Emperor Charles V to repress the Reformation. Finally, who can conceive of the call for a broadly conceived reform and expansion of education and literacy for both boys and girls, for the Catholic Church's own reform that called for reduction in corruption and for spreading their message to the whole world, without the issues raised and the pressure brought to bear by Luther? Who would have been the target of the anathemas expressed at Trent without a counterpoise in Luther and his offshoots? And to whom, directly or indirectly, would subsequent movements be indebted, such as the Baptists, Methodists, and Pietists of various sorts, if not to Luther? Even the Second Vatican Council with its proclamations and elevation of the laity owes many of its theological underpinnings and rationales at least indirectly to the reformer.

So Luther's influence holds great sway. But it was not always so. When he wrote and posted his *Ninety-Five Theses on Indulgences*, we find an initially reluctant and narrowly focused reformer, one who was no rebel but who had specific problems in focus. After all, the indulgences were poisoning his flock, reducing their penance to a mere mockery. Luther saw the threat and threaded the needle with ninety-five somewhat angry statements sharply formulated (as customary) for the purpose of an academic disputation. These statements were neither mere bombast nor simple broadsides—rather, there was a precision to these assertions that worked to separate surgically the error of abusive indulgences from what Luther regarded as a prior valid use. Luther sought to expose the pastoral problem and combat the destruction of souls wrought by the indulgence preachers. Furthermore, he proposed as remedy the reform of these abuses and the instatement of corrected policies to build up the flock and to promote their salvation and Christian life. It is these *Theses*, together with their immediate and long-term effects, that will form the core of this chapter. Here Luther gradually becomes a reformer of Christendom, but the *Theses* simply represent a first step. In large part it was the negative response of the Roman Church that precipitated his further reforms, which were often expressed in ways that were more theologically positive and less critical in tone. What we see in the *Theses* is the inception of the broader work, directed at a narrowly focused problem, but hardly incorporating or even anticipating its later fruition. That was pounded into Luther through broken promises and further immersion in God's Word. Here we see little evidence of radical breaks, but rather an audacious yet scriptural and practical approach to specific problems.

Yet the *Theses* also represent a positive concern for the faith and lives of Christians. Luther's main purpose was to remove from his people the risk of despair and damnation that could be caused by the errors he condemned. Here we find only slight direct emphasis on the central, positive message of the Gospel. What the *Theses* did assert was that Christians, as true believers in the faith found in the Gospel of Christ, should be taught that they needed to live their lives, maintain their households, and love their neighbors, and only from any excess resources focus their energy on fund-raisers for unnecessary projects such as building St. Peter's Basilica in Rome. Therefore, Luther did not shy away from addressing how the believer should handle his money and worldly possessions when faced with building churches and receiving indulgences. It was this final issue that garnered the attention of the Church authorities, for Luther's radical solution was to love the neighbor and one's own household first, by concrete and monetary means, essentially cutting off the funding to Rome that was broadly and deeply resented especially in Germany.

Ninety-Five Dividers and Unifiers

Dissemination of Martin Luther's *Ninety-Five Theses on Indulgences* marked the beginning of a major historical period in a way few other actions by an individual have. Major trends often creep into the picture. Not so with the Reformation. While there were people who were thinking similar thoughts and considering similar actions, it was Luther's *Theses* that galvanized an unmistakable movement, in a manner unintended by their author. This granted Luther both a fame and a notoriety that he neither sought nor expected.

Scarcely two months earlier, Luther had penned what he considered much more damaging and theologically direct theses, against Scholasticism. This was the core medieval system of forming theology, and so he was surprised that there was virtually no response. For several years he had taught in his classes that people were saved by the grace of God, through faith in Christ crucified, rather than by their own works, no matter how pious. This had not brought out the authorities, and he had not even been reproved for his work. What, then, was so different about the *Ninety-Five Theses* that they touched such a nerve with their readers and made them so viscerally either pro- or anti-Luther? Why did they polarize people and institutions so greatly? In what ways did the *Theses* constitute a watershed moment?

This chapter will first explore the reasons Luther was uniquely equipped to address the problems of the Church and its practices in his generation, providing needed context. Second, the *Theses* themselves will be explored, through a fresh translation of selected examples with a view to understanding the problems, issues, and the audience Luther bore in mind when penning them. Third, the question of how they were actually received by these groups will be addressed. Fourth, I will address the question of how the *Theses* might be useful today. Finally, I will take up what events in his early career as a reformer caused Luther to broaden his focus and take on major issues faced by the Church of the day.

Crucial to all these questions is whose issues Luther took up in the *Theses*. It was not his intent to generate a broad controversy, and the *Theses* represented a typical invitation to an academic debate, but there were particular interest groups whose problems and concerns he addressed and certain groups whose behavior he vigorously attacked. If we can understand whom Luther intended to write for and against as well as how he crafted his argument to meet those groups' proclivities, it will become clearer and more comprehensible what caused the *Theses* to have such an impact. An important factor here is that the people who read or heard about the *Theses* were frequently already of a mind either to favor them or to view them as a threat. Many people were already well on their way to thinking the way Luther thought but could not express so clearly what bothered them. They shared his critiques and eventually found relief in the same things that brought him comfort and solace with God. This dispelled the fog they felt in their lives and contributed to making his writings so immediately understood and popular.

Luther's Doggedness Fosters Reform

Many who followed Luther viewed him as a German Hercules, cleaning up the Augean stables of Rome. To the Roman Catholic establishment who took the *Theses* as a threat, Luther was a kind of Frankenstein's monster that they had inadvertently cobbled together. He was portrayed by his foes as a seven-headed beast. Following the production of the *Theses*, Luther produced so many high quality, biblically based writings in such a short time that his opponents concluded that he could not be one man, but must have been a consortium of humanists (more on this group later). His great productivity was in part due to his indisputable genius, but his intensely disciplined life also contributed. He had been reared in a relatively strict, better-off-than-average household of peasant stock, yet as a youth and young man he became highly educated, with a bachelor's degree and master's degree in general studies (the liberal arts), and a master's degree and doctorate in theology. Here was an honest man who had taken his monastic oaths and the discipline of the cloister so seriously that on several occasions he might have died of exposure, sickness, and hunger. He had learned to live and thrive on three or four hours of sleep a night. He was ordained a priest and became a serious and pious preacher who proved very popular with his parishioners. In addition, he was granted local supervisory responsibilities for his district in the Augustinian order. If that were not enough, he was appointed professor of the Bible (*Lectura in Biblia*) and brought to this charge brilliant insights and innovation. While there were others who held the title of doctor of theology and were versed in the Bible, Luther used his chair in a unique way, to lecture solely on the biblical text. Furthermore, he eliminated much of the then-dominant philosophy of Aristotle from the curriculum at Wittenberg and, soon after Erasmus's Greek text of the New Testament became available, he learned Greek and later Hebrew. It had become apparent to him that the customary and Church-endorsed Latin Vulgate lacked the precision required for sound biblical study. Luther was also becoming known among the circle of Renaissance humanists, and they helped to disseminate his work. In fact, Luther was well-acquainted with their craft and used humanistic studies extensively to structure his own work and sharpen its appeal. In addition, he was something of a teaching superstar (although Philip Melanchthon, after his arrival in 1518, turned out to be even more popular as a professor). Luther was considered indispensable to the newly founded Wittenberg University and had his doctorate fees paid for by none other than Prince Frederick the Wise, who in effect became his patron and sponsor. Suffice it to say that in Luther we find a man of great piety and fear of God, who worked extremely hard and brought tremendous gifts and self-discipline to the task of bringing his renewed understanding of the scriptural Gospel to both the elites and the masses. In a few days' time, Luther penned the *Ninety-Five Theses* and perhaps posted them to the door of the Castle Church (written in Latin, with the door playing the customary role of bulletin board for the university). What is certain is that he sent them to his archbishop and perhaps some other area bishops as well. He also shared copies with some of his humanist associates and friends. From these initial contacts the *Theses* spread, and within six months their forceful ideas were felt throughout much of Europe.

As to his personality, again things worked in his favor. He was gregarious and hard working. Not above physical labor, he was a person who could be trusted with one's secrets and sins, yet he was able to win over princes, burghers, scholars, and peasants with his genuine humor and rustic brilliance in

Latin and especially German. Although he was also prone to periods of depression, he would find his remedy in the Scriptures, the cross, his brothers in Christ, and eventually in his wife, Katie, and his children. (When two of their children died, he grieved terribly.) Luther was a person with whom one could enjoy a beer, who was sometimes rustically crude, but he was a person whom, despite his rougher edges, you could count on to show tremendous love, trust, and forgiveness.

A Somewhat Insignificant Posting

There was nothing particularly significant about posting theses on a bulletin board, and it was no great matter to send them to the archbishop, Albert of Mainz. The latter action was considered both a courtesy and a necessity, as the abuses being protested were occurring in Albert's lands. Luther's actions were not particularly revolutionary as he did not distribute the *Theses* in German, but rather in Latin, calling for a scholarly debate of their propositions. Even the few people who could read (much less in Latin) would probably have needed an academic background to understand them. Neither was the content of the *Theses* particularly novel. Very few of them were directly about the Gospel of Christ, as Luther at the time was coming to understand it. They mostly focused on pastoral problems Luther faced because once his people had purchased an indulgence, they no longer considered the seriousness of their own guilt and their impenitent attitudes. Luther's prince, Frederick the Wise, had himself prohibited the indulgence preachers from entering Electoral Saxony, as they would compete with his own display of relics on All Saints' Day, a church fund-raiser that provided 1,902,202 years and 275 days off purgatory.[1] Luther does not even mention the prince's relics, which he does not find at this point to be at issue. Furthermore, in the *Theses* he does not, as he would later, protest against the notion of purgatory itself. Rather, Luther takes the position that the indulgence hawkers were making unfounded and reckless promises about what sins and guilt the pope could or could not remit. In particular they made false statements that penalties for sins imposed in the afterlife (purgatory) could be forgiven even without contrition on the part of the sinner. This would set up Luther's later problem with sacraments being effective *ex opere operato* (by the very doing of the thing, it is completed).

---

1 Roland Bainton, *Here I Stand: A Life of Martin Luther* (Peabody, MA: Hendrickson, 2010 [originally published 1950]), 53.

This teaching that grace was imparted through sacraments and other means whether or not a person actually had faith led to many insincere practices in the Church. For Luther it was not indulgences themselves that were at issue, but the inflated promises that were associated with them. Unaware of the deal that had been struck between the pope and Archbishop Albert to sell these indulgences, Luther attempted to insulate the pope from the abuse of the indulgence hawkers' false claims, believing him ignorant of the situation. Here we find Luther arguing not that there can be no indulgences, but rather that any indulgence granted must be limited to penalties of this world imposed by the Church. So although there were many potentially inflammatory expressions in the *Theses*, their content remained theologically conservative. They argued for a restoration and improvement of the preaching of Christ rather than a false piety found in reliance upon corrupt forms of indulgence. Ironically, about a year later, the pope himself would weigh in on the matter in the bull *Cum postquam*, largely affirming Luther's position (but not his contribution) and quashing the worst of the abuses.

In addition, contrary to popular lore, the initial spread of the *Theses* was not particularly rapid. At first they went to the archbishop, and later perhaps Luther sent copies to some of the local bishops as well as to some of his humanist associates. To give an idea of the actual pace of events, it took about a month before the *Theses* reached Archbishop Albert, who then sent them on to Rome, where they arrived several weeks later. There was the intention, mentioned in the brief preface, to have a debate, but as nobody stepped forward to engage the questions directly, a significant correspondence developed among various parties, not always involving Luther himself. He later makes the comment that within two weeks all of Germany was involved,[2] but the evidence speaks otherwise, and the respected Luther biographer Martin Brecht indicates that this statement refers to two weeks after the printers actually had the document in hand. It was not until early 1518 that Luther noticed any real trouble. Johann Tetzel, the Dominican preacher of indulgences, was newly minted a doctor of theology based on theses against Luther's position that were in fact written by Konrad Koch (also known as Wimpina).[3] Having this abruptly conferred academic credential, Tetzel affirmed that he would see to it that Luther would be burned at the stake in short order. Ironically, he would soon recant his own teaching and, as in the interim he had fallen gravely ill, would beg Luther's forgiveness, which

2 Martin Brecht, *Martin Luther: His Road to Reformation 1483–1521*, trans. James L. Schaff (Philadelphia: Fortress, 1985), 205.

3 Brecht, *Luther: His Road to Reformation*, 207.

the friar of Wittenberg gladly granted. Once the *Theses* were both published and translated into German, they caught fire in the minds and hearts of those who supported Luther's ideas as well as among those who considered them heretical and blasphemous.

Whose Problems Did Luther Address in the *Theses*?

Before concerning ourselves with the reception of the *Theses*, it is both appropriate and illuminating to answer the question of whose problems Luther had in mind and how he specifically addressed their concerns through these statements. As a part of this section I will work up a description of each party involved, their significance to Luther and the cause of reform, and how he addressed their issues either through specific references or more indirectly.

As I have been studying the *Theses* in Latin, there are two points that should be made from the outset. First, the authoritative Weimar edition of Luther's writings does not number the theses from 1 to 95. Instead, it numbers them in three groups of twenty-five each and a fourth group of twenty. Therefore, in the text of the chapter I have listed the numbers in the modern, customary numbering, while in the footnotes I have employed the Weimar edition numbering.

The second point is one that will require more research, but I believe will be borne out through subsequent study. Luther uses two different terms for indulgences, and it appears to me that he uses them differently in rather specific ways. In the case where he is speaking about them as a proper matter without distortion or error, he calls them *indulgentias*, which should obviously be rendered "indulgences." Where he is speaking about the abuse of indulgences, he uses the term *veniarum*, from the Latin for forgiveness, which should be rendered "forgiveness things," but in view of the fact that Luther considers their current marketing an abuse could also be seen as "trivial forgiveness" or "vain things." This term has typically been translated "indulgences" as well, doing a disservice to the distinction Luther is likely making and as a result weakening the thrust of his argument. I will be rendering *veniarum* as "vain things," "specious or trivial things," or in other similar ways, while sometimes placing the word "indulgences" in square brackets for clarity.

Renaissance Humanists and Their Concerns

Renaissance humanists, who have already been mentioned several times, are a party that Luther addresses in the *Theses* in part by sharing them with some members of the humanist group, who then disseminated them further in educated circles. Humanist stylistic concerns and nuances are reflected in the document. It is therefore important to understand who and what the humanists represented and why Luther was naturally allied with them.

Quite often people become confused between modern secular humanists and the humanists of the Renaissance. The secular humanists arose out of the eighteenth-century Enlightenment and often held that God (if He existed at all) was at most unconcerned about human endeavors and at worst was a fraud perpetuated by the authorities to keep down the masses. Luther would have had nothing to do with this sort of thought, and his Reformation was dedicated to the proposition that God is both personal and loving toward His creatures and especially toward those who believe the Gospel of Jesus Christ. For him, therefore, the concept of a mechanistic, distant, or disinterested God, or the idea that there is no God, would be inconceivable—a narcissistic attempt to enthrone mankind in God's place.

Renaissance humanism, on the other hand, was quite different. It concerned itself with the *studia humanitatis* (study of the humanities, the liberal arts), which involved the use of copies of ancient texts as authorities and models for life, government, and behavior. These in turn superseded more recently developed medieval traditions. In fact, the whole concept of the Middle Ages was developed by the Renaissance thinkers, who believed that their new efforts represented the rebirth of the ancient phoenix of learning after a long, dead "middle age." Renaissance means "rebirth." Nobody awoke in the Middle Ages and thought, "Eureka, I think I live in a middle age! The Renaissance is coming!" This label and idea originated with the subsequent Renaissance, and the concept of a "middle age" amounted to a kind of flyover zone—a demeaning term applied to the intervening period.

These Renaissance humanists believed in God and in Christ. Their concern was what they saw as the thicket of ignorance that had been developing through the work of medieval scholasticism, which they believed argued extensively while arriving at few truths. The humanists pursued the ancient Roman concept of virtue, which, when applied to thought and education, meant esteeming streamlined arguments that led to definite answers. This practice of arriving directly at the truth through pointedly stylized argument was called *rhetoric*, a word whose meaning has largely changed today as it now usually connotes argument for the sake of argument or even just plain lousy (weak) arguments dressed up in fancy language. In the classical and Renaissance periods, rhetoric was considered the most advanced of the basic trio of studies (along with grammar and dialectic) expected to be mastered by every student, which was called the trivium.[4] Rhetoric comported well with Renaissance scholars, who believed direct argument toward truth was the most effective means to promote the faith and advance society. This would have resulted in the lament of the humanists against Aristotle and his scholastic followers. For Renaissance humanists, Plato and his ideas of certainty, truth, and eternity largely displaced the medieval standard of study based on Aristotle or, to be more fair, at least his scholastic promoters.

Ancient texts were highly esteemed by the Renaissance humanists, and although these had been dutifully copied and stored in monastic libraries by countless generations of monks, it became the humanists' unique task to make new copies available and disseminate them. The cry of "*Ad fontes*"—"To the sources!"—was a regular part of their vocabulary. In addition, they cultivated first a fine antique Latin and later a Greek style of composition, eschewing the linguistic corruptions that had taken hold in the Middle Ages. What use was respecting ancient texts if one did not have the rhetorical skills to understand and emulate their nuances? Who could truly appreciate their nuances without having the skills to compose at a similar level? The ultimate style modeled was that of Cicero, the great orator of the golden age of Rome; the ultimate rhetoric, that of Quintilian, whose exhaustive treatment was considered the greatest of the ancient age.

Although Renaissance humanism was not included in Luther's direct curriculum at Erfurt University, where he had studied for his undergraduate and initial master's degree, he participated in many extracurricular classes, seminars, and discussions on this subject. He was well-acquainted with the work of Desiderius Erasmus—perhaps the greatest Renaissance humanist ever and certainly the most prominent in Luther's day—and other lesser lights such as Rudolph Agricola, who had the temerity to introduce Hebrew as an academic language for study of the Bible. One of Luther's favorite humanist authors was Lorenzo Valla, whose no-holds-barred writing and criticism appealed to the reformer. Valla's keen textual analysis in the late 1400s had revealed the *Donation of Constantine* as a forgery and exposed consequent exaggerated papal claims to European lands as fraud. Luther made extensive use of humanist rhetorical methods and sometimes apologized for not being more "stylish" in his letter writing as he hurriedly dashed something off.

Luther's early correspondence demonstrates this affinity in several ways. In his more formal letter writing he tended to imitate the classical grammatical

4 The advanced studies—geometry, arithmetic, astronomy, and music—formed the quadrivium and were taken up only after the trivium was mastered.

forms more closely—with verbs moving to the ends of sentences, the appearance of ablative absolutes (an advanced classical construction), and the length of sentences significantly extended. Furthermore, he often employed subtle classical allusions to obscure yet highly pertinent ancient characters, probably relying on the work of the humanist Erasmus taken from his *Adages*. He also made use of classical nicknames during the early years, styling himself when he formed his new reliance on the Gospel as *Eleutherius*, "The Freed Man" in (Latinized) Greek. His emphases on literacy and education and the publication of the biblical text as the sole arbiter of theology and in the language of the people also places him in the direction this camp was headed by further disseminating in translation the source text of Christianity. Had Luther not been remembered as a monumental reformer, he would nonetheless likely be recognized as a significant Renaissance humanist.[5]

So aside from the fact that members of this movement likely took upon themselves the distribution of the *Theses*, how does Renaissance humanism manifest itself in the document? First, the style of argument takes no hostages and is an unambiguous assertion of truth against slippery moral and ethical values. Here we see the assertion of not only ancient Greek and Roman but also Germanic virtue. Scholastic pussyfooting around is excluded. While Luther took captive a form of scholasticism—theses—he endowed it with humanist priorities. For example, in Thesis 1 Luther asserts, "In saying, 'Do penance, etc.,' our Lord and Savior Jesus Christ willed that the entire life of the believer be one of repentance."[6] In Thesis 62 he states, "The true treasure of the Church is the most holy Gospel of the glory and grace of God."[7] Again in Thesis 79 he tells us, "To say that the cross with papal insignia and arms is equivalent to the cross on which Christ hung is blasphemy."[8] Here there is no beating around the bush; we have clear and direct arguments in pursuit of truth, a truth arrived at by delving into the sources (*ad fontes*) and based, at least indirectly, on the ancient text of the Bible.

Sometimes rhetorical nuance, which would also have appealed to the humanists, is displayed, as in the subtler arguments in Theses 81–88. Luther's

---

5 For more on these matters, see Timothy P. Dost, *Renaissance Humanism in Support of the Gospel in Luther's Early Correspondence: Taking All Things Captive* (Aldershot: Ashgate, 2001).

6 WA 1:233, Thesis 1: "Dominus et magister noster Iesus Christus diciendo 'Penitentiam agite &c.' omnem vitam fidelium penitentiam esse voluit."

7 WA 1:236, Thesis 12: "Verus thesaurus ecclesie est sacrosanctum euangelium gloria et gratie dei."

8 WA 1:237, Thesis 4: "Dicere, Crucem armis papalibus insigniter erectam cruci Christi equivalere, blasphemia est."

introduction to these theses reflects a cushioned approach to the thorny problem of telling his superiors things they might not want to hear, things that could easily get him into trouble. In Thesis 81 we read: "This licentious and empty preaching makes it not so easy for learned men to sustain the reverence due the Pope against false charges, to say nothing of addressing certain astute questions from laymen."[9] There follow seven highly caustic propositions about indulgences that had been floating around, from which Luther has effectively insulated himself.

Other examples are evident where humanists would have appreciated Luther's source-based approach. He sometimes subtly weaves in biblical texts to make his point, inventing nuanced parallels. In Theses 92 and 93 we read: "Depart, therefore, all those prophets who say to the people of Christ, 'Peace, peace,' and there is no peace. [93]—But all those prophets are well led who say to the people of Christ, 'Cross, cross,' where there is no cross."[10]

Here we can see a parallel to the book of the prophet Jeremiah in which he laments:

> "For from the least to the greatest of them, everyone is greedy for unjust gain; and from prophet to priest, everyone deals falsely. They have healed the wound of My people lightly, saying, 'Peace, peace,' when there is no peace. Were they ashamed when they committed abomination? No, they were not at all ashamed; they did not know how to blush. Therefore they shall fall among those who fall; at the time that I punish them, they shall be overthrown," says the LORD.[11]

This scriptural context worked well with Luther's general theme throughout the *Theses* that there would be severe consequences for people who ignored the truth and exploited the people of God. The lack of shame on the part of these false preachers made them doubly guilty.

Luther's Concerns for His Ecclesiastical Superiors

A second important constituency were the members of the church hierarchy, essentially Luther's ecclesiastical superiors, to whom the *Theses* appealed for the correction of abuses. Luther was unaware at the time that Archbishop

---

9 WA 1:237, Thesis 6: "Facit hec licentiosa veniarum predication, ut nec reverentiam Pape facile sit etiam doctis viris redimere a calumniis aut certe artutis questionibus laicorum."

10 WA 1:238: "17 Valeant itaque omnes illi prophete, qui dicunt populo Christi 'Pax pax,' et non est pax. 18 Bene agant omnes illi prophete, qui dicunt populo Christi 'Crux crux,' et non est crux."

11 Jer. 6:13–15 (ESV).

Albert himself, in a secret deal with Rome, had contributed to the problem of the indulgences in his lands. In order to secure an indulgence of his own so that he could become a pluralist[12]—both the archbishop of Mainz and the archbishop of Magdeburg—Albert had promised payment of 10,000 ducats (gold coins) to the pope.

Roland Bainton humorously characterizes the negotiations:

> Knowing the role they would ultimately play, Albert turned to them [the Fuggers] for the initial negotiations. He was informed that the pope demanded twelve thousand ducats for the twelve apostles. Albert offered seven thousand for the seven deadly sins. They compromised on ten thousand, presumably not for the Ten Commandments. Albert had to pay the money down before he could secure his appointment, and he borrowed the sum from the Fuggers.[13]

The money had been borrowed from the local bankers, the Fuggers of Augsburg, at steep interest, with the proceeds to be recovered by the sale of a plenary indulgence in the territories in question. This plenary indulgence granted forgiveness to an individual or a dead relative at the time of purchase and at the hour of death, and it could cover any sin. It was even proclaimed that should one want to violate sexually the holy Virgin Mary, he would be forgiven. Luther was well aware of this preaching, as in Thesis 75 he states, "It is an empty opinion that these papalesque indulgences can forgive the sins of a man even if he could do the impossible and violate the God-bearer. This is madness."[14] Needless to

12 A pluralist was someone who held more than one office in the Church. The problem arose when the individual was unable to carry out the duties of his ministry. Apart from the impossibility of knowing and actually shepherding the people in their charge, quite often they would farm these duties out to others and would profit off the difference in monetary proceeds between the income of their offices and what they paid their vicars.

13 Bainton, *Here I Stand*, 58. Although Bainton's figures are essentially correct, he has simplified the history considerably. Martin Brecht gives a better idea of the true picture of things. The archbishopric was already in debt to the tune of about 20,000 ducats because two previous archbishops had been ordained in recent years and had to include first year's fees as part of their ordination. Therefore, the amount involved had grown to at least 21,000 ducats, including Albert's new fee. When the Fuggers' profits are considered, Brecht mentions a debt of 52,286 ducats. The proceeds of the indulgence were to be divided equally, with half going to repay the Fuggers and half to Rome. Luther was unaware of this level of corruption when he penned the *Theses* and mailed them to Albert. See Brecht, *Luther: His Road to Reformation*, 178–79.

14 WA 1:237, Thesis 25: "Opinari venias papales tantas esse, ut solver possint hominem, etiam si quis per impossibile dei genitricem violasset, Est insanire."

say, once one had purchased such an indulgence it is difficult to envision why one should ever again take seriously sin, penance, or forgiveness.

Luther, unaware of the arrangement between Albert and the pope, writes in full hope and faith that his objections will be heard fairly by the parties in question, that the pastoral issues of impenitence will come to the fore, and that his superiors will marshal their powers to rein in the outrageous claims of the indulgence preachers. It is essential to understand here that rather than their complete abolition (that would come only later), Luther focuses his critique on what he views as the abuse of indulgences. He believes he is informing his superiors of abuses of which they must be unaware. Little did he know that they would soon turn against him, viewing him as an upstart monk who, on the basis of Scripture, was challenging both their financial arrangements and the authority of their teaching.

Luther's Defense of the Pope

What follows are some examples to illustrate the points above, beginning with Luther's defense of the pope. Thesis 38 says, "Neither the remission nor the participation of the Pope is condemned by this in any way (as I have already said), as it simply represents a declaration of the divine remission."[15] Here Luther indicates that the pope is simply doing what God is also doing, so under the circumstances there is no real issue. In fact, the Word of God is echoed and fulfilled through this proper proclamation of indulgences. Far from condemning the practice, by declaring the pope's work parallel to the work of God, Luther clearly allows for it.

Thesis 53 indicates, "They are enemies of both Christ and the Pope, who on account of this insignificant preaching [of indulgences] order the actual Word of God silenced in other churches."[16] Here Luther puts the pope in a good light by placing him alongside Christ. Those who preach wrongly in the name of the pope or Christ are both in the same boat of condemnation. The pope remains, for Luther, Christ's representative on earth.

Thesis 55 says, "It is necessarily the mind of the Pope, that, if these trifles [indulgences] (which are the least of things) are celebrated with one bell, one pageant, and one ceremony, the Gospel (the greatest thing) should be preached

15 WA 1:235, Thesis 13: "Remissio tamen et participation Pape nullo modo est contemnenda, quia (ut dixi) est declaration remissionis divine."

16 WA 1:236, Thesis 3: "Hostes Christi et Pape sunt ii, qui propter venias predicandas verbum dei in allis ecclesiis penitus silere iubent."

with a hundred bells, a hundred pageants, and a hundred ceremonies."[17] Here we have an insight into Luther's projection of what the pope has "in mind" regarding the ceremonies that surrounded the abusive preaching of the indulgence peddlers. Mockery is present in the sarcasm expressed here. The ceremonies are fancy and impressive and used to market the indulgences at some expense of both time and effort. Luther projects that the pope would think the Gospel a hundred times as glorious and deserving of a hundred times the ceremony of these puny indulgences. Here Luther was not actually saying that this scenario represented the ideal; rather, he was employing hyperbole to indicate that if one wants to stack up trivial ceremonies, the honor due the Gospel should be much higher than that for indulgences.

Theses 69 and 70 declare:

> Bishops and other church officials are obligated to receive the lightweight "apostolic" commissars [of indulgences] with all due reverence. [70] But they have a greater obligation to keep every eye peeled, keep every ear alert, so that these men don't preach their own dreams in place of what the Pope has actually authorized.[18]

In this case Luther is making an oblique reference to the thought of a passage of Jeremiah, the lamenter against false prophets. Jeremiah 23:28 says (translating the Vulgate), "Let the prophet who has a dream tell the dream, and he who has My Word, let him speak My Word, for what has straw to do with wheat? says the Lord." In the Vulgate, which Luther would likely have used at the time, the parallel is even clearer: "Propheta qui habet somnium narret somnium et qui habet sermonem meum loquatur sermonem meum vere quid paleis ad triticum dicit Dominus." Here we find the same word for the dreamy, inaccurate prophet—"somnis"—as is found in the theses in question. When combined with Luther's contempt for indulgence preachers, the parallels are clear. Although Luther probably did not have the ability to read it for himself at the time, the Hebrew of the text is even clearer about these matters. The first phrase indicates that the person should chat about the dream he has. The second essentially says, "Let the prophet whom I have worded, word My word." There is a very strong difference in emphasis that comes out even in the Latin translation, and Luther is

17 WA 1:236, Thesis 5: "Mens Pape necessario est, quod, si venie (quod minimum est) una campana, unis pompis et ceremoniis celebrantur, Euangelium (quod maximum est) centum campanis, centum pompis, centum ceremoniis predicetur."

18 WA 1:236: "19 Tenentur Episcopi et Curati veniarum apostolicarum Commissarios cum omni reverentia admittere. 20 Sed magis tenentur omnibus oculis intendere, omnibus auribus advertere, ne pro commissione Pape sua illi somnia predicent."

making a sophisticated point about the noisy chatter of the indulgence preachers with their made-up dreams when compared to the profound preaching of God's Word articulated by His true prophets.

Thesis 80 says, "Reason itself will condemn the Bishops, Curates and Theologians who permit such sermons to be freely heard among the people."[19] Here we have a more nuanced defense of the pope. In essence, Luther places the blame for the problems at hand on underlings who have not correctly carried out their duties. Officials at any level whatsoever who permit these abuses, as well as theologians who justify them, will be condemned. Here the "reason" of the theologians, a scholastic specialty, becomes Luther's chosen judge and executioner. This represents a parallel to the Book of Proverbs in the Bible, in which reason cries out to the foolish ones to abandon their folly and come to their senses, another biblical parallel obliquely noted by Luther.[20]

Indulgence Preachers Receive No Quarter

Third, there were the indulgence preachers themselves. Forgiveness in exchange for gold was their credo. Luther had no truck with these hucksters, pointing out that they denigrated the Gospel by their false priorities; their imaginative sins; their watered-down grace; their poor, external view of piety; and their false teaching on indulgences and purgatory. Luther's parishioners had been stopped from securing these documents locally by Prince Frederick's decree, prohibiting the activity of the indulgence preachers in his territories. Still, they traveled to the nearby towns of Jüterbog and Zerbst[21] to hear the spellbinding bombasts of the Dominican Tetzel and others. Upon returning to their home parish, they often showed contempt for their family and other responsibilities, indicating that they would be forgiven at the hour of their death no matter what they did. For this reason, confession to their priest, Luther, was no longer needed. This placed at risk not only the individual but also the entire social structure. Furthermore, the indulgence preachers' false teaching in the pope's name defamed the pontiff and brought into question the proper

---

19 WA 1:237, Thesis 5: "Rationem reddent Episcopi, Curati et Theologi, Qui tales sermons in populum licere sinunt."

20 The nuance may go even deeper. There is the possibility that it refers to the unselfish and tattered depiction of Philosophy personified as a woman who came to Boethius as he awaited execution in the prison of Theodoric and with her searing use of reason asked what caused him to be so disappointed. She was the main protagonist or antagonist, depending on perspective, in Boethius's famous *Consolation of Philosophy*. This was one of the most read books of the Middle Ages.

21 Brecht, *Luther: His Road to Reformation*, 183.

authority of both the papacy and the Church itself. As an illustration of these abuses, there was a story of a poor knight who went to Tetzel and purchased an indulgence. He and his men then went down the road Tetzel would be traveling and waylaid him and his party, stealing the indulgence monies. When Tetzel protested that the thieves would certainly go to hell for their impious boldness, the knight simply laughed and produced the letter of indulgence recently procured, stating that, according to Tetzel's own preaching, they had nothing to worry about.[22]

Here it is important to understand that a great many of the *Theses* dealt with the issues of this false preaching in oblique and indirect ways. Therefore, I will confine myself to the most obvious examples:

> 20 Therefore the Pope, when he speaks about the remission of all penalties, doesn't mean this to be understood in the simplest sense, but rather only with reference to those penalties he himself has imposed.
>
> 21 Therefore those preachers of indulgences are in error when they say that indulgences free and save a man from all penalties.
>
> 22 Moreover, he cannot remit to the souls in purgatory penalties which the canon laws indicate have to be endured.
>
> 23 If there are any possible cases in which the remission of all penalties could be granted at all, it is certain that this would only be granted to the absolutely most perfect, i.e., most few.
>
> 24 It follows upon these points that the vast majority of the populace is fooled by those imprecise and overblown promises to save them from these penalties.
>
> 25 The selfsame power that the pope has over purgatory generally, each and every priest and pastor holds in his diocese or parish specifically.
>
> [26] The pope does most excellently when not by the power of the keys (which nobody holds) but rather through the way of devout prayers he grants remission to spirits.
>
> [27] It is simply human preaching, that immediately after the coins clink in the coffer, the spirit is told to fly out [of purgatory].
>
> [28] It is certain, however, that as soon as the coins clink in the coffer covetousness and avarice are allowed to increase; but when prayers increase things rest in the hands of God alone. . . .

---

22 Carter Lindberg, ed., *The European Reformations Sourcebook* (Malden, MA: Blackwell, 2000), 32.

[32] Eternally damned are those, along with their teachers, who through these empty letters believe they have secured their own salvation.

[33] Guard carefully against those emptily prattling that this Papal gift is such an inestimable gift of God that it can reconcile people to God.

[34] The grace of those vain letters therefore only applies to sacramental satisfactions that have been made up by men.

[35] They do not preach Christianity who teach that contrition is not necessary for those who will purchase souls or confessional things [indulgences].[23]

23 WA 1:234–35:

> 20 Igitur papa per remissionem plenariam omnium penarum non simpliciter omnium intelligit, sed a seipso tantummodo impositarum.
>
> 21 Errant itaque indulgentiarum predicatores ii, qui dicunt per pape indulgentias hominem ab omni pena solvi et salvari.
>
> 22 Quin nullam remittit animabus in purgatorio, quam in hac vita debuissent secundum Canones solver.
>
> 23 Si remissio ulla omnium omnino penarum potest alicui dari, certum est eam non nisi perfectissimis, i. e. paucissimis, dari.
>
> 24 Falli ob id necesse est maiorem partem populi per indifferentem illam et magnificam pene solute promissionem.
>
> 25 Qualem potestem habet papa in purgatorium generaliter, talem habet quilibet Episcopus et Curatus in sua diocesi et parochia specialiter.
>
> 1 Optime facit papa, quod non potestate clavis (quam nullam habet) set per modum suffragii dat animabus remissionem.
>
> 2 Hominem predicant, qui statim ut iactus nummus in cistam tinnierit evolare dicunt animam.
>
> 3 Certum est, nummo in cistam tinniente augeri questum et avariciam posse: suffragium autem ecclesie est in arbitrio dei solius. . . .
>
> 7 Damnabuntur ineternum cum suis magistris, qui per literas veniarum securos sese credunt de sua salute.
>
> 8 Cavendi sunt nimis, qui dicunt venias illas Pape donum esse illud dei inestimabile, quo reconciliatur homo deo.
>
> 9 Gratie enim ille veniales tantum respiciunt penas satisfactionis sacramentalis ab homine constitutas.
>
> 10 Non christiana predicant, qui docent, quod redempturis animas vel confessionalia non sit necessaria contritio.
>
> I thank David Maxwell of Concordia Seminary, St. Louis, Missouri, for his assistance in the translation of Thesis 10.

Here is a significant attack on the indulgence preachers, which nonetheless maintains a defense of the pope and the proper preaching of indulgences. Claims made by the preachers are both overblown and misleading. Furthermore, they misrepresent the power of the indulgences by claiming that indulgences can forgive penalties that not even the pope has the authority to forgive. Luther makes it clear that prayers are more effective and important than indulgences. He affirms that the pope's authority to forgive is also held by the ordinary parish priest and that there is nothing superior about forgiveness through an indulgence. Particularly scathing is the attack on money in the trade of indulgences. Here he makes a pun on the tinny sound of the coin and the coffer. When the coin is trapped in the chest, there is no evidence that the soul is released from [or "soul flies out of"] purgatory. However, there is a guarantee that greed and avarice increase to such a degree that the preacher of such nonsense may be trapped by his own greed and avarice, sins that could send a person to hell. Too much was being claimed about indulgences, and the results of these assertions were both false and misleading. The indulgence preachers needed to repent, for they were leading the people to a false faith that did not save.

Addressing Concerns of Educated and High-Ranking Laypeople

Another important group was the educated laity, particularly figures such as Frederick and members of the burgher and professional classes, whose piety as well as charity were affected by the ruinous indulgences and their preaching. When dealing with the concerns of these upper classes, Luther indicated that it was difficult to defend the honor of the Church and pope against their keen criticisms. Remember that, for Luther, Frederick represented a rare prince of real piety, who really did not accept bribes and was actually concerned for his eternal life and the salvation of his subjects. Furthermore, Frederick greatly admired Luther, although perhaps he met him only once at his doctoral graduation (for which Frederick paid the fee). Later, he became better acquainted with Luther through correspondence directed through his court chaplain, George Spalatin. This insulated relationship would work well later, for when, following the Diet of Worms, Frederick was asked where Luther was, he could reply, "I really haven't seen him." Of course, by the time of the late Middle Ages, there was a whole class of townsfolk—laypeople such as doctors, artisans, lawyers, notaries, and city officials—many of whom could read Latin or could find someone to translate for them. Their criticisms could be brutal and proved difficult, if not impossible, to refute.

What follows are a few prime examples:

> [81] This licentious and empty preaching doesn't make it easy for learned men to sustain the reverence due the Pope against false charges, as well as certain astute questions from laymen:
>
> [82] They ask, "Why does the Pope not evacuate purgatory on account of most holy love and the ultimate necessity of the souls involved, which would be the most just of all causes? Rather, he releases an infinite number of souls because of most insubstantial money to build a Basilica, a most insignificant purpose."
>
> [83] Or, "Why should funeral and anniversary masses for the deceased continue, and why are the fees that support these [masses] not returned, or allowed to be returned, to those who endowed them, since it is wrong to pray for those now already redeemed [by indulgences]?"
>
> [84] Or, "What kind of novel piety is this by God and the Pope, that an impious and inimical person can, on account of grudgingly conceded money, redeem a soul, who is both pious and a friend of God, and yet because of its own need this same pious and favored soul cannot be saved simply through the love found in grace?"[24]

For Luther, the exchange of grace for money was the main issue here. People were asking, "If the pope is a good person and has the ability claimed by the indulgence preachers to liberate souls from purgatory for coin, why doesn't he just do so out of the goodness of his heart and for the sake of Christian charity?" The answer had to be either that the pope was ignorant of what was occurring (which at this point Luther believed was the case), that the pope was not a good man, or that the pope did not enjoy this power over the afterlife that some had claimed for him. Luther had earlier addressed this point by indicating that the pope neither had such power nor would he claim to have it.

---

24 WA 1:237:

> 6 Facit hec licentiosa veniarum predicatio, ut nec reventiam Pape facile sit etiam doctis viris redimere a calumniis aut certe argutis questionibus laciorum.
>
> 7 Scilicet. Cur Papa non evacuat purgatorium propter sanctissimam charitatem et summam animarum necessitatem ut causam omnium iustissimam, Si infinitas animas redimit propter pecuniam funestissimam ad structuram Basilice ut causam levissimam?
>
> 8 Item. Cur permanent exequie et anniversaria defunctorum et non reddit aut recipi permittit beneficia pro illis instuta, cum iam sit iniuria pro redemptis orare?
>
> 9 Item. Que illa nova pietas Dei et Pape, quod impio et inimico propter pecuniam concedunt animam piam et amicam dei redimere, Et tamen propter necessitatem ipsius met pie et dilecte anime non redimunt eam gratuita charitate?

Another aspect of the money issue is the matter of Masses that had been endowed for the dead. If, as the indulgence preachers claimed, the soul was immediately released from purgatory upon payment, wouldn't it be right to refund the money that was paid to endow those ongoing Masses, as they were now at best useless and possibly even injurious to those saying them? In Thesis 84 Luther makes the case that, in the view of those preaching indulgences, money is more important than either attitude or character. The word "grudgingly," which I have added for clarity, is implied in the term "conceded." Here we have a person who did not want to give the money even to free his lost relatives, but did so because to do otherwise would create a bad appearance. This was a highly vain, superficial, and unethical reason to do so. On the other hand, the pious soul who was a friend of God and in need of His grace had to be saved by such a selfish sort. Were this the case, God would no longer be a just judge. Here the generosity of God is contrasted with the stinginess of man.

Five more theses conclude this section dealing with various complaints: if the penitential canons for indulgences are expired and out of date, why doesn't the pope, a very rich man, pay for St. Peter's himself? What about those who are already truly pious and don't need indulgences? Why not give out this forgiveness for the sake of goodness and for free? If salvation of souls is the goal, why not suspend the current indulgence letters? It is no wonder that when asked by Frederick the Wise what Luther did to deserve so much wrath, Erasmus responded, "Two crimes Luther has committed. . . . He has attacked the crown of the pope and the bellies of the monks." According to Bainton, in response "Frederick laughed."[25]

Priorities of the Monks

Then there were the educated yet humble monks among the readership. Among these were found both supporters and critics. In general, the Dominicans—the great medieval heresy hunters and preachers—ended up on the attack against Luther while many of the Augustinians with their learned bent and some of the Franciscans with their practical charity would prove supportive, although many of the latter group could not go along with the notion of salvation by grace alone without works. Aspects of humility and service are present in the *Theses*, and these, as well as Luther's overall learned approach, would have been appreciated by many in the monastic communities.

---

25 Bainton, *Here I Stand*, 164.

Here are some examples of theses that would appeal to the humility prized by the monastic community:

> 3 [Penance] is not meant here in only an interior sense, for interior penance is nothing at all, unless it operates outwardly through various mortifications of the flesh. 4 Thus the penalty remains, as long as hatred of self remains (which is the true internal penance), that is, until we go into the kingdom of heaven. . . .
>
> 19 It is not established that all those [in purgatory] are certain and secure in their blessed salvation, even if it seems certain to us. . . .
>
> [39] It is extremely difficult for even the most learned Theologians in the same breath to extol the superior greatness of these empty things [indulgences] and true contrition in the hearts of the people. [40] The truly contrite ask for and love the penalties [for their sin], whereas the great empty letters make men indolent and hateful of these opportunities for salvation. . . .
>
> [94] Christians are exhorted that they should study to follow their head Christ through penalties, deaths, and hells, [95] and let them be more confident of entering heaven through many tribulations rather than through a secure peace.[26]

Luther was at the time involved in one of his theological stages of development now known as his "theology of humility." This would have appealed greatly to many of his monastic brethren, as the more serious monks believed this attribute was essential to their progress in salvation. Although these theses were designed to make Luther's case about interiority and the importance of a proper attitude in order to foster a sound belief in Jesus Christ, they would especially have appealed to the monastic class with its emphasis on zeal, humility, study, and sacrifice. In addition, many monks would have chafed at the vanity of these

---

26 WA 1:23, Thesis 3: "Non tamen solam intendit interiorem, immo interior nulla est, nisi foris operetur varias carnis mortificationes. 4 Manet itaque pena, donec manet odium sui (id est penitentia vera iustus), scilicet usque ad introitum regni celorum."

WA 1:234, Thesis 19: "Nec hoc probatum esse videtur, quod sint de sua beatitudine certe et secure, saltem omnes, licet nos certissimi simus."

WA 1:235: "14 Difficillimum est etiam doctissimis Theologis simul extollere veniarum largitatem et contritionis veritatem coram populo. 15 Contritionis veritas penas querit et amat, Veniarum autem largitas relaxat et odisse facit, saltem occasione."

WA 1:238: "19 Exhortandi sunt Christiani, ut caput suum Christum per penas mortes infernosque sequi studeant, 20 Ac sic magis per multas tribulationes intrare celum quam per securitatem pacis confidant."

indulgences when compared to the rigors of suffering the ascetic life in the footsteps of Jesus. In their view, the substance of what was actually required dwarfed the specious character of a faith grounded in improper and false piety generated from overblown claims about pieces of paper. Christians should have cultivated an attitude that the good way of life was the hard way, the path of humility and suffering with Christ.

Appeal to Early Nationalism

Another group were those who sought a culturally and linguistically united Germany. Political unity was out of the question at the time, as more than four hundred territories made up what we today call Germany. These early "nationalists"[27] included members of the knightly class and people who simply resented the drain of coin and prestige that seemed constantly headed to Rome. It was the feeling of many that, for Rome, piety was a commodity for export. Would not a homegrown German faith and life result in a condition as good as or better than the results obtained when money was constantly headed out of the country in exchange for a false, external religion? Luther himself had experienced this problem on his visit to Rome in 1510. Here there were plenty of religious sites, designed to free souls from purgation, but there were also brothels reserved for priests only and plenty of impious rushing of Masses for the dead. Many Germans saw Rome as a kind of religious mass production system that satisfied nobody, but simply brought in copious funds. Taken alongside the wealth of the Borgia and Medici clans, both of whom had recent popes from their ranks (to name only the most prominent families), there was plenty of potential for abuse. The theses we have already examined provide evidence that establishes these points.

Although Luther was aware of these nationalistic matters, he was largely quiescent on this subject in the *Theses*. This is probably because taking it up would have effectively detracted from his main argument. In a certain sense, although the *Theses* were not specifically antipapal, their general tenor on first reading could be seen as a pro-local response to the issues at hand. There are, however, places where some anti-Roman ideas inadvertently leak out. Here are a couple of examples, including a good example from Luther's critiques made by the astute laypeople, where one of the main complaints was that there was plenty

---

27 I use the terms "nationalists" and "nationalism" advisedly, as the situation differs starkly from the nation building that would later occur in the Enlightenment, Romantic, and Modern periods. One might better term what occurs here "culturalism," but that term also has its problems as it does not express political aspects of the issue.

of money in Rome and that the cathedral could easily be paid for by the Italian families who often bought and controlled the papacy:

> [51] Christians should be taught that the Pope wishes, if necessary, to sell (if it were complete) the Basilica of St. Peter, and even give of his own funds, to many of those from whom the peddlers of vanities conjure money. . . .
>
> [86] Moreover: Why doesn't the Pope, whose accumulated stuff today is most opulent compared even to the crassest of Crassuses, from his own great fund of money, rather than the impoverished believers, construct this Basilica of St. Peter?[28]

Although Luther has scrupulously avoided criticizing the pope on the matter of his handling of indulgences, this does not mean that there was nothing to be said about the matter of how he handled the financing of St. Peter's. Clearly, Luther did not consider it fair that the lands called Germany footed the bill for a construction project that could easily have been handled out of the papal treasury or by the families that vied for papal control. Others who were of a less charitable bent might apply the term "racket" to what was going on, and might view the people not from Rome as pious and upright compared to the manner in which the churchmen of Rome seemed to peddle indulgences as commerce.

Concern for the Piety of Ordinary Laypeople

Our final category of theses will be those directed to the individuals charged with the care of ordinary Christians—in other words, priests and others who preach the Word of God to the faithful. Luther had significant comments on this matter, born from his experience as a parish priest and monk, and he had firsthand experience dealing with his own crisis of faith as well as the doubts and struggles of others.

> [36] Whatever Christian is truly contrite already has full remission from both punishment and guilt, without having been granted vain letters.

---

28 WA 1:235, Thesis 1: "Docendi sunt christiani, quod Papa sicut debet ita vellet, etiam vendita (si opus sit) Basilica s. Petri, de suis pecuniis dare illis, a quorum plurimis quidam concionatores veniarum pecuniam eliciunt."

WA 1:237, Thesis 11: "Item. Cur Papa, cuius opes hodie sunt opulentissimis Crassus crassiores, non de suis pecuniis magis quam pauperum fidelium struit unam tantummodo Basilicam sancti Petri?"

[37] Whatever Christian there is, whether alive or dead, already has participation in all the benefits of Christ and the Church, without empty letters, and has been given these benefits by God Himself. . . .

[40] True contrition seeks out and loves these penalties, but the empty indulgences greatly relax people and make penalties odious to them, according to the occasion.

[41] These venial apostolic letters should be proclaimed cautiously, so the people neither falsely understand them nor prefer them to other good works of charity.

[42] Christians should be taught that the Pope is not of a mind that vain letters should in any way be compared to works of mercy.

[43] Christians should be taught that whoever gives to the poor or lends to those in need does better than if he buys vain letters.

[44] For through works of charity, charity increases and makes a man better, but through empty letters nothing becomes better in him except his ability to be free of penalties.

[45] Christians should be taught that whoever sees someone in need and fails to give to him, and instead buys himself an indulgence, has not purchased a Papal indulgence but procured God's wrath.

[46] Christians should be taught that unless they have a superfluous abundance beyond what they need to maintain their household, they should keep their money and under no circumstances waste it on vain letters.

[47] Christians should be taught that they are free to purchase indulgences, not that it is required.

[48] Christians should be taught that, more than vain letters and immediate cash, the Pope both needs and desires their pious prayers on his behalf.

[49] Christians should be taught that vain Papal letters are only useful if they don't rely on them, but are toxic if they lose the fear of God through them.

[50] Christians should be taught that if the Pope knew of the exactions of the preachers of vanities, he would pound the Basilica of St. Peter into ashes rather than see it built on the skin, flesh, and bones of his sheep.

[51] Christians should be taught that the Pope wishes, if necessary, to sell (if it were complete) the Basilica of St. Peter, and even give of

his own funds, to many of those from whom the peddlers of vanities conjure money.[29]

Here we find down-to-earth advice to pastors for advising their flocks. People needed to spend their money on their homes, their families, their neighbors and others rather than waste money on indulgences. People should not be seeking to avoid the penalties of their sins, but rather rejoice in the discipline of the Lord who makes them stronger and better individuals in the Christian life by chastisements. Love and its works should govern all actions that grow out of the Gospel of Jesus Christ, and the fruit of that growth would be good Christian

---

29 WA 1:235:

11 Quilibet christianus vere compunctus haet remissionem plenariam a pena et culpa etiam sine literis veniarum sibi debitam.

12 Quilibet verus christianus, sive vivus sive mortuus, habet participationem omnium bonorum Christi et Ecclesie etiam sine literis veniarum a deo sibi datam. . . .

15 Contritionis veritas penas querit et amat, Veniarum autem largitas relaxat et odisse facit, saltem occasione.

16 Caute sunt venie apostolice predicande, ne populus false intelligat eas preferri ceteris bonis operibus charitatis.

17 Docendi sunt christiani, quod Pape mens non est, redemptionem veniarum ulla ex parte comparandam esse operibus misericordie.

18 Docendi sunt christiani, quod dans pauperi aut mutuans egenti melius facit quam si venias redimeret.

19 Quia per opus charitatis crescit charitas et fit homo melior, sed per venias non fit melior sed tantummodo a pena liberior.

20 Docendi sunt christiani, quod, qui videt egenum et neglecto eo dat pro veniis, non indulgentias Pape set indignationem dei sibi vendicant.

21 Docendi sunt christiani, quod nisi superfluis abundent necessaria tenentur domui sue retinere et nequamquam propter venias effundere.

22 Docendi sunt christiani, quod redeptio veniarum est libera, non precepta.

23 Docendi sunt christiani, quod Papa sicut magis eget ita magis optat in veniis dandis pro se devotam orationem quam proptam pecuniam.

24 Docendi sunt christiani, quod venie Pape sunt utiles, si non in eas confidant, Set nocentissime, si timorem dei per eas amittant.

25 Docendi sunt christiani, quod, si Papa nosset exactiones venialium predicatorum, mallet Basilicam s. Petri in cineres ire quam edificari cute, carne et ossibus ovium suarum.

1 Docendi sunt christiani, quod Papa sicut debet ita vellet, etiam vendita (si opus sit) Basilica s. Petri, de suis pecuniis dare illis, a quorum plurimis quidam concionatores veniarum pecuniam eliciunt.

citizens who take care of their faith and their livelihoods rather than squandering their money on vain things such as indulgences. Luther believed that the pope cared about such people and that, were he aware of the abuses, he would put a stop to them and pay for St. Peter's himself. Luther's major concern here was the loss of piety and the fear of the Lord that accompanied the cheapest and least authentic kind of grace heralded by the indulgence preachers. This destruction of piety endangered the souls of believing Christians who knew no better. It should be noted that Luther did not consider himself to be converting people to Christianity but rather removing the misery imposed by the lies being preached, thereby eliminating a danger to the souls of believers who might otherwise be led astray.

How Various Groups Responded to the *Theses*

What were the responses, where they can be determined, of the various groups Luther had in mind as he penned the *Theses*? As far as the humanists in Germany were concerned, as they were not all of one mind on the question of what constituted proper faith and yet tended to eschew scholasticism, most were with Luther. In fact, they worked to spread his teachings, and Luther both reached out to them and sometimes received letters that were both enthusiastic in tone and full of questions. Luther also worked with John Lang, known as a humanist, who early on helped him with Greek exegetical problems. Of course, there was also the faculty at Wittenberg University that, at Luther's urging, had embarked a few years earlier on a course of curriculum reform that involved bolstering the study of Greek and Hebrew while reducing the customary reliance on Aristotle. Several faculty were retired as a part of this process, replaced with members amenable to the humanist way of learning. As we know, the faculty in general gladly received the *Theses*, and members such as Andreas Karlstadt, as well as Philip Melanchthon, who joined the faculty about a year later, were certainly supportive of this early stage of Luther's program. Melanchthon would become a lifelong supporter. Karlstadt and Luther would have a falling out over the pace of change as well as over Karlstadt's willingness to dissent from the theology generally promoted at Wittenberg. "Brother Andreas" would soon be numbered with the radicals.

Another person of interest is Desiderius Erasmus (ca. 1467–1536), who as far as Renaissance humanism is concerned may have been the greatest figure of all. Certainly Erasmus took an initial interest in the progress of the

Reformation under Luther and defended him on various occasions, as when he corresponded with Frederick the Wise. As so many others, Erasmus had his own ideas about reform. While it appeared that Luther was advancing these ideas, Erasmus did little to hinder Luther's work. Yet Erasmus never really provided public support. This angered Luther, who would soon find himself under the gun (or, rather, facing the stake). In addition, Erasmus prevented his publishers from printing Luther's writings after he found they had published one of the reformer's early works. On the other hand, Erasmus sent a copy of the *Theses* to Thomas More, a well-known humanist and rising adviser to Henry VIII, and by this means abetted their spread to England. More, in his turn, was likely a significant contributor of advice to Henry VIII's pamphlet against Luther, which won the monarch the papal title "Defender of the Faith." I think Lewis Spitz had it right when he said about many of the figures who were humanists that those who were younger than Luther tended to follow his cause while most of those older than Luther did not, possibly out of concern for their need for security in their old age.[30]

What was the response of the second group, Luther's ecclesiastical superiors? The archbishop of Mainz, to whom Luther sent the *Theses* with a long letter exhorting him to stamp out the abuses of the indulgence traders, passed the buck by sending the letter and its attachments on to Rome. It took about a month for the *Theses* to reach Albert, and then probably another month for them to reach Rome. The papal response was multifold. First, when it became apparent that the *Theses* had some bite and were cutting into the revenues of the campaign to build St. Peter's, Luther was to be confronted and to recant or to be essentially muzzled. In this regard, the pope dispatched Cardinal Cajetan, the foremost scholar of the day on Thomas Aquinas, to meet with Luther. While the reformer expected a hearing at which he could have his questions answered from Scripture by one of the best intellects of the day, the encounter rapidly broke down, with Cardinal Cajetan demanding that Luther simply recant his teachings. For his part, Luther's questions left Cajetan, unfamiliar as he was with Luther's line of thought, befuddled. Of course, others were sent to negotiate with and attempt to bribe the elector (implying that Luther could be named a cardinal, perhaps with an eye to promoting Luther into silence) by granting Frederick the Golden Rose, a kind of princely merit badge of honor from the pope. The rose itself had significant value, as it was typically made from between four and eight pounds of gold (at the time valued at perhaps $70,000 to $140,000,

30 Lewis Spitz, *The Religious Renaissance of the German Humanists* (Cambridge, MA: Harvard University Press, 1963), 291, 292.

depending on the purity of the metal as well as the weight).[31] Frederick was judicious enough to refuse the bribe. Furthermore, Luther enjoyed a real advantage with the elector, as he was able to write to him in German and during the dusty tedium of business often made him laugh by peppering his letters with little jabs at his opponents. Later, Luther debated his views at Leipzig and was eventually excommunicated. Ultimately, following his appearance at the Diet of Worms, he was declared an outlaw in the empire. None of these tactics were worthy of Luther's affirmative defense of the pope, but simply drove him to the conclusions of his thinking to such a degree that he would soon repudiate his early statements found in the *Theses* as too soft. For example, instead of debating indulgences, he would later dismiss the entire notion of purgatory as unscriptural and counterproductive to the message of grace found in the Gospel.

Monastic orders would also respond to Luther in various ways. His own order, the Augustinians, was largely supportive, as many of the concerns Luther held were not entirely foreign to the teaching of Augustine. He was welcomed to defend his teachings at the Augustinian cloister in Heidelberg, a venue at which not only members of his order but also other interested parties were in attendance. There he produced and discussed twenty-eight theological and twelve philosophical theses that represented a more positive presentation of his reform message. The theological theses were indirectly against Aristotle or, to be more specific, the medieval scholastic positions that had arisen from Aristotle's ethics. In addition, Luther advanced a theology of the cross in which God's Word was the essential criterion for judging what constituted the good and the bad, the saved and the damned, rather than judgments arrived at by means of a theology of glory founded on worldly appearances and standards. The twelve philosophical theses were written directly against the philosophical positions of Aristotle.

Luther had the most difficulties with the Franciscan and Dominican orders. Many of the Franciscans were discontented with the ideas Luther expressed that might hinder the works of charity they so loved. Ironically, Luther's teaching in fuller form would not have interfered with these at all, as he believed that justification by grace through faith in Christ changed persons so that they were prone to producing good works from their new nature. The Dominicans were definitely against Luther and his teachings. These preachers and heresy hunters saw in Luther a fresh target. Johann Eck and Luther had been introduced prior

---

31 I have been unable to find the exact weight of the rose awarded Frederick. The bribe was actually to sway the prince elector to vote for Francis I, the papal candidate for Holy Roman emperor. Frederick instead supported Charles I of Spain, who subsequently become Emperor Charles V.

to the reform controversy and had previously been on relatively good terms. But when Eck attacked Luther's teaching and later unfairly declared himself the victor after the Leipzig Debate (the Leipzig faculty was not supposed to render a verdict, according to the terms agreed upon, but they did anyway), Luther's disgust with him became visceral. Luther excoriated Eck in many of the letters he penned in the time between Leipzig and the Diet of Worms, after which time he appears to have left the matter behind. There was little or no direct response from the monks to Luther's "theology of humility" statements in the *Theses*.

What of the German nationalists? Here Luther received much support. First, there were the knights who supported Luther: Ulrich von Hutten and Franz von Sickingen. The term "nationalism" here has to be taken with a grain of salt, as it does not represent the nationalism that binds everybody together under allegiance to one state that was later a hallmark of the nineteenth and twentieth centuries. Rather, here we see a kind of people's nationalism, a resentment toward foreign influences and a pride in German culture. Hutten had extensively supported such positions and became an ardent Luther supporter. Sickingen was an active knight and offered the support of himself and his men in protecting Luther and promoting the cause of reform through military means. The reformer refused the support, instead choosing to rely on God, something that worked in his favor as the knights were soon wiped out in battle, and Hutten soon after died of syphilis. There were many other supporters among the common people who were sick of foreign influences and saw in Luther a way of having their own grievances heard. Luther discovered this paradox of his popularity and notoriety both in the great reception he received from strangers as he journeyed to Worms in April 1521 and much later in the peasants' disappointment over Luther's condemnation of their actions during the Peasants' Revolt of 1524–25.

One of the best ways to understand the reception of Luther's ideas by the educated laypeople was the rapid acceptance of the Reformation in many cities and towns. By the late Middle Ages towns and cities had important legal privileges. As a result, their citizens did not readily fit into the three traditional strata of clerics, nobles, and peasants. Having obtained charters from the local nobles, free towns and cities expressly made the wishes of their communities known by their adoption or eschewing of the new reforms. In many cases the lay burghers of these towns and cities readily accepted the teachings of the Reformation, and in fact the magistrates and council members of these municipalities—often lawyers and other educated individuals—moved rapidly for the conversion of the churches from papal traditions to the new way.

In the case of the princes themselves the waters are a bit murkier, especially as to what their actual motives (as opposed to their stated ones) may have been for adopting the Reformation. In their case there was a tremendous incentive to adopt the new faith, as it resulted in the closure of monasteries and the return of control of those lands to the prince. In many cases Rome would make offers to princes—for example, to levy taxes on the Church in their territories—in order to counter this Reformation pressure. It is not that there were not princes who sincerely believed the teachings of Luther's *Theses* and the Reformation, but determining why particular territories signed up for the movement is not simple.

In the case of ordinary laypeople, the picture is clouded by a lack of records. However, it can be said from the general picture painted by visitors, such as the emissaries who attempted to issue the bull of excommunication for Luther, that the vast majority of people from all walks of life favored Luther, and the remainder were against the pope. A good sign of the general reception of Luther's works among the average people, the *Ninety-Five Theses* included, was that Luther was in 1521 declared to be an outlaw and could have been killed with impunity, but he lived without a bodyguard until he died twenty-five years later, in his old age, of natural causes.

Furthermore, we know that the clergy were often listening and receptive to Luther. When he later declared that clergy should be able to marry and that celibacy was optional, almost immediately those priests who had been living with women in "clerical marriage" (a euphemism for clerical concubinage) regularized their families by openly marrying. Many others who had lived in celibacy, like Martin Luther himself, also eventually married. Consideration must be given to the fact that it was somewhat depressing to conceive of a God of such difficult standards of purity or to believe in long-term purgatorial punishments. The *Theses* broke the ice for Luther's later writings that more clearly and centrally stated that Jesus Christ is compassionate and that God graciously favors those who have faith in Him.

But what of the more purely academic responses to Luther? An interesting case is found in the correspondence between Luther and Dungersheim von Ochsenfurt. Luther began to receive letters from Dungersheim in late 1519. Exhaustive treatments, chock-full of citations from medieval and ancient fathers, would be the best way to describe them. They are extensive, as many as twenty pages long in print, with a total of seven exemplars in all, only two of which are printed in the Weimar edition, providing the correspondence applicable to

Luther's replies.[32] Luther was at first cordial and congratulates Dungersheim on taking his positions seriously and attempting an answer, but after the second letter, he rather unceremoniously dismisses his opponent's epistles, indicating that they are actually volumes and that he did not have time to answer them. Besides, he said, they missed the point of the Gospel, as though stacking up innumerable wrongheaded statements made them stronger. The point here is that there were people in academia who were really trying to understand Luther and to convert and reconcile him again to the papal church, and he in turn was charitable to them, to a point.

Another issue is the unanticipated effects of the *Ninety-Five Theses*. Luther had opened a kind of Pandora's box of revolutionary results. This is the case in the work of other reformers Luther inspired, some of whom he would later repudiate. Many visions of what would constitute an ideal reformation emerged, particularly in the light of the doctrine of *sola scriptura*. The problem was well characterized by none other than Johann Eck, who warned that if there were not one interpretation of the Scriptures, made by the pope, there would be a myriad of different interpretations by individuals. Many, like Karlstadt, came to the conclusion that the slow pace of Luther's Reformation caused sin in the people. Others, like Thomas Müntzer, thought Luther not socially radical enough, and they ended up waging a disastrous war for the Word of God. Erasmus thought that Luther went too far and was too bold and too concerned about inner matters rather than focusing on sincere piety and a purer practice. The French reformer John Calvin, later active in the city of Geneva, considered himself Lutheran in that he believed he sincerely followed Luther's teaching (particularly through the lens of Luther's most extensive theological book, *On the Bondage of the Will*), yet Lutheranism would eschew Calvinist teachings as too coldly rational and as not properly considering the tensions found in Scripture. And who can forget Huldrych Zwingli, the reformer of Zurich, whom Luther characterized at the Marburg Colloquy (1529) as having a different spirit. Many scholars believe that Zwingli walked his own path but at the very least was inspired to walk that path by the groundbreaking work of Luther. In each of these cases, the *Ninety-Five Theses* broke the ice, and subsequent writings caused varying responses. Many walked along the road with Luther for a time, but broke with him when they discovered that Luther's vision of the Reformation did not match their own. For his part, Luther also changed the application and emphasis of his message

32 The two examples from Dungersheim to Luther in the Weimar edition of Luther's correspondence are eight and twenty printed pages, respectively. See WA Br 1:517–24, 574–94. Luther's replies to Dungersheim appear at WA Br 1:566–68 and 601–3.

in response to various considerations and opinions that arose. For example, he was prepared to delay practicing the Mass in German for the sake of the political position faced by Frederick until after the prince's death in 1525. He was also ready to place greater emphasis on ordination as a mark of the Church's approval than he had early on—in his *Babylonian Captivity of the Church*, in which he largely dismisses ordination as not a sacrament—when he saw the challenges to an orderly church life occasioned by the rise of the radical reformers.

Relevance of the *Ninety-Five Theses* Today

So how can we receive Luther's Reformation, and more specifically the *Ninety-Five Theses*, today? It is certain that the same issues that vexed the Church at the time of the Reformation are still present today. At the core of Luther's complaint was that people were seeking comfort in the wrong things. This certainly remains a significant pastoral issue today. Churches often wrongly prioritize their obligations, accenting worldly ideas and priorities over truly sound, biblically based faith and hope—a concern Luther also brought to the fore in his day. Leadership problems can also be found in many places, and there are still people who, unlike Luther, will not give the authorities the benefit of the doubt until the true facts come to light. We can see Luther doing this in his *Theses* through his defense of the pope, a matter on which he would later reverse his position. It is certainly also true that there remain those who repent of nothing, as they do not believe in the depths of their depravity. Moreover, many have little appreciation for the Gospel as the power of God for salvation to all who believe.[33] Certainly there are some issues in the *Theses*—in particular various technical concerns about indulgences—that have been "corrected" by those who still believe in purgatory. Luther would later deprive the argument for indulgences of oxygen by eliminating purgatory as unbiblical and redefining in a scriptural manner the relationship of the saints (all believers in forgiveness through Christ) to eternal life.

Other broader issues could also be raised. Matters of academic and personal protest and the ability of Luther as an individual to survive the onslaught he faced and to thrive under it have certainly inspired others to speak out on various causes. Although Luther would not have approved of much of what has subsequently occurred, his bold approach has certainly inspired many. Rights of the individual to protest have been greatly expanded since Luther's day, in part

33 Rom. 1:16, paraphrased.

because of his modest yet outraged protest against the misery and impiety he witnessed some five hundred years ago. And so there is still relevance to Luther's protest, even at a time so far removed from his.

THE AFTERMATH OF THE *NINETY-FIVE THESES* AND THE DEVELOPMENT OF A REFORMER

Luther experienced a period of relative calm in the immediate aftermath of the distribution of the *Theses*. After about six months, however, the hiatus caused by slow communications ended, and Luther found himself on quite a hot seat. Tetzel, the Dominican preacher of indulgences, had armed himself with a largely ghostwritten set of theses he defended in a contrived disputation. He was declared a doctor, however, and so was theoretically able to debate Luther on these matters. He immediately produced propositions of his own against the reformer. Luther responded with explanations of his own theses. At this juncture, Luther was asked to make the dispute private and not engage in public debate on the matter. This he agreed to do, provided his opponents did the same. When they did not comply (which happened almost immediately), Luther felt free to air his views again and again.

Luther held several advantages that were not typical for his day. His prince, Frederick the Wise, was an elector in the Holy Roman Empire and so could not be easily invaded or sanctioned politically, except in a case such as gross apostasy. For this reason he remained Roman Catholic and preserved the Latin Mass in his territory, sheltering the newly founded Reformation. Once he had decided to protect Luther, therefore, not much could be done to dislodge the new movement from his realm. Frederick held such sway that the pope himself recommended him along with Francis I, king of France, to replace Holy Roman emperor Maximillian, who had died in 1519. Frederick refused the massive bribes being offered by both sides in the succession process and so won the trust of all. He basically chaired the meeting at which the papal candidate Francis was unanimously rejected in favor of the Spanish Habsburg sovereign, Charles. As a result, Charles owed Frederick a major favor and willingly listened to his advice. When the matter of Luther's trial came up, Frederick broached the possibility and advantages of holding the proceeding in Germany rather than in Rome. This would help to redress the imbalance between pope and empire, adding to imperial prestige and authority. By keeping the matter in a secular court and settling it at a diet (congress) of the empire, the pope would not completely have his way and the emperor could bolster his authority in a concrete and public manner.

In addition, there was Luther's incredible popularity, of which he was mostly ignorant until he journeyed to Worms in the spring of 1521. It was extremely difficult for Luther's opponents to make any headway in the lands that supported him. Bainton comments on this when he says, "Aleander, the papal nuncio in Germany, reported that nine tenths of the Germans cried, 'Luther,' and the other one tenth, 'Death to the Pope.' This was unquestionably an exaggeration."[34] Luther also enjoyed an advantage with his prince as he was both one of his favorites and could correspond with him in German, including inside jokes to spice up his letters. It is easy to see how the sometimes ribald quips would engage Frederick in ways that the dry, translated Latin from the papal emissaries could not. Furthermore, Luther's colleagues ran interference for him, and so the Reformation in important ways amounted to a team effort, of which he was the inspirational and guiding force at Wittenberg. Significant contributions were made early on by both Karlstadt and, after he arrived, Melanchthon. Luther was both protected and supported by many and was so revered that even after he was placed under the death warrant at Worms, he lived out his natural life without a bodyguard, though always within the protection of his prince's and other supporters' lands.

Of course, of great interest to many is the reformer's theological development. From our study of the *Ninety-Five Theses* it becomes evident that Luther was, at this early stage of his career, loyal to the papal church. He attacked only what he considered abusive elements and limited those attacks to particular issues. General reformation was not really evident in this early document. Because Luther's positions were ignored and eventually largely rejected, his thought crystallized, and he became more and more willing to abandon and condemn what he regarded as practices questionable and contrary to Scripture. Eventually he embarked on a positive program of establishing a Reformation Church.

First, Luther wrote to clarify the indulgence question, penning explanations for each of the *Theses*. He was asked to silence himself after this document was produced, and he did for a time, until his opponents began writing again. Soon, at the Heidelberg Disputation, he presented a stunning case against the appearance-driven theology of Aristotle, which he styled a theology of glory. This he replaced with the "Word as Christ crucified," a theology driven by the writings of the apostle Paul and others, which he termed the theology of the cross. External goodness and success might hide actual evil and failure, but those who sought the will of God through a cross-based appropriation of God's Word were able to work the truly good and gracious will of their Lord and receive and

34 Bainton, *Here I Stand*, 130.

promote His kingdom. Furthermore, Luther would confuse and flummox one of the most skilled theologians of the day with his use of the new scriptural theology. Cardinal Cajetan was supposed to interview Luther and grant him a hearing. It had all been arranged with Prince Frederick. Instead, over a multiday period, Luther was repeatedly ordered simply to recant even as he kept asking for scriptural evidence of where he was wrong. Cajetan finally stormed out of the interview in frustration, wrote a scathing report to Frederick, and intended to order Luther to face trial in Rome. Luther, for his part, responded that there really was no interview and that only one command passed the cardinal's lips: "revoco," or "recant" in English.

Another development, somewhat surprising to the reformer, was his locking of horns with Johann Eck. The two had been introduced earlier and had been on at least cordial terms. Karlstadt, Luther's colleague and friend, had accepted an invitation to debate Eck, and Luther was also to appear. However, this invitation was altered, rescinded, and reinstated several times over the next six months. Luther smelled a rat and prepared himself for the debate by deeply studying many of the texts of the early church fathers, as well as by deepening his study of Scripture. He had been right in guessing that he was going to be dragged into the debate, for once it was ruled that Karlstadt could no longer use the books he had brought, he began to falter. Luther was then pressed into service in a debate that most believe was more or less argued to a draw (over about two weeks). The terms of the debate had called for two neutral universities (Paris and Erfurt) to render a verdict as to the victor. But the University of Leipzig declared Eck the winner, and he paraded this news that he had bested Luther the heretic, something that vexed the reformer to no end. In the more than 190 letters Luther answers over the next two years, Luther insults or belittles Eck in many of them. After the Diet of Worms, he drops the matter, as there were other fish to fry.

The Leipzig Debate, more than any other event, amounted to a turning point for the reformer. At this point he knew that his opponents would stop at nothing to destroy the new Gospel message and to silence its messenger. He declared that he would protect himself with nothing but the Word of God. Here was a moment of pure dependence. Luther's "discovery of the Gospel" might be seen, therefore, as a process in which the reformer discovered various parts of the Gospel in various stages or through various insights. Certainly, there were aspects of the Gospel that he had already understood and taught in his lectures on the Psalms from 1513, but that was just the beginning of a deeper appreciation that would come only through the hardships of danger and rejection. Luther waged an emotional, highly personal battle for the Gospel that would last his entire life. There was one occasion when Katie (whom he married in

June 1525) dressed herself in funeral garb because Martin had been despondent for about a month. He asked her tenderly who had died, and her response was that obviously God had, and she wanted to join him in his mourning. In terms of repentance and the monastic life he had taken on, reform came slowly as well, and Luther did not remove the cowl and give up praying the canonical hours until about the time of the Diet of Worms. Forensic justification, the teaching that one is saved by and created a new person through being declared righteous by God rather than by one's own effort, was not fully developed until the arrival of his young colleague Philip Melanchthon. Lowell Green has credited his influence with that element of Luther's doctrine.[35] What was different after Leipzig was that Luther, with a mature personal and intellectual understanding of the Gospel and the Scriptures, now depended more or less solely upon them. So he rejected the help of German knights who offered him their protection. This is also the period when he questioned and rejected ideas such as purgatory and the cult of the saints, as well as many other popular and long-standing traditions of piety. However, he eliminated them gently, not forcing people to immediately give up the practices themselves. Rather, by feeding them through the Word of God, they would eventually outgrow and eschew these weak habits.

The aftermath of the Leipzig Debate also represented a time of great creativity for the reformer. At least four great reformation treatises were produced in 1520 alone. And he preached on the two kinds of righteousness in a sermon. Here he expresses the idea that there are actually three kinds of things people call righteousness, but the first, generated by human sacrifices and works, is false. The first true, or proper, kind of righteousness is Christ's righteousness that He has freely offered the penitent sinner by His sacrifice on the cross. In this type, God's gracious character is the sole reason that the sinner finds salvation. Luther therefore styles it a passive righteousness, a term that indicates not passive behavior but rather the received quality of the salvation. From this emerges a second true kind of righteousness, for the renewed person then is able to conduct himself freely in life as a new creation, doing good works for the neighbor and making acceptable sacrifices to God. Because the Christian still has a sinful nature, he is seen as *simul iustus et peccator*, at the same time saint and sinner. Although the Christian is a sinner, this does not hold back the new nature from also doing good, being compelled by Christ's love to do so willingly.

In *The Freedom of a Christian*, Luther recapitulates the teaching of two kinds of righteousness. The tract itself begins with an open letter to Pope Leo X

35 See Lowell Green, *How Melanchthon Helped Luther Discover the Gospel: The Doctrine of Justification in the Reformation* (Fallbrook, CA: Verdict Publications, 1980), 213–50.

in which Luther requests that the pope not listen to those around him who have misrepresented Luther's positions, but rather act to clean up the corruption of Rome and to use the accompanying tract as a guide to reform. The tract itself expresses Luther's famous propositions that the "Christian is the true lord of all, subject to none; and that the Christian is the dutiful servant of all and subject to all."[36] These paradoxical statements are then proven scripturally—first, by discussing the renewal of people through justification, then by discussing their new justified life and its attendant good works. Finally, Luther cannot resist getting into the worship wars of his day, decrying both those enthralled with truly empty ceremonies and people who constantly wanted to change everything, including practices that were at the least harmless and perhaps even salutary and useful. Here he proposes the use of the classical "golden mean," asking his hearers not to fall into either the ditch of iconoclasm or the ditch of empty ceremony. In the end, the Christian is freed by Christ to serve God and the neighbor. That the freedom is without limits is not evident in this world, but can only be perceived through the eyes of faith. Here we labor and suffer.

Furthermore, Luther wrote *On the Babylonian Captivity of the Church* concerning the sacraments of the Church. Beginning with the argument that no intelligent person would quibble over how many sacraments there actually are (the medieval period had theologians who listed as many as forty), he ends up determining two or three, depending on what part of the tract he is writing. Sacraments typically have an element and were always instituted by Christ Himself. This left Baptism and the Lord's Supper—and, if one ignored the element requirement, Absolution or the forgiveness of sins. Confirmation, ordination, matrimony, and extreme unction were rejected as sacraments, but the first three were encouraged as practices so long as they were performed in conformity with the Scriptures. Extreme unction would require a complete revamping to be acceptable as a practice by scriptural standards.

Finally, there was the *Address to the Christian Nobility of the German Nation concerning the Amelioration of the State of Christendom*. In this document, Luther appealed to the German nobles (hundreds of leaders of territories in the Holy Roman Empire) to do what they had done in the past—reform or bring improvement to the Church. Here Luther laid out the doctrine of the two realms or kingdoms in which he balanced the sacred and secular spheres and declared that each sphere must enhance the other or, when it was out of line, bring it into check. His argument was that there is a priesthood of all believers. Therefore, even secular governments could be called upon to make some

36 WA 7:21, 49 (my translation; cf. AE 31:344).

ecclesiastical decisions, redressing imbalances when abuses had arisen and the normally responsible authorities, the bishops, refused to act. He then provided concrete proposals for matters that should be reformed in Christendom, especially regarding the structure of the Church and its message.

Soon the reformer would be excommunicated, although the process took six months rather than sixty days, as there was no printer who would publish the papal bull against Luther. After this, Luther was given an opportunity for a trial at Worms. Here, when presented with his works, he took his stand and refused to take back the truth of God's Word as he had written about it. He was eventually rejected by the diet and declared an outlaw, meaning that anybody who encountered him could kill him with impunity. Frederick arranged with his court chaplain, Spalatin, to have Luther spirited away to the Wartburg Castle. There Luther began the real task of building a new evangelical movement for reforming the Church, particularly by translating the entire text of the New Testament from Greek and his memorized Latin, as well as producing two volumes of model sermons (postils) to better demonstrate evangelical preaching. Much more could be said about his later life, but suffice it to say, by now he was unmistakably a reformer of Christendom.

The *Ninety-Five Theses* were Luther's opening attempt at reform, but they were a limited salvo against certain specific and identifiable abuses. It was not his program at that time to reform the entire Church and change much of its theology of sin and grace. The papal church's response to his initial attempt at improvement was what led him down the path of reformation and protest that would eventually lead to the development of the Lutheran Church. Many other reform movements also rose from the work of Luther, owing their establishment and identity either to identification with his teachings or opposition to them. The *Theses* alone may be surprisingly non-reformational in some of their themes, such as their defense of the pope, but they did indicate a new willingness to critique and change some practices of the Church, changes that would be amplified and broadened by subsequent events. Luther would not compromise on his beloved Scripture and was ready to lay down his life for the cause of the Gospel. Had not others intervened, this would likely have been the course of events, but they did, and so, as I have already indicated, without a bodyguard, Luther the reformer died of the diseases of advanced years, and not because he was condemned by the Church.

The Reformation Message: Luther's Reform and Wright's Redefinition of Justification

Jonathan Mumme

Friends or Foes: A Real Challenge to the Reformation's Main Message?

In the year 1545, an aged Martin Luther noted in the preface to his collected Latin works that the watershed juncture of what would come to be known as the Reformation had to do with divine and human righteousness, that is, with the righteousness of God and human standing with God in His righteousness.[1] As he reflected on events of more than twenty-five years previous, Luther described that he had once pursued matters pertaining to salvation "with all seriousness . . . in dread of the last day . . . from the depth of my heart want[ing] to be saved,"[2] yet not in a way that could set his conscience at rest.[3] A personal and theological metamorphosis transpired when he moved from understanding the righteousness of "the righteous God who punishes sinners"[4] as a righteousness according to which God Himself is just and scourges that which is not, to grasping this righteousness as a righteousness which God gives, a "passive righteousness

1 *Preface to the Complete Edition of Luther's Latin Writings* (1545), AE 34:327–38, WA 54:179–87.

2 AE 34:328, WA 54:179.24.

3 AE 34:336f., WA 54:185.21–186.2.

4 AE 34:336, WA 54:185.23f.

with which merciful God justifies us by faith."[5] This insight into the writings of Paul and the whole of the Sacred Scriptures, which Luther described as a personal rebirth,[6] would eventually contribute to a reconfiguration of Europe and a restructuring of the Western Church.

The reform movement beginning with Luther and moving out from Wittenberg, though influenced also by other factors, had, irreducibly, to do with something called "justification." The attestation of colleagues,[7] the attempted appropriation by students and heirs,[8] and the anathematization by opponents[9] all affirm the centrality of the doctrine of justification in and for the Reformation. "The article of justification is the master and prince, lord, ruler and judge over all kinds of doctrines. It preserves and governs all ecclesial doctrine and raises up our conscience before God. Without this article the world is nothing but death and darkness," said Luther.[10] Of the confrontation with the papacy and scholastic theology that was reshaping the Western Church Luther could say, "We . . . taught and urged nothing except this doctrine of justification."[11]

The Reformation's main message had, without a doubt, to do with the doctrine of justification and specifically with that doctrine as taught by the apostle Paul. Thus, when a new or revised interpretation of Paul's teaching on justification is offered, it can stand as a challenge to the teaching that was at the heart of Luther's reform movement or it can outright score cutting-edge scholarly points by calling "the Reformation doctrine of justification"[12] into question. The so-called New Perspective on Paul has posed just such a challenge, and its most

---

5 AE 34:337, WA 54:186.7f.

6 AE 34:337, WA 54:186.8.

7 Philip Melanchthon, *Melanchthon on Christian Doctrine: Loci Communes, 1555*, trans. and ed. Clyde L. Manschreck (Grand Rapids: Baker, 1965), 151.

8 E.g., FC SD III 67.

9 E.g., the Council of Trent's canons concerning justification, especially nos. 9 and 12–14; see Norman P. Tanner, ed., *Decrees of the Ecumenical Councils* (London: Sheed & Ward, 1990), 2:679f.

10 *Die Promotionsdisputation von Palladius und Tilemann* (1537), WA 39/1:205.2–5.

11 *Lectures on Galatians* (1535), AE 26:223, WA 40/1:356.16–18.

12 On the question whether there was a uniform Reformation doctrine of justification, see Berndt Hamm, "What Was the Reformation Doctrine of Justification?" in *The German Reformation: The Essential Readings*, ed. C. Scott Dixon (Oxford: Blackwell, 1999), 56–90; David C. Fink, "Was There a 'Reformation Doctrine of Justification'?" *Harvard Theological Review* 103, no. 2 (2010): 205–35; and Korey D. Mass, "Justification by Faith Alone," in *Reformation Theology: A Systematic Summary*, ed. Matthew Barrett (Wheaton: Crossway, 2017), 511–48.

prominent proponent, N. T. Wright, offers a perspective on Paul's understanding of justification that is "fresh" (at least according to Wright himself) precisely in differing from Luther and the "Lutheran" reading of Paul.

Granting that for Luther justification and salvation are rather synonymous, a step that will be explained below, this article will take N. T. Wright as a representative of the New Perspective on Paul and argue that Wright does offer some improvements to Luther's understanding of Paul's doctrine of justification. However, Wright's rejection of Luther's teaching on justification is based as much on a misreading of Luther as it is on any cutting-edge reading of Paul. Further, it will be demonstrated that, holistically considered, Luther's soteriology—that is, his understanding of how human beings are saved—corresponds to and aligns with Wright's own presentation of Pauline soteriology to a surprising degree. This suggests that, despite Wright's constant attempt to score points with his fresh perspective on Paul by using Luther as part of his foil, these ostensible foes actually have the potential to be fast friends who mutually sharpen each other's reading of Paul. Thereby this article means to take Wright's "Luther" out of his hand and in turn to open Wright's work to Lutheran readers of Paul.

Turning first to Wright, an attempt will be made to summarize his understanding of Paul's doctrine of justification and how this differs from the standard, classic, or, as he says, "Lutheran" reading of Paul. Thereafter observations about Luther's doctrine of justification will be offered, before finally discussing the grand overlap between these two systems and the possibility for mutual amelioration.

Wright on Rightly Reading Justification against the "Lutheran" Wrong

The so-called New Perspective on Paul, as self-avowed New Perspective scholars readily admit, actually includes multiple perspectives on Paul.[13] However, a leading and unifying characteristic of this school of interpretation is the intention and effort to read and understand the apostle Paul in his proper historical context, especially within the Second Temple Judaism of the first century. Paul, New Perspective theologians argue, did not understand Judaism as a religion of legalism, to which Christianity, a religion of grace, was the right alternative.[14]

13 N. T. Wright, *Justification: God's Plan and Paul's Vision* (Downers Grove, IL: IVP Academic, 2009), 28.

14 N.T. Wright, *Paul: In Fresh Perspective* (Minneapolis: Fortress, 2005), 147.

Rather, Paul thought in and worked with Jewish categories or doctrines in his presentation and proclamation of Jesus the Messiah. The New Perspective's main criticism of the so-called Old Perspective on Paul, which it associates generally with the Protestant Reformation, is that the traditional reading of Paul has de-Judaized his message,[15] thereby marginalizing or even silencing overarching themes such as Israel, the covenant, the Law as Torah, salvation history, and eschatology, substituting for them an individualized, modern, Western reading of Paul that speaks in the main to how this or that person gets saved and goes to heaven. The main trajectory of the New Perspective is set down by James D. G. Dunn and N. T. Wright, with both building on the work of E. P. Sanders. Although Dunn, Wright, and other New Perspective scholars can and do disagree on many points of Pauline interpretation, the main lines of this school's interpretation are as follows: (1) First-century Judaisms were not legalistic but were characterized by "covenantal nomism," which entailed salvation by grace and obligation to follow YHWH's ways. (2) Since first-century Jews were not espousing "works-righteousness," Paul is not opposing such a legalism in his letters. (3) The matter in question, then, is not of works-righteousness versus grace but of who belongs to the people of God and thus inherits the promises made to Abraham, and how such identity is known. (4) Paul does not differ from most Jews on grace, faith, and works in regard to salvation; rather, what distinguishes Paul's message is his conviction that Jesus is Israel's Messiah and the Lord of all creation, and that salvation is now defined by belonging to Christ rather than by the Torah.[16]

As Wright, arguably the New Perspective's most prominent proponent and certainly its most prolific author, is pulled out from this chorus of voices for a solo performance, a few caveats must be noted. Wright himself is not, finally, interested in promoting "the New Perspective" over against "the Old Perspective," much less in conquering the latter by the former.[17] Rather, he understands himself to be offering a reading of Paul that preserves decisive convictions of the reformers refined by the results of recent Pauline studies, thus offering a clearer picture of Paul's theology and with it his understanding of justification. Further, Wright, a modern-day exegete, refers to the doctrine(s) of justification born of the Reformation and to Luther in very, very general terms. This essay, on the other hand, means to dialogue with Wright from a very specific

15 Wright, *Justification*, 194–97.

16 Kent L. Yinger, *The New Perspective on Paul: An Introduction* (Eugene, OR: Cascade, 2011), 30f.

17 N. T. Wright, *Paul and the Faithfulness of God* (Minneapolis: Fortress, 2013), 1038.

perspective, namely, through Luther's thought alone on the basis of primary sources. Hopefully this specificity offers a fresh perspective and some new insights on the perceived antagonism of two rather unacquainted but potentially fast friends.

As he approaches Paul's writings, Wright is careful to define "justification" and related terminology[18] according to what these terms *denote* in Paul's writings, thereby bearing in mind important distinctions between justification terminology and other soteriological vocabulary in these letters. This, he asserts, Luther failed to do. Justification and salvation are related but distinct, and certainly are not synonymous or simply interchangeable. "Justification is God's declaration that someone is in the right, is a member of the sin-forgiven covenant family, while salvation is actual rescue from death and sin."[19] Salvation, in Paul's theology, indicates "rescue from death and all that causes it."[20] According to Wright, justification is a central emphasis of Paul's soteriology, nested in a redefined Jewish doctrine of God's election, with justification's forensic element being "one important and non-negotiable facet of the whole."[21] Election is what shapes Paul's soteriology; in God's choosing people to be part of His single family, He rescues them from death and all that leads to it. This soteriology can, according to Wright, be observed according to seven broad and interdependent emphases: (1) justification, (2) anthropology, (3) being in Christ, (4) salvation history, (5) apocalyptic, (6) transformation/deification, and (7) covenant.[22] The last of these—covenant—Wright claims as the controlling category in the mix, unfolding an understanding of covenant as God's single plan through Abraham

---

18 Chiefly the verb *dikaioō*, the noun *dikaiosynē*, and the adjective *dikaios*. On this terminology, see James B. Prothro, "The Strange Case of Δικαιόω in the Septuagint and Paul: The Oddity and Origins of Paul's Talk of 'Justification,'" *Zeitschrift für die neutestamentliche Wissenschaft und die Kunde der älteren Kirche* 107, no. 1 (2016): 48–69. On the movement from this Greek vocabulary into the Latin "*iustificare*," "*iustitia*," "*iustus*," as well as on the conceptual difficulties posed by the divergent-looking English terminology ("justify," "righteousness/justice," and "righteous/just"), see Alister McGrath, *Iustitia Dei: A History of the Christian Doctrine of Justification*, 3rd ed. (Cambridge: Cambridge University Press, 2005), 1–54.

19 Wright, *Justification*, 170; cf. *Justification*, 71, 79–92, and 137. See also Wright, *Paul and Faithfulness*, 927.

20 Wright, *Justification*, 240.

21 Wright, *Paul and Faithfulness*, 934; cf. *Paul and Faithfulness*, 782 and 925.

22 Wright, *Paul and Faithfulness*, 774–82. Chapters 9–11 of this work are a detailed development of Wright's shorter exposition of Paul's redefinition of the Jewish doctrines of monotheism, election, and eschatology around the twin poles of Messiah and the Spirit in *Paul: In Fresh Perspective*; see esp. 153 there.

(and thus Israel) for the restoration of the whole creation.[23] Although especially in the Western tradition justification has been made to do larger duty, measured on Paul's own writings justification is a facet of the larger soteriology that runs under covenantal election. Justification terminology, although it is "related closely to the whole theme of human salvation," does not "*denote* that entire sequence of thought."[24] Justification's specific place in the soteriological sequence has to do with status, which, at least as presented in Paul's Epistle to the Romans, has its place in a "lawcourt" setting.[25] "Righteousness" denotes the status that a person has not based on moral character, but declared and effected when the lawcourt finds in that person's favor. To be righteous is to be *in the right*, which for a plaintiff means vindication, for a defendant means acquittal, and for a guilty defendant means pardon. A person stands righteous and has the status of righteousness when he or she is "justified." The Greek word *dikaioō*, "to justify," does not indicate a transformation, nor does this verb denote any shaping or change of a person's character; rather, "to justify" denotes a declaration that grants the status of righteousness.[26] This terminology of justice or righteousness Paul regularly refers back to God's covenant with Israel.[27]

Although Wright also draws on 1 and 2 Corinthians, Ephesians, and Philippians to delineate Paul's teaching of justification, his interpretation of this subset of Paul's election-driven, covenantal soteriology can be sketched through his reading of Galatians and Romans. Here, as elsewhere in Paul's letters, justification has its "home" in a redefined election, which can be summarized under three points: (1) God's purposeful choosing of Israel, (2) with the purpose of this choosing being the "setting to rights" of the whole creation, which (3) is brought forward—future into the present—with the "setting to rights" of human beings.[28]

Along these lines the issue in Galatians is the redefinition of the people of God through the faithfulness of Jesus the Messiah and not according to works of

---

23 Wright, *Justification*, 97: covenant is "the single-plan-of-the-creator-through-Abraham-and-Israel-for-the-world."

24 Wright, *Justification*, 87 (emphasis Wright's).

25 Wright, *Justification*, 90.

26 With the move to *iustificare* as "to make righteous" in the post-Augustinian, Latin-speaking West, Wright sees a changing of scene from legal to medical, from the lawcourt to hospital: *Justification*, 90–92.

27 Wright, *Justification*, 92–100.

28 See Wright, *Paul and Faithfulness*, 925.

the Torah.[29] What constitutes belonging to God's people—the keeping of works of the Torah or belief in Jesus the faithful Messiah? Paul understands election and salvation according to the latter, with faith in Jesus the Messiah now standing as the badge of who belongs to God's people, His covenant family. Abraham is evoked (Galatians 3) not as an example of how individual salvation happens, but to point to God's single, purposeful plan (the covenant) to rescue and liberate the whole human race through him.[30] Over against a modern Western tradition of individualized interpretation about personal salvation, Wright stresses that "the doctrine of justification by faith was born into the world as a key doctrine underlying the *unity* of God's renewed people."[31] Justification is, first, a collective category.

"The righteousness of God,"[32] to which Luther pointed in his 1545 preface to his Latin writings, Wright understands as God's (covenant) faithfulness. As in Galatians, so, too, in Romans Wright finds Paul taking up justification now in its particular forensic, lawcourt setting (Rom. 3:21–26) against the backdrop of redefined election (Rom. 1:18–3:20). The message of Rom. 3:21–26 is that "God's covenant faithfulness is revealed, through the faithfulness of Messiah, for the benefit of all who believe, Jew and Gentile alike."[33] "God's righteousness" is His faithfulness to the promises made to Abraham (Romans 4), which were made with the whole world in view. The backdrop for the forensic treatment of justification in Romans 3 is the final judgment indicated in Rom. 2:1–8. The present verdict, pronounced over faith, anticipates the verdict of the Last Day. Faith, which is delivered through the preached Gospel and results "out of sheer grace," is the badge that marks those who belong to the people of God; it "indicates the presence of genuine, humble, trusting, and indeed we might say image-bearing humanity."[34] In this mix, Rom. 3:28 has to do with acquittal, forgiveness,

---

29 Wright reads "*dia pisteōs Iēsou christou*" ("through the faithfulness of Messiah Jesus") and "*ek pisteōs christou*" ("of Messiah's faithfulness") (Gal. 2:16) as indicating Christ's own faithfulness; with "*eis christon Iēsoun episteusamen*" ("we have believed in Messiah Jesus"), Christ also remains the object of these Christians' faith. Works of the Law/Torah are not "the moral good works done to earn justification (or salvation)" but instead "the peculiar commandments and ordinances which kept Jew and Gentile separate from one another" (Wright, *Justification*, 172, summarizing Dunn).

30 Wright, *Justification*, 114–40.

31 Wright, *Paul: In Fresh Perspective*, 113 (emphasis Wright's).

32 Rom. 1:17, cf. 3:5, 21f., 25; 10:3.

33 Wright, *Paul: In Fresh Perspective*, 119.

34 Wright, *Justification*, 210 and 209 respectively.

and being cleared. This "locuted"[35] acquittal sets the stage for the discussion of Abraham, not as a "decovenantalized" example of the believing individual, but as the foundation of God's covenantal promise-giving and the nonreckoning of sin to His family. On the basis of the covenant given to Abraham for the whole world Paul mounts "a single great argument for *assurance*" in Romans 5–8, in which "being in Christ" is "rooted in, and fully dovetails with, the doctrine of justification."[36] The result is a soteriology according to which people are not "saved *from* the world of creation, but saved *for* the world of creation (Romans 8:18–26)."[37]

So, as Wright reads Paul, the doctrine of justification is not about how people are converted or become Christians; it is not even, at least not directly, about how individuals are saved. Instead justification has to do with being able to tell, in the present, who belongs to God's people, His family. God's declaration of family status, of belonging, is one made over faith.[38] This doctrine of justification, which is forensic (as in Romans) but not *only* forensic (as in Galatians), is nested in and inextricable from Paul's doctrine of salvation, which itself is not about dying and going to heaven but about resurrection to life and renewal of the creation, an eschatological consummation already breaking into the present.

Wright overtly gives the impression that, in the main, what has just been summarized is quite removed from and even at odds with what Luther taught regarding God and human beings with respect to salvation and justification. When Wright does directly mention him, Luther stands as the stereotypical, overly anxious, great-grandfather of a Reformation tradition that is after an individualized answer to an unhelpful question, namely, "How can I find a gracious God?"[39] With this ubiquitous but dubious assumption about the impetus of his theology,[40] Luther is taken as the point of departure for a whole tradition of "inward-looking soteriologies," which incorrectly assume that "we are . . . the center of the universe."[41] Although he writes of Luther as if he is directly

35 Wright, *Paul and Faithfulness*, 945.

36 Wright, *Justification*, 224–40, quotation at 225 (emphasis Wright's).

37 Wright, *Justification*, 234 (emphasis Wright's).

38 Wright, *Paul: In Fresh Perspective*, 159f.

39 Wright, *Justification*, 23. Cf. Wright, *Paul and Faithfulness*, 916; and Yinger, *New Perspective on Paul*, 23, 56, 98.

40 On this question see Jonathan Mumme, *Die Präsenz Christi im Amt: Am Beispiel ausgewählter Predigten Martin Luthers 1535–1545* (Göttingen: Vandenhoeck & Ruprecht, 2015), 291–97.

41 Wright, *Justification*, 25 and 23 respectively.

familiar with his thought, citations of Luther's own writings in Wright's works are very sparse.[42] His chief "Lutheran" exposure—to a degree favorable—seems to be with Ernst Käsemann, but Rudolf Bultmann's "Lutheran" existentialism is simply odious.[43] A reader familiar with Luther gets the sense that Wright's picture of the reformer is influenced or even shaped by his interaction with his own critics, who seem mainly to be of a modern American Evangelical tradition which, though historically heir of other Reformation movements, nonetheless often lays claim to "Luther's doctrine of justification." It is understandable that after decades of discourse with disparagers of his New Perspective on Paul, Wright has a certain interpretive foil in mind as he pointedly and often playfully puts forward his interpretation of the apostle's theology. Wright's foil for a familiar but fundamentally faulty reading of Pauline justification presents a message about how individuals are converted, saved, and obtain safe passage to heaven. This happens when some "thing" called "righteousness," which Christ has morally achieved through His perfect, active obedience, is imputed to the believer, of course, by faith.[44] Wright is well acquainted with the work of modern Evangelicals defending Reformation slogans about justification by faith alone without works; for example, he responds directly to the modern American Evangelical John Piper. However, anyone honestly familiar with Luther may certainly question whether speaking of a "traditional reading" that includes "everyone from Luther to John Piper" is not, so far as Luther is concerned, itself "a straightforward category mistake" on par with that of a transferable, thing-like righteousness that Wright attributes to this ostensibly unified tradition.[45] So

42 Wright, *Justification*, 112 mentions "Luther's wonderful and deeply flawed commentary on Galatians," which the reader assumes he has read. Wright (in *Paul and Faithfulness*, 915 n. 386) seems pleasantly surprised to learn, via a secondary source, that Luther understood the Gospel as a story about Christ.

43 On Käsemann: see Wright, *Paul: In Fresh Perspective*, 15, 18, 41, 51 ("one of my own heroes"); Wright, *Justification*, 65, 205, 249. On Bultmann and/or existentialism: see *Paul: In Fresh Perspective*, 18; *Justification*, 131: "romantic or existential individualism" that seduces "old perspective diehards"; Wright, *Paul and Faithfulness*, 1016.

44 E.g., Wright, *Justification*, 46, 92, 105, 158, 206, 217; and Wright, *Paul and Faithfulness*, 916, 929, 951f. Wright refers to this transferable, thing-like righteousness as "ontologized": *Paul and Faithfulness*, 947, 951.

45 Wright's *Justification* was written in large part as a response to John Piper's *The Future of Justification: A Response to N. T. Wright* (Wheaton: Crossway, 2007); quotations from *Justification*, 158 and 232 respectively.

construed, Luther, "Lutheran," and "the Lutheran tradition" come to be almost a shorthand way of saying "poor exegesis" and "curtailed soteriology."[46]

Luther's Doctrine of Justification as Christologically Applied Soteriology

To track Luther's understanding of justification three things are necessary: one must become familiar with its terminology, catch its essential contours, and, finally, recognize its basic pattern. In what follows, Luther's doctrine of justification will be presented as a teaching about salvation brought about and effected for humans by the God-man, Jesus Christ. For this, Luther's understanding and use of Pauline terminology will be traced, before the crucial contours of his thinking are explored in more detail. Finally, the basic pattern of how Luther understands salvation will be delineated.

Although other factors were involved, Luther's famed "Reformation turn" was certainly influenced by his reading of Paul. Insights for what can be called his "theology of covenant"[47] were won through lectures at the University of Wittenberg on Romans (1515–16) and Galatians (1516–17 and again in 1531). In the prefaces on these Epistles written for his German New Testament, Luther sought to share with others the central conviction that human beings could be certain of their salvation and right standing before God. In his preface to Romans (first published in 1522) readers meet an understanding of justification that is borne along by some essential Pauline vocabulary: "law," "sin," "grace," "faith," and "righteousness."[48] In seeking to help people read Paul rightly, Luther shows Paul's talk of the Law to indicate a divine maker of demands, which pertain not only to external actions but to the inner motives of human hearts. "The law," which "itself is good and just and holy"[49] in demanding that the heart will what is good and find pleasure in it, requires the impossible. This impossible requirement serves to multiply sin and to make the human heart hate the

46 See, e.g., *Justification*, 65, where "Lutheran" is used as the antipode of "good exegete." On the now overused and nary-defined "Lutheran" along with suggestions for clarified use, see James B. Prothro, "An Unhelpful Label: Reading the 'Lutheran' Reading of Paul," *Journal for the Study of the New Testament* 39, no. 2 (2016): 119–40.

47 Carter Lindberg, *The European Reformations*, 2nd ed. (Chichester: Wiley-Blackwell, 2010), 60–69.

48 *Preface to the Epistle of St. Paul to the Romans* (1546, 1522), AE 35:366–72; WA DB 7:2.17–13.26.

49 AE 35:367, WA DB 7:5.37.

Law.[50] The Law, then, both reveals and multiplies sin, which means "not only the outward works of the body but also all activities that move men to do these works, namely, the inmost heart, with all its powers."[51] In view of the bearing and motivations of the heart, Luther closely associates grace and faith with the Law and sin. According to God's grace, which is His "favor, or the good will which in himself he bears toward us, by which he is disposed to give us Christ and to pour into us the Holy Spirit with his gifts,"[52] God "does so much that we are accounted completely righteous before God."[53] Faith, "a living, daring confidence in God's grace,"[54] is worked by God Himself and is given to human beings. This confidence or trust is counted by God "as righteousness for the sake of Christ our Mediator." "Righteousness," concludes Luther, "is such faith."[55] Faith, the opposite of the root cause of all sin, namely unbelief, keeps the Law, both in terms of the heart and in terms of external action.[56]

In construing this Pauline terminology, Luther makes statements that became formulaic for summarizing his understanding of human righteousness before God. "Faith alone makes a person righteous and fulfills the law."[57] "The right way by which a person must be justified and saved" is that "they must be justified without merit . . . through faith in Christ, who has merited this for us by his blood, and has become for us a mercy-seat by God."[58] Such pithy statements from his preface to Romans are consistent with Luther's most careful—indeed, testamentary—professions of his teaching, at whose heart was the conviction that "this faith alone justifies us."[59] Thus, in its simplest, most formulaic mold, Luther's understanding of justification holds that human beings come to enjoy

---

50 AE 35:366f., WA DB 7:3.20–5.28.

51 AE 35:369, WA DB 7:7.27–29.

52 AE 35:369, WA DB 7:9.10–12, showing trinitarian activity.

53 AE 35:370, WA DB 7:9.18f.

54 AE 35:370, WA DB 7:11.16.

55 AE 35:371, WA DB 7:11.28–30.

56 AE 35:368f., WA DB 7:7.20–26.

57 AE 35:368, WA DB 7:7.20f.; cf. AE 35:369, WA DB 7:7.34f.

58 AE 35:373, WA DB 7:15.25–29. Note the hendiadys "be justified and saved," which equals "be saved."

59 SA II I 4; cf. SA III XIII 1. See also *Confession Concerning Christ's Supper* (1528), AE 37:365, WA 26:505.16–17: "There remains only one way" of salvation, "faith in Jesus Christ." Luther's personal confession at the end of this his last response to the Sacramentarians in the controversy over the Lord's Supper in the 1520s, structured by the three articles of the Creed, does not discuss salvation as justification but as redemption, similar to SC Creed 4; AE 37:362 and 363, WA 26:502.20f. and 504.12.

a status of justice or righteousness before God not by anything they themselves do, but solely on the basis of what God has graciously done and gives in Christ, received by faith alone.[60]

Simple formulas are useful and make for easy, shorthand reception, but they still invite the familiar question of Luther's Small Catechism: "What does this mean?" And one will not get to the meaning of something like "justification through faith alone" without observing all the different elements of what Luther indicates with his talk of justification. On the one hand, his *concept* of righteousness and justification is closely associated with specific terminology of Paul's letters.[61] This Pauline basis for Luther's doctrine of justification can, on an overarching exegetical level, look like a door too narrow for the passage of all theology. If, as his perhaps infamous definition claims, the whole of theology is about the God who justifies sinners,[62] is not Luther trying to stuff, yank, and haul the whole camel of the Holy Scriptures through an impossible needle's eye? This question must be honored on an exegetical level. However, in order to exegete or interpret Luther in an honest fashion, one must recognize that he often speaks of justification as a sort of synonym for salvation.[63] That "justification" and "salvation" in Paul's writings at least *denote* different though related things does not seem to concern Luther. Not only on an exegetical level but also on a systematic-theological level this can prove very frustrating; the reformer sometimes seems to throw specific terminology about in a rather haphazard, willy-nilly fashion, running hues and colors together in a fascinating, somewhat impressionist way ill-suited to the technical diagramming of systematic-theological categories. This means, however, that when Luther is talking about "righteousness" and "justification," he may well be referencing some aspect of Paul's thought, such as God reckoning someone righteous (cf. Romans 4), but he may also be speaking of the overarching whole of the Creator's setting His creation right, about the whole kit and caboodle, the big shebang of what today would most likely be labeled a Christian metanarrative. By Luther's own

60 Lindberg (*European Reformations*, 67) states that "justification by grace alone through faith alone" is Luther's "metatheological proclamation."

61 See above, p. 59 n. 18.

62 *Commentary on Psalm 51* (1538), AE 12:311, WA 40/2:328.17–20.

63 Hendiadys-like pairings of justification and salvation: *Palladius und Tilemann*, WA 39/1:226.6f.13, 251.10f.; see also above, p. 65 n. 58, and below, the quote at p. 67 n. 66; *Enarratio Psalmorum LI . . . et CXXX* (1538), WA 40/3:335.21, 347.25f. Similar pairings of justification and regeneration: *Palladius und Tilemann*, WA 39/1:234.19.23, 241.6–10. In both of Luther's major confessions, justification terminology washes around with talk of redemption and/or reconciliation; see above, p. 65 n. 59, and below, p. 67 n. 64.

associations—whether we approve of them or not!—understanding Luther's doctrine of justification means not only grasping his explanation and appropriation of Pauline terminology but also giving attention to his often ad hoc and incidental explications of the whole of God's restorative interactions with His creatures and with all His creation as self-giving Trinity.[64]

Having traced Luther's basic justification terminology and having noted that with "justification" language Luther can be indicating nearly any aspect or indeed the whole of salvation, the stage is set to trace some key contours of Luther's soteriology. In what follows, the essential contours of Luther's doctrine of justification will overlay and build on one another to form the unified whole of a soteriologically applied Christology. These are (1) the complementary motifs of nonimputation of sin and indwelling/union, (2) anthropology weighed in view of creation, (3) Christ as "form" and "person," (4) eschatology, and (5) the polar application of the Office of the Keys.

When the breadth and depth of Luther's theological associations with justification are kept in mind, reception of his rather holistic thought can be rescued from fixating piecemeal on specific points. What "justified by faith in Christ" (Gal. 2:16) might all mean and entail is a case in point. A given reading of Luther's doctrine of justification by faith in Christ, holding high particular points of an almost omnipresent conflict with certain elements of scholastic theology,[65] can rightly find grounds for understanding justification as a reality or status into which sinners-become-believers are pronounced and proclaimed. The article or doctrine of justification is simply "that we are pronounced righteous and are saved solely by faith in Christ, and without works,"[66] rather than "by love."[67] On account of faith in Christ, which is created and sustained solely by God's Word, God imputes righteousness and reputes the sinner a righteous person.[68] The righteousness whereby the sinner-become-believer is justified is

---

64 *Confession Concerning Christ's Supper* (1528), AE 37:366, WA 26:505.38–506.12. Cf. SC Creed 1–6: an unmerited relationship with the Creator as Father, wrought by faith in the Son as Redeemer, is mediately effected by the Holy Spirit. For God as essential Self-Giver, see LC Ten Commandments 25 and Lord's Prayer 56.

65 *Lectures on Galatians* (1535), AE 26:122–36, WA 40/1:217.26–238.34; AE 26:172–76, WA 40/1:290.32–295.34; AE 26:276–91, WA 40/1:432.17–452.26.

66 *Lectures on Galatians* (1535), AE 26:223, WA 40/1:355.25f.

67 *Lectures on Galatians* (1535), AE 26:137, WA 40/1:240,20f.; see also AE 26:123, WA 40/1:218.18–20; cf. AE 26:143, WA 40/1:250.10f.

68 *Lectures on Galatians* (1535), AE 26:4, WA 40/1:41.15f. See also AE 26:6, WA 40/1:43.24; AE 26:123, WA 40/1:218.19f.; AE 26:229, WA 40/1:363.30 (commentating on Gal. 3:6 and quoting Gen. 15:6). Cf. "*reputandam iustitiam*" ("reputed righteousness"),

an alien righteousness[69] that he does not have on his own or produce by his efforts, though the justified reality and status does result in good works,[70] which do not contribute to justification but are theologically subsequent. The chief focus of this reading is on faith as trust, separate from any works, as that which brings about salvation for the sinner-become-believer. Related, but an important shade or two removed from this reading, is what we might call the standard position of sole-forensists of the classically Protestant, now "Old," Perspective on Paul, according to which sinners-become-believers have no righteousness of their own, but, because of faith, have the righteousness of God or Christ imputed to them by God.[71]

Another reading of "faith in Christ" according to Luther, nourished by the selfsame sources, focuses not so much on the "in" that marks justifying faith's object (as with "faith in Christ" in the sense of "to believe in Christ"[72]) as on the "in" that marks a somewhat mystical located-ness of Christians in Christ, whose reciprocal reality is Christ's being *in* the believer.[73] According to this reading, justification has to do with Christ's presence in faith, in the believer; Christ Himself, being the "form" of faith, is the believer's righteousness.[74] Righteousness is, thereby, not a category simply alien or solely imputed to believers, but one belonging to them by way of union with Christ.[75] Thus the focus of this reading is on the salvific union of Christ and the Christian. Further steps along this

---

WA 40/1:388.23. On imputation of righteousness as the nonimputation of sin, see below, p. 79 n. 139.

69 *The Disputation Concerning Justification* (1536), AE 34:153, WA 39/1:83.24f.; cf. AE 34:177f., WA 39/1:108.24–109.3.

70 *Lectures on Galatians* (1535), AE 26:226, WA 40/1:359.13f.

71 See Piper, *Future of Justification*, 73–80. Cf. Wright, *Justification*, 46: "If 'imputed righteousness' is so utterly central . . . so standing-and-falling-church important . . . , isn't it strange that Paul never actually came straight out and said it?"

72 *pisteuō* + *epi* (e.g., Rom. 4:24; 9:23; 10:11) or *pisteuō* + *eis* (e.g., Gal. 2:16; Phil. 1:29).

73 As with *pisteuō* used with *en* (e.g., Eph. 1:13; cf. 1:15); reading also *pistis christou* as a subjective as opposed to an objective genitive (Rom. 3:22; Gal. 2:16; 3:22; Phil. 3:9), thus indicating the faithfulness of Christ. See also Rom. 8:1; 12:5; 2 Cor. 5:17; Gal. 2:20; 3:26, 28; and Col. 1:27. See especially Luther's commentary on Gal. 2:20 (1535), AE 26:166–79, WA 40/1:280.13–300.22.

74 *Lectures on Galatians* (1535), AE 26:129f., WA 40/1:228.27–229.21 (229.15: "in this faith Christ is present"). See Tuoma Mannermaa, *Christ Present in Faith: Luther's View of Justification*, trans. Kirsi Stjerna (Minneapolis: Fortress, 2005).

75 See *Lectures on Galatians* (1519), AE 27:227, WA 2:495.4f.; *Treatise on Christian Liberty* (1520), AE 31:349–51, WA 7:53.15–55.6; *Lectures on Galatians* (1535), AE 26:166, WA 40/1:282.21f.; AE 26:167–70, WA 40/1:283.18–288.21 (see above, n. 73).

path of interpretation have led some to expound Luther's doctrine of justification as a form of, or at least compatible with, theosis, that is, salvation by way of divinization.[76]

Even if the "sole-forensist" reading of Luther does not ignore aspects of indwelling and union in Luther's theology, it is suspicious of any human works getting too close to justification itself. Similarly, a reading that highlights the union of Christ and the believer, though not rejecting reckoned or imputed righteousness, is reticent to see Christ's righteousness *remaining* alien to or outside the Christian. The polar pitfalls in both readings of "justification by faith in Christ" are avoided by attending to both the Object of saving faith and the Indweller of Christians: by attending to "justification by faith *in Christ*."

Luther, a charismatic figure sometimes given to ad hoc, hyperbolic emphasis, did state that justification is "the principle locus of our salvation," "the *summa* of all Christian doctrine and the sun that illumines the church. For when this doctrine stands the church stands, but if it falls, the church also falls."[77] This "one article concerning justification even by itself creates true theologians,"[78] whereas "if the doctrine of justification is lost, the whole of Christian doctrine is lost."[79] However, "justification by faith" was not simply *the* thing that ran his theology, as a few, perhaps less hyperbolic, words on Christology show: "For in my heart this one article reigns, namely, that of faith in Christ, from whom, through whom, and unto whom all my theological cogitations flow back and forth, day and night."[80] The article on Christ "is the chief [article] in our religion."[81] Significantly, the chief article of Luther's foremost confession of faith and doctrine bears no title.[82] Taking up matters that "pertain to the office and work of Jesus Christ or our redemption" (*so das Ampt und Werk Jesu Christi oder unser Erlosung betreffen*), the first article in Part II of the Smalcald Articles throws out a string of Scripture references specifying the redemptive work of Christ and titles related to it, digested by way of Rom. 3:23–25: " 'All have sinned,' and 'they

76 See Risto Saarinen's summary of the Finnish school's interpretation in "Justification by Faith: The View of the Mannermaa School," in *The Oxford Handbook of Martin Luther's Theology*, ed. Robert Kolb, Irene Dingel, and Ľubomír Batka (Oxford: Oxford University Press, 2014), 254–63.

77 *Psalm 130* (1532–33), WA 40/3:335.21, 351.33–35.

78 *Disputation Concerning Justification*, AE 34:157, WA 39/1:87.3f.

79 *Lectures on Galatians* (1535), AE 26:9, WA 40/1:48.28f.

80 *Lectures on Galatians* (1535), WA 40/1:33.7–9.

81 *Enarratio 53. capitis Esaiae prophetae* . . . (1544), WA 40/3:704.8f.

82 SA II I is simply titled "the first and chief article."

are now justified without merit by his grace, through the redemption that is in Christ Jesus . . . by his blood.'" Moving on by way of Romans 3 Luther states, "Now because this must be believed and may not be obtained or grasped otherwise with any work, law, or merit, it is clear and certain that this faith alone justifies us."[83] The form and content of this article, the heart of his confession, begs the question whether it is about Christ's office and work of redemption or about justification. The ambiguity is pointed: the office and work of Christ and justification are one; redemption and justification are inseparable. And indeed elsewhere Luther demonstrates that he understands Christ's person, Christ's office and work (redemption), and justification as a single article,[84] for the person and two natures of Jesus Christ cannot be properly and fully considered without considering His office or work, which is salvation or justification, and vice versa. Similar to the Second Article of the Nicene Creed, the personal union of the Son of God (divine nature) and the Son of Mary (human nature) transpires "for us men and for our salvation."

Operating as a soteriologically applied Christology, Luther's doctrine of justification understands Christ as the object of that faith in view of which sins are not imputed to the believer and according to which Christ with His righteousness dwells in the believer and the believer with his sins dwells in Christ. Inasmuch as this articulation of salvation has to do with the God-*man* it also bears some profound anthropological insights. An enigmatic passage from *The Disputation Concerning Man* (1536) shines strange but intriguing light on the depth and possibility of justification in Luther's thinking. Asking what it means to be human, Luther notes a concise, and unified, philosophical definition: "man [is] an animal having reason, sensation, and body,"[85] a definition that leaves human beings ignorant of their source (efficient cause) and purpose (final cause) and confused about their souls (formal cause). A unified *theological* definition of man, however, is not so quickly at hand. Man is "a creature of God consisting of body and a living soul,"[86] but Luther's discussion deals with man's pre- and post-lapsarian conditions in view of the inherent contradiction posed by the mortality that divides body and soul. Theological analysis of prelapsarian man notes that he was, from the beginning, made "*ad imaginem dei*" ("into God's image").[87] Such is man in view of his efficient cause, his "font," God,

83 SA II I 4 (Kolb-Wengert, 301, *BSLK* 415.14–17).

84 See *Lectures on Galatians* (1535), AE 26:282–85, WA 40/1:441.13–444.29.

85 *Disputation Concerning Man* (1536), AE 34:137, WA 39/1:175.3f.

86 *Disputation Concerning Man*, AE 34:138, WA 39/1:176.7–9.

87 *Disputation Concerning Man*, WA 39/1:176.7–9; cf. AE 34:138.

his Creator.[88] Such is man also in view of his purpose and the intent that the Creator yet has for him, even in his post-lapsarian condition. "His future form" is to be the "reformed and perfected image of God."[89] The connection between man's pre-lapsarian state, with creation as it once was, and his divinely intended super-lapsarian future, with creation as it will be when the effects of the fall are overcome and its futility is replaced by full purpose, comes with the only proper definition of true human being that can be given in the current fallen state: "*hominem justificari fide*," "[to be] human is to be justified by faith."[90] Here, in the midst of a theological anthropology being weighed in view of creation, stands justification by faith. Is this merely Luther as a one-trick pony, doing what he always does, a garage-band theologian playing the same three-cord progression because it is the only one he knows? Or is there some true music happening here? It must be noted that justification by faith as it appears in *The Disputation Concerning Man* does not serve to shut down or replace creationology, anthropology, or indeed eschatology (more on that below), but it serves to explore, unfold, and harmonize them. For to be justified by faith means finding oneself involved in the Creator's process of forming material toward His willed purpose and therefore its proper end. In the case of the man being justified by faith, this means inclusion in God's process of re-forming *ad imaginem dei*—into the image of God. Several of Luther's theses warrant full citation:

> 35. Thus man in this life is nothing but the material of God into life in his future form.[91]
>
> 36. In the same way also all creation (*tota creatura*), now subjected to vanity, is for God material into its glorious future form.
>
> 37. And as earth and heaven in the beginning were to the form completed after six days, that is, its material,
>
> 38. such is man in this life into his future form, when the image of God will be reformed and perfected.[92]

---

88 *Disputation Concerning Man*, WA 39/1:175.37.

89 *Disputation Concerning Man*, WA 39/1:177.9f.; cf. AE 34:140.

90 *Disputation Concerning Man*, WA 39/1:176.34f.; see Oswald Bayer, *Martin Luther's Theology: A Contemporary Interpretation*, trans. Thomas H. Trapp (Grand Rapids: Eerdmans, 2008), 155–58.

91 For this translation consult Wilfried Härle, Johannes Schilling, and Günther Wartenberg, eds., *Martin Luther Lateinisch-Deutsche Studienausgabe* (Leipzig: Evangelische Verlagsanstalt, 2006), 1:669.11–12.

92 *Disputation Concerning Man*, WA 39/1:177.3–10.

Is this noise best left in the garage or is it music whose symphonic structures suit it to the proper halls of theology by ringing in the essential tones of Christianity's overarching story? The talk of "image" and "form" that Luther ties to justification as he weighs what it means to be human hints that something symphonic is afoot here. For these terms belong inextricably to the creation narrative that sets the stage for the whole of Christian theology.[93] However, the recognition that "form" and "image" are also essential *christological* terminology[94] must certainly deliver Luther from relegation to the status of garage-band bandit and instead place him as a proper composer whose work still deserves a serious theological hearing. The object of justifying faith—namely, Christ who is in one undivided person fully and distinctly God and fully and distinctly man—drives, carries, and finally completes Luther's doctrine of justification. As previously noted, the office or work of Christ—that is, the saving, redeeming, justifying activity of the God-man—is the single and unified hub around which the whole wheel turns.

The anthropological contour just observed, explicated under "form," aligns precisely with one of Luther's chief disagreements with scholastic soteriology in his 1535 Galatians commentary: the *form* of justifying faith. The form of justifying faith has to do with what makes faith *justifying* faith. The scholastics argued that love is what makes faith justifying faith; thus love was the *form* of faith, and only as formed by love does faith justify. Against this Luther repeatedly asserts that Christ, the object of faith, is Himself the "form of faith." Christ, faith's object, is what makes faith justifying. Thus not simply faith formed by something, but that faith whose very form is Christ Himself justifies.[95] Initially, being human meant being formed *ad imaginem Dei*, into the image of God. Now being human means being justified by faith. The incarnate Christ, who is the image of the invisible God, is the form that justifying faith has and possesses, which form sees to the final re-formation of the image of God in the believer.[96]

Scratching now the surface of a doctrine of justification that operates as soteriologically applied Christology, a further point of contact shows the intimate connection between justification and Christology in Luther's thinking,

---

93 See Gen. 1:26f. (image) and 2:7 (form).

94 See, e.g., Phil. 2:6–7: "form of God" and "form of a servant," as well as Col. 1:15: "image of the invisible God."

95 *Lectures on Galatians* (1535), AE 26:129f., WA 40/1:228.18–229.35; AE 26:167–69, WA 40/1:283.20–286.21; AE 26:268–70, WA 40/1:420.6–423.31; AE 27:28–31, WA 40/2:34.8–39.15; cf. AE 26:137, WA 40/1:240.13–16; AE 26:161, WA 40/1:275.10–15.

96 *Lectures on Galatians* (1535), AE 26:259, WA 40/1:407.13–15: justification's opposite is the refusal "to be justified by a divine blessing and formed by God the Creator" as "merely passive matter."

namely, Luther's use of "person" in the Galatians commentary. The freight "person" carries in Christology after Chalcedon can hardly be overestimated,[97] ensconced as it is even in the Athanasian Creed. Luther knew and theologized deeply through and in the Chalcedonian categories; the personal union of Christ's two natures formed, for example, the foundation for Luther's rather pointed conclusions about the communication of their attributes.[98] Christ, as "divine and human Person," is not a "private person." It is not simply that He does not do what He does for Himself, asserts Luther, but that He is not who He is for Himself, but rather "for us."[99] Christ's substitutionary role in salvation is, in Luther's understanding, not limited to doing works left undone by human beings or simply paying the penalty for sinful human actions by Christ's human suffering. He did not simply take up the sin of sinners; He took upon Himself "our sinful person,"[100] so that He "bore the person . . . of all sinners."[101] Further, the "wondrous duel" fought between sin and righteousness and between their effects—namely, life and death—takes place in the person of Christ,[102] and the defeat of sin and death "in the unique person of Christ" points to the victory of righteousness and life that will change the whole creation or total creature (*tota creatura*) through His person.[103] Being "justified by faith alone" involves a "felicitous exchange" of persons, according to which the divine and human Christ, through a willed act of self-emptying, assumes the mask, or *larva*, of sinful human beings in order to overcome sin and death and "[give] to us His innocent and victorious person" as a liberating reality and identity in which Christians are clothed.[104] Not simply some moral attribute of Christ, such as righteousness, is given to the believer—rather, the fullness of Christ's person, which is completely

---

97 For the Chalcedonian Definition, see Tanner, *Decrees of the Ecumenical Councils*, 1:86–87.

98 See, e.g., Oswald Bayer and Benjamin Gleede, eds., *Creator est Creatura: Luthers Christologie als Lehre von der Idiomenkommunikation* (Berlin: de Gruyter, 2007).

99 *Lectures on Galatians* (1535), AE 26:287, WA 40/1:448.14–19. Cf. comments on the Nicene Creed, above, p. 70.

100 *Lectures on Galatians* (1535), AE 26:284f., WA 40/1:443.23f.

101 *Lectures on Galatians* (1535), AE 26:277, WA 40/1:433.20f. Cf. the creationological, paternal imperative in the Father's sending of the Son: "Be the person of all men" (AE 26:280, WA 40/1:437.25).

102 *Lectures on Galatians* (1535), AE 26:280f., WA 40/1:438.32–440.13; quotation AE 26:281, WA 40/1:439.31f.

103 *Lectures on Galatians* (1535), WA 40/1:440.26–30; cf. AE 26:282.

104 *Lectures on Galatians* (1535), WA 40/1:443.23–44.18; cf. AE 26:283f.

righteous and the victor over both sin and death.[105] Accordingly, Christian faith entails a rejection of one's own person. Stating that "Christian righteousness" is "that righteousness by which Christ lives in us, not the righteous that is in our person," Luther claims that this person must be rejected and "Christ and my conscience must become one body, so that I am looking at nothing but Christ crucified and resurrected."[106] "So far as justification is concerned, Christ and I must be so closely attached that He lives in me and I in Him."[107] A "cementing and inhering"[108] take place through faith, according to which a Christian is not to view his person as distinct or separate from Christ's person, but precisely as one single, inseparable person with Christ.[109]

As might be expected, any consideration of Christ's person carries with it both divine and human implications. An implication, one might say, from the divine side of these considerations is that Christ is the fully operative agent in all that pertains to human salvation. On the one hand, there is here a clear crossing of swords with the scholastic theology that preceded Luther. Luther claims that, by attributing some or any part of human salvation to the operations of fallen human beings, the scholastics deny the divinity of Christ,[110] rob Him of titles such as "Savior" and "Justifier,"[111] and make human beings out to be true God "by nature,"[112] that is, in their humanness. However, corresponding to a closely related clash over original sin, if human beings are indeed dead under the curse of sin, then the conquering of sin and death can be attributed to no man except Christ, who by His divinity overcomes them in His person; any attributing of such a work to humanity amounts to a denial of Christ's divinity.[113] On the other hand, the divinity of Christ is of import for rightly thinking

105 Opposite here are not righteousness given/reckoned to the believer/sinner and Christ given to/for the believer/sinner; opposite instead is the sinner attempting to give himself to or come to the Son of God; see *Lectures on Galatians* (1535), AE 26:176, WA 40/1:295.35–296.22; cf. SC Creed 6.

106 *Lectures on Galatians* (1535), WA 40/1:282.16–22; cf. AE 26:166.

107 *Lectures on Galatians* (1535), AE 26:167, WA 40/1:284.20–22.

108 *Lectures on Galatians* (1535), WA 40/1:284.24f; cf. AE 26:167.

109 *Lectures on Galatians* (1535), WA 40/1:283.20–25, 285.15–17 and 24–26; cf. AE 26:167f.

110 *Lectures on Galatians* (1535), AE 26:127, WA 40/1:224.28–34.

111 *Lectures on Galatians* (1535), AE 26:154, WA 40/1:265.13–15 (here regarding a form of monastic absolution).

112 *Lectures on Galatians* (1535), AE 26:283, WA 40/1:442.24.

113 *Lectures on Galatians* (1535), AE 26:282f., WA 40/1:441.13–33; and AE 26:165, WA 40/1:281.19. See also Luther, *Disputation Concerning Justification*, AE 34:156, WA 39/1:86.10–13.

about the works that Christians do in fact perform. Luther understands Christ to be the actor in or agent behind the good works that Christians carry out. It is not by some moral necessity or obligation that justifying faith cannot be without good works; justifying faith cannot be without good works given the personal presence of Christ in the person of the believer, also according to His divinity. Although it is possible for man, at least fallen man (even in his most significant undertakings), to be "idle,"[114] idleness is, to Luther's mind, simply a contradiction of the nature of God. God cannot, as God, be idle, and thus God perpetually works wherever He is.[115] If the fully divine person of Christ is given to the believer, it is not *ethically or morally* impossible that the Christian fail to bring forth good works; it is *theo*-logically impossible, and thus it is a *theological* necessity of the most encouraging and enabling variety that Christ will work good in and through all Christians. For this same reason Luther understands it to be a *theological* contradiction to talk about works needing to be added to faith in Christ in order for faith to be justifying faith, for wherever faith has Christ as its object, Christ Himself is present with the fullness of His perpetually active and efficacious divine nature. One cannot add works to justifying faith, for inasmuch as Christ is present in this faith such works are already there. Good works are not an addendum to justification but are soteriologically distinct aspects of a single, incarnational, gracious movement of God toward man. That which "comes from heaven," "in the flesh," rescues human physicality, sensory perception, and embodied activity from being "of the flesh."[116] As Luther, against his scholastic opponents, weighs distinctions between "abstract" or "absolute" faith and "composite" or "concrete" faith along christological lines,[117] he states that the former can and must be considered alone in its divine, justifying function, but the latter is an incarnational reality.

> Therefore faith perpetually justifies and vivifies, and nevertheless it does not remain alone, that is, idle. It is not that it does not remain

---

114 See the Book of Ecclesiastes.

115 See above, p. 74 n. 111. See also Luther, *Lectures on Galatians* (1535), AE 26:129f., WA 40/1:228.27–229.26; AE 26:155, WA 40/1:265.31f.; AE 26:272f., WA 40/1:427.11–14; as well as AE 26:278, WA 40/1:434.21–28: Christ as but an example and thus, at least to some extent segregated from sinners, is "useless." A man can be imitated; imitation of God is idolatry. Cf. Luther, *On the Bondage of the Will* (1525), AE 33:242, WA 18:753.28–36; as God, God works all things in all things (1 Cor. 12:6).

116 *Lectures on Galatians* (1535), AE 26:171, WA 40/1:289.16–30; see also AE 26:172, WA 40/1:290.30f.: "In short, this life is not the life of the flesh, although it is a life in the flesh; but it is the life of Christ, the Son of God, whom the Christian possesses by faith."

117 *Lectures on Galatians* (1535), AE 26:261–68, WA 40/1:409.30–419.21.

> alone in its own station and office, because perpetually it alone justifies, but [*faith*] *also becomes man*, that is, it does not remain idle or without love.[118]

What is predicated of justifying faith's object guides what may be predicated of faith itself. Just as "man" is a new word when taken in composite fashion as joined with divinity, so also are "working" and "doing" new words when joined with faith. "Let faith always be the divinity of works . . . . Thus faith is universally the divinity in the work, the person, and the members of the body, as the one and only cause of justification,"[119] Christ, the divine object of justifying faith, is also human, and works as such.

In addition to these anthropological and creationological components of a doctrine of justification wherein Christ as form and person makes complementary the motifs of nonimputation of sin and indwelling, Luther's soteriology also entails an eschatological contour that emerges from the humanity of Christ. Christ justifies or saves, perpetually, in a fashion that never loses the downward God-to-man motion of His incarnation and subsequent humiliation. In Himself, in His person, Christ drove the destructive nonentities of sin, death, and the curse *in nihilum*, "to nothing."[120] This reductive motion is experienced by a person in regard to his own nature or substance: brought to the recognition that his nature is entirely corrupted by sin, all of man's righteousness is reduced "to nothing."[121] To know oneself—to hear of oneself as sinner and nothing but sinful—is to know and say "that we are nothing at all, just as we have been created out of nothing."[122] Where Christ reduces sin to nothing, where man's righteousness is reduced to nothing, the stage is set for the Creator's restorative work.

Precisely in discussing justification as the Creator's restorative work, Luther comes to his famous statement about the subject of theology: "The proper subject of theology is man guilty of sin and condemned, and God the Justifier and Savior of man the sinner. Whatever is asked or discussed in theology outside this subject,

118 *Lectures on Galatians* (1535), WA 40/1:427.11–14; cf. AE 26:272 (emphasis added). Cf. citation above, p. 71 n. 90.

119 *Lectures on Galatians* (1535), AE 26:266, WA 40/1:417.15f and 26f.

120 *Lectures on Galatians* (1535), WA 40/1:441.13–33 (quote at 24); cf. AE 26:282.

121 *Commentary on Psalm 51*, WA 40/2:327.15–26.

122 *Disputation Concerning Justification*, AE 34:156, WA 39/1:86.14f.; cf. AE 34:191, WA 39/1:122.11f.: ". . . the mercy of God makes nothing out of all sin, just as out of nothing he makes all things."

is error and poison."[123] In addition to the hendiadys of "Justifier and Savior," the grand scope of association with justification becomes clear from the context of Luther's exposition of Psalm 51. According to the Gospel, the sinner hears that God "restore[s] man through Christ," who belongs to sinners.[124] "All Scripture points to this, that God commends His kindness to us and in His Son restores to righteousness and life the nature that has fallen into sin and condemnation."[125] The future, eternal life has to do with "the God who justifies, repairs, and makes alive and with man who has fallen from righteousness and life into sin and eternal death."[126] Justification thus entails a restoration of man's nature, and this restoration Luther presents as a present-tense, eschatological category.

In a 1537 disputation for the promotion of two doctoral candidates, Luther's thesis that "the justification of the Law must be fulfilled in us through the Son of God" is challenged on the grounds that this would then equate, at least in some respect, justification with regeneration.[127] Given that believers' regeneration is imperfect, would this not make justification imperfect? Luther does not respond to this argument by pointing out how his interlocutor has misunderstood his thesis, but by saying, "It is true, *I concede the whole argument.*"[128] Justification, in Luther's holistic consideration, entails regeneration. The perceived contradiction of justification and regeneration Luther handles with the present-tense application of a future reality, namely righteousness. Regeneration takes time, and a Christian finds himself at the intersection of two epochs. "The time of grace" and "the time of Law" are overlapping realities,[129] experienced simultaneously, according to which the Christian is *simul iustus et peccator*—at the same time righteous and a sinner.[130] The time of grace is an in-breaking of full and restored time into the broken, mortal time indicated by the Law—an in-breaking of restored creation into the fallen world of fallen creatures. Christians as

---

123 *Commentary on Psalm 51*, AE 12:311, WA 40/2:328.17–20. Cf. Luther, *Palladius und Tilemann*, WA 39/1:222.16: "the having-mercy God"; and *Preface to Luther's Latin Writings*, AE 34:337, WA 54:186.7: "merciful God."

124 *Commentary on Psalm 51*, AE 12:311, WA 40/2:327.30.

125 *Commentary on Psalm 51*, AE 12:311, WA 40/2:328.20–22.

126 *Commentary on Psalm 51*, WA 40/2:328.26–28; cf. AE 12:311.

127 *Palladius und Tilemann*, WA 39/1:204.1f.

128 *Palladius und Tilemann*, WA 39/1: 234.18–23 and 235.1f. (AI) (emphasis added).

129 *Lectures on Galatians* (1535), AE 26:340–42, WA 40/1:523.20–527.27.

130 *Lectures on Galatians* (1519), AE 27:231, WA 2:497.13. *Lectures on Galatians* (1535), AE 26:232, WA 40/1:368.26. Along the same lines see the repeated "this life" and "meanwhile" in *Disputation Concerning Man* (Theses 3–5, 8, 35, 38, 39), AE 34:137–40, WA 39/1:175–77.

Christians—that is, believers in Christ as believers in Christ—have in themselves the firstfruits of the new creation,[131] whose full harvest is coming; they enjoy a leavening,[132] which will yet leaven fully. Their incipient righteousness awaits full, perfect righteousness.[133] Simultaneously, as corrupted by and perpetuators of sin, Christians experience in themselves a contradiction to this new creation.[134] Christians, as those who are both just and sinners, are those who are to be justified through a justification that God Himself is absolutely and certainly bringing about;[135] they are those underway, on a journey.[136] Faith is an absolute eschatological beginning that is consummated in death.[137] God's way with the believer now is mercy, forgiveness, which is shown to the Christian as one in and covered by Christ.[138] God's way with sin in this present conflict between the Law and grace, between sin and righteousness, is to *not reckon or*

---

131 *Palladius und Tilemann*, WA 39/1:235.2–9 (AI). See also *Disputation Concerning Justification*, AE 34:152, WA 39/1:83.14f. Paul applies the term *aparchē* ("firstfruits") to Christ (1 Cor. 15:20), to persons/believers (Rom. 11:16; 16:5; 1 Cor. 16:15; 2 Thess. 2:13), and to both together (1 Cor. 16:15), associating firstfruits with the Spirit (Rom. 8:23); see also James 1:18 and Rev. 14:4.

132 *Lectures on Galatians* (1535), AE 26:351, WA 40/1:538.23–26. See Matt. 13:33/Luke 13:21 and Rom. 11:16, which associates the motif of leaven with firstfruits. Cf. 1 Cor. 5:6–8 and Gal. 5:9.

133 *Lectures on Galatians* (1535), AE 27:22, WA 40/2:25.20–23. *Palladius und Tilemann*, WA 40/1:241.24–27.

134 *Lectures on Galatians* (1535), AE 26:288, WA 40/1:448.35–449.19—experience themselves, "substantively," as sin and the curse itself.

135 See the thoughts on conscience, certainty, and comfort below, p. 81.

136 *Disputation Concerning Justification*, WA 39/1:83.16–21: "23. For we perceive a man to be justified [*Iustificari . . . hominem*] is not yet a righteous man, but is in the very movement or journey toward righteousness. 24. Therefore, whoever is being justified is also still a sinner, and yet he is, as it were, considered fully and perfectly righteous by God pardoning and having mercy. 25. Moreover, our God pardons and has mercy on us in view of Christ, our advocate and priest, interceding and sanctifying our beginning [*initium*] of righteousness." Cf. AE 34:152f. The Vulgate uses *initium* for *aparchē* at James 1:18; see above, n. 131.

137 *Lectures on Galatians* (1535), AE 26:229, WA 40/1:364.14, cf. 360.24: "faith consummates divinity."

138 For the theme of mercy as it appears in *Palladius und Tilemann*, see WA 39/1:203.5–13, 210.16f., 215.20, 221–22, 223.9f., 225.6–9.21f., 228.8f., 230.16–20, 232.4–233.13, 235.17, 235.35–236.15, 236.20f., 238.3–9, 241.19f., 242.13–23, 246.26f., 247.2–5.23, 249.8–15, 254.3–15, 255.18f., 256.9f.; in Thesis 42 (204.30f.) Christ is named "our mercy seat." Jeffrey G. Silcock, who produced the forthcoming translation for AE 72, aptly concludes in his introduction: "The only thing 'necessary'" for justification "is God's mercy."

impute sin to the believer, which is the import of Luther's talk of "imputation."[139] To the believer, in whom the work of justification has by faith begun, is now reckoned that full righteousness that he will substantially[140] enjoy after death, the final absolution,[141] as a resurrected new creation.[142] This present-tense nonimputation of sin happens through Christ, who fulfills the Law, who is the Law's fulfiller not simply in time past but now, in the believer, in whom He is being formed and who, being in Him, is being formed in His image. The presence of Christ *in* the believer (Gal. 2:20; Col. 1:27) is tied throughout to what is reckoned to the believer and being effected in the believer, namely, salvation as a fully right and just standing and identity with God. Christ's being in believers pairs with believers being "in Christ." This New Testament baptismal language (Rom. 6:3; Gal. 3:27; cf. Rom. 8:1, 2 Cor. 5:7) nourishes Luther's understanding of the nonimputation of sin, for Christ is a shelter and shade to believers against the wrath of God, who does not see their sin *in Christ*.[143] Solely by the mercy of God righteousness is reckoned and worked now, so that the believer may be fully righteous in the future.

Faith justifies because its object, Christ, justifies. Faith that has Christ as its object has and thus is the restoration of the proper, right, just relationship between Creator and creature, wherein man reckons rightly to God what is God's, thereby recognizing God as God, and God so recognized, recognizes man as man.[144] As in the person of Christ, so also in justifying faith God and

---

139 *Lectures on Galatians* (1519), AE 27:227, WA 2:495.2–5; AE 27:232, WA 2:497.37f.; *Psalm 130*, WA 40/1:348.30–350.22 (here "repute" and "impute" are, as elsewhere also, used as synonyms); *Theses Concerning Faith and Law* (1535), AE 34:123, WA 39/1:55.32–35; *Disputation Concerning Justification*, AE 34:153, WA 39/1:83.7f.; AE 34:166f., WA 39/1:96.24–98.14; AE 34:180, WA 39/1:111.10–12; AE 34:190, WA 39/1:121.26f.; AE 34:191, WA 39/1:122.8–15; AE 34:194f., WA 39/1:125.1f.; *Palladius und Tilemann*, WA 39/1:204.25–38, 249.15–19.

140 Cf. purgation in *Palladius und Tilemann*, WA 39/1:236.21–23, 247.26–27; and *Disputation Concerning Justification*, AE 34:168, WA 39/1:99.22–27; AE 34:177, WA 39/1:108.5–15; AE 34:182f., WA 39/1:113.25–114.5; with sin having no substance of its own, God through Word and Sacraments purges the substance that is corrupted by sin, namely, the substance of the person himself; cf. above, p. 78 n. 134.

141 *Lectures on Galatians* (1535), AE 26:232, WA 40/1:368.14.

142 *Palladius und Tilemann*, WA 39/1:203.16–19, 235.9–236.5 (AI), 241.18–27, 242.22f. See also *Against Hanswurst* (1541), AE 41:218, WA 51:520.25–29.

143 *Disputation Concerning Justification*, AE 34:153, WA 39/1:83.2f.; *Lectures on Galatians* (1535), AE 26:232, WA 40/1:367.22.

144 *Theses Concerning Faith and Law* (1535), AE 34:113f., WA 39/1:48.7–30. *Lectures on Galatians* (1535), AE 26:229f., WA 40/1:363.28–364.17. See also Luther, *Christian*

man are at last united and finally distinct. In justifying faith man finally ceases his attempt to be God and is again man, a creature. Luther's doctrine of justification is essentially the soteriological application of Chalcedon's Christology.[145] With this in mind Luther's (re-)definition of theology's subject[146] is not really a redefinition. Rather, in saying that theology is about man the sinner and God the Justifier, Luther did what he was oft wont to do, namely, treat an issue in an ad hoc fashion, saying what he did as a corrective to a specific error. For Luther, too, *God* is the subject of theology, but for God alone to be God and not to be displaced by a humanly produced amalgam of self-justifying man's own creation, God brings man to recognize that he is a sinner and that God alone is his Justifier. Only in this way is God truly God and so the proper subject of theology. Justifying faith, a human trust, is, therefore, nothing other than the proper attribution of divinity to God, according to which God also reckons man as fully man, attributing to him full humanity and not the corrupted humanness of his sinful nature. In this restored relationship stands the end game of justification according to Luther: God is "all in all, and marvelous in His saints," and man is "His perfectly pure creation."[147]

A final contour keeps this rounded and holistic presentation of salvation from ever going static. Luther's doctrine of justification lives in a radically polarized application of Law and Gospel,[148] which in the lived experience of believers and the on-the-ground reality of the Church plays out in the ministerially exercised Office of the Keys. Justification, along with its counterpart condemnation, happens when the Gospel and the Law are preached, when the Sacraments are administered or withheld, when sins are forgiven or retained.[149] In this

---

Freedom (1520), AE 31:350f., WA 7:53.34–54.30; and *Lectures on Genesis* (1535–45), AE 8:193, WA 44:720–23f. On justification as recognition, see Oswald Bayer, *Living by Faith: Justification and Sanctification*, trans. Geoffrey W. Bromily (Grand Rapids: Eerdmans, 2003), 1–8.

145 See above, p. 73 n. 97. The counterpart to the inseparability of the believer's person and Christ's person (an anti-Nestorian motif, see above, p. 74 n. 109) is that in a fallen world only in the person of Christ are God and man distinct and not being mixed up by man's attempts to be God (an anti-Eutychian motif).

146 See above, pp. 76–77 n. 123. Cf. Oswald Bayer, *Theology the Lutheran Way*, trans. Jeffrey G. Silcock and Mark C. Mattes (Grand Rapids: Eerdmans, 2007), 17–21; and Bayer, *Martin Luther's Theology*, 29–43.

147 *Palladius und Tilemann*, WA 39/1:203:36f.

148 See, e.g., SA III IV and III XIII 3 with III III 42–45. See also *Lectures on Galatians* (1535), AE 26:129f., WA 40/1:228.27–229.21; *Palladius and Tilemann*, WA 39/1:245.19–246.11, 249.8–15; *Disputation Concerning Justification*, AE 34.161, WA 39/1:91.23–25 (R^1).

149 See Mumme, *Die Präsenz Christi im Amt*, esp. 335–52.

important regard justification is not first and foremost a doctrine but an event, an encounter. As a mediately delivered encounter, any perceived discrepancy between the external, alien righteous of Christ for Christians and the internal, proper righteousness (of Christ) in Christians is quite easily diffused.[150] What Christ salvifically works in the heart—namely faith—He works through the external means of His Word and Sacraments delivered by ministers He Himself has sent.[151] On what the triune God so mediately and thereby surely does and says, the conscience may firmly rely.[152] The certitude and assurance of right standing with God, of being in His favor, stands as a hallmark of Luther's theology that one encounters at nearly every turn.[153] It is a mistake, however, to take this simply as some individualized, subjective, and therefore perhaps merely psychological conviction. The certitude of consciences that find their rest in Christ is effected by Christ Himself setting them at rest by having His Word preached and His Sacraments administered to them. Care of souls (*Seelsorge*) in a tradition taking bearings from Luther is therefore nothing less than mediately delivered and fully polarized application of Law and Gospel, the former reducing persons to nothing and the latter creating and giving life out of this nothing. This ministers do in the stead of Christ, who Himself humbled Himself to the nothingness of death so that His resurrection might itself be the shared reality of His fellow human beings.

Having traced the terminology of Luther's doctrine of justification and explored its key contours, a basic pattern of his soteriology is offered as a navigational tool with the following points:

1. Justification has to do with the setting right of the fallen creation; "justification" terminology is used alongside and interchangeably with other soteriological terminology such as redemption.
2. Human beings, created in or into the image of God, are fallen creatures, fully corrupt in their sin, and thereby incapable of righting their state of affairs and their relationship with their Creator.[154]

---

150 See *Disputation Concerning Justification*, AE 34:153, WA 39/1:83.22–25; AE 34:177f., WA 40/1:108.24–109.3; and *Theses Concerning Faith and Law*, AE 34:110, WA 39/1:27–34. See above, pp. 67–69 and nn. 65–76.

151 See *Confession Concerning Christ's Supper*, AE 37:366, WA 26:506.8–12; SA III VIII 3–13.

152 *Lectures on Genesis*, AE 8:185, WA 48:714.11f.

153 Summarized in Lindberg, *European Reformations*, 60–69.

154 Justification takes place without human works or merit. Human beings can do nothing to get right with God.

3. Justification is entirely God's work; it is an act of merciful *divine* monergism carried out by and in the *person* and therefore through the *humanity* of Jesus Christ.[155]
4. Jesus Christ, the God-man, alone justifies, that is, sets things right between men and God, by His death and resurrection.[156]
5. Human beings are justified solely by faith.[157]
6. Faith, which is trust in Jesus Christ as Savior and Justifier, saves because of its object, which is the God-man, Jesus Christ.
7. This faith is worked and sustained by the Holy Spirit who encounters people with Christ by way of the preached Word and administered Sacraments.
8. Justification is an eschatological reality being worked in the present, where sins are not reckoned to the believer for the sake of Christ; to the believer, likewise for the sake of Christ, is presently reckoned the full righteousness that he will finally come to be after death in the resurrection.
9. Faith in Christ entails Christ being and acting in the believer, and the believer being in and sheltered under Christ.
10. Being justified entails the renewal of the proper form of human being through the restoration of the image of God in human beings, which image Christ is.

This soteriology is what Luther presented as his doctrine of justification. Is it "curtailed"?[158] Is it fundamentally at odds with the great story of the Christian faith that N. T. Wright wishes to tell? Or must Luther not be curtailed and foiled to act as the "old" counterpart of a perspective that wants to be "new"?

Luther and Wright on Salvation: The Actual Friendship of Alleged Foes

Holistically operating as the doctrine of Christ's person and work employed for understanding and presenting human salvation, Luther's doctrine of justification hardly falls prey to the charge of being about how people get saved and go

155 Justification happens by God's mercy or grace alone (*sola gratia*).

156 *Solus Christus.*

157 *Sola fide.*

158 See above, p. 64 n. 46.

to heaven by having some *thing* called "righteousness" imputed to them, despite what Wright's comments would have his readers believe. Although the merits, and demerits, of Luther's exegesis can certainly be debated, the notion that the nature and scope of his soteriology begins and ends with the forensic transaction of an "ontologized" righteousness is simply farcical. The contours traced above are, even in their basic form, nothing nearly so flat as that. Justification according to Luther is about totally corrupted human beings receiving a divine-humanly delivered, salvific, tangible-though-hidden, ongoing encounter with the Son of God become man, who, as fully active and effective God and fully passive and obedient man, faithfully restores in the eschaton what He promises now, namely, human being made right with the Creator. Surprisingly, what is usually cast as a feud between Wright and Luther can, upon closer examination, be read as a broad soteriological friendship, wherein differences obtain that make for mutual sharpening of thought between pupils of Paul.

Possibilities for a mutual sharpening of thought must wait until the broad congruity of Luther's and Wright's soteriologies is shown, but first two points must be ceded, at least to a degree. First, did the covenant made with Abraham and the purposeful election of Israel for the rescue and renewal of the world play omnipresent roles in Luther's articulation of justification as they do in Wright's? No, at least not to the same degree. This admission relates to a difficulty long since recognized by Luther's modern biographers, historians, and would-be systematizers of his thought: Luther's understanding of the Jews was problematic. And if more work has been done on Second Temple Judaism in the last generation than in the previous millennium, as Wright claims,[159] one may not realistically expect a sixteenth-century Augustinian to produce the same results as a twenty-first-century New Testament scholar. Second, Luther is, according to what Wright demonstrates from Paul, guilty of expounding "justification" in a way that takes in too much data. As demonstrated above, he tosses the term around as a sort of synonym for "salvation" that is also interchangeable with other soteriological terminology. Luther is not, however, guilty of shrinking the soteriological data to fit the term "justification." He does not, in contradistinction to claims of some modern-day self-proclaimed heirs of his doctrine, speak of justification as the strict imputation of righteousness that as such excludes facets of transformation or being in Christ, a doctrine of justification that is thereby safely quarantined from ecclesiological and (to borrow a word from his friend Wright) *redefined* ethical considerations.[160] Here something very

159 Wright, *Paul: In Fresh Perspective*, 3.

160 Cf. Wright, *Paul and Faithfulness*, 913f.

mundane is ceded: Luther, an Observant Augustinian with one foot planted in the Middle Ages even as the other was ever treading into modernity, applied the term "justification" as the Western tradition had for more than a millennium, that is, broadly and without great concern for what justification terminology (as opposed to salvation terminology or redemption terminology, etc.) precisely denotes in Paul's writings.[161] This hardly means, however, that Luther's soteriology is as flat as a farmer's field in central Illinois.

To substantiate the claim of surprisingly broad coincidence between these alleged foes, one might ask Luther and Wright to play a couple hands of soteriology, with Wright dealing the cards or even stacking the deck, just to see if the old reformer can follow his new suit. For the first hand, Luther must follow the "seven broad emphases" that, Wright says, modern exegetes recognize in Paul's doctrine of salvation.[162] And for the second hand, Wright's own seven-point sequence of thought about the shape of Paul's doctrine of justification will serve as the dealing of the cards.[163]

First, the seven broad emphases of Paul's soteriology: (1) justification, (2) anthropology, (3) being in Christ, (4) salvation history, (5) apocalyptic, (6) transformation/deification, and (7) covenant.[164] As to justification, the specific topic that is at issue here, Luther's somewhat imprecise use of the term has already been noted. Nevertheless, Luther and Wright agree that justification is forensic, but it is not only forensic. Further, Wright and Luther agree that insofar as justification is forensic, what is happening is forgiveness, acquittal, and a nonreckoning of sin. Indeed, Luther's teaching about imputation is first and foremost about what is *not* imputed, namely sin. On another level, Luther presents the future, full, and final righteousness of the believer being reckoned to the believer in the present, but this is not Wright's bogeyman of God imputing someone else's thing-like righteousness of moral virtue to the believer. In general Luther's present-tense reckoning of eschatological righteousness is supported by Wright's interpretation of Romans. The notion that an "ontologized" righteousness of Christ or God, as moral attribute with a sort of existence of its own, gets reckoned to the sinner is rather hard to come by in Luther, despite Wright's generalized caricature of the reformer's teaching.[165] An imputed fulfilling of the Law "through Christ" does not, according to Luther, equal the imputing of an

161 See above, p. 59 n. 18.

162 Wright, *Paul and Faithfulness*, 777–82.

163 Wright, *Paul and Faithfulness*, 925–66.

164 See above, p. 59 n. 22.

165 Wright, *Paul and Faithfulness*, 947, 951.

alien and unreal moral quality, but rather points to the real work that Christ has Himself accomplished and absolutely will accomplish in believers, also as a collective, the Church.[166] The anthropology of Luther's soteriology, as sketched above, is robust, with its guiding star being a Chalcedonian Christology rather than some modern Western form of individualism. Luther's soteriological anthropology is christological and ontological, with any existentialist impulses taking a backseat to these driving forces. As to the Pauline emphasis of being *in Christ* (*en Christo*), along with its counterpart, Christ's presence in the believer, this, too, plays strongly in Luther's understanding of salvation, aligning with and even undergirding categories of identity and nonimputation of sin on the one hand (i.e., believer in Christ), and of renewal, good works, love, and vocation on the other (i.e., Christ in the believer), none of which are safely quarantined from justification and salvation in Luther's polar application of theology. Wright tethers the temporal considerations of salvation history to a redefined eschatology ubiquitously present in his writing on Paul, and this redefined eschatology Wright believes carries Paul's sequence of thought on justification.[167] Luther is not without his salvation-historical insights, but there does seem to be some noticeable difference between Wright and Luther in regard to this particular soteriological emphasis. However, Luther's soteriology is also loaded with eschatological and chronological considerations inasmuch as the Christology that propels his anthropological insights and the incorporative dimensions of his doctrine of justification is a Christology of the full divinity and therefore the full eternality of Christ, "who was, and is, and is coming" (Rev. 1:8). The tension between the now and the not yet of Christian existence and the inherent contradiction of the simultaneity of being saints and sinners are broken and resolved only by the final exulted coming of Him who once humbly came as the Son of Mary. Passing over the apocalyptic emphasis for a moment, one may also note a similarity to Wright's theme of transformation or deification.[168] Clearly Luther's doctrine of justification entails change, regeneration—and this on a level more profound than augmentation of moral behavior or even moral character. There is a restoration of the image of God in the works here. Luther, however, at least in his later writings, does not think of or present this change so much in the way of human beings being made divine as he does in the way of human beings being made human through the proper humanity of Jesus Christ; this is more

166 Luther, *Palladius und Tilemann*, WA 39/1:250.5–11, and *Against Hanswurst* as p. 79 n. 142 above.

167 See above, p. 59 n. 22; p. 84 n. 164.

168 See above, p. 68 n. 74; p. 69 n. 76.

a humanification or anthroposis than a divinization or theosis.[169] Covenant, Wright's unifying theme among the seven, can do what it does by highlighting God's faithfulness to and actualization of His promises. Luther may not lace the boot of "the single-plan-of-the-creator-through-Abraham-and-Israel-for-the-world"[170] quite as tightly as Wright would like, but there is scarcely a category so essential to and at work in Luther's theology as promise, being as it is for him a synonym of the efficacious Gospel.[171] And finally apocalyptic: on the one hand, it is common knowledge that Luther viewed the world apocalyptically; he thought the end of the world very near. The way he looks at the world is shaped not only by the Old Testament prophets and John the Baptist in the Gospels but also by an apocalyptic element of Paul that Luther associates with the ministerial exercise of the Office of the Keys.[172] When Christians interact with their ministers, according to Luther, this is interacting with Christ; this is the in-breaking of His gracious or, if need be, His devastating rule in personal and certainly collective Christian life.[173]

Seven for seven: Luther has played a hand of soteriology, not only following thematic soteriological plays, but even coming up with the same trump card as the dealer.

On to the second hand: Wright now deals Luther a straight sequence of justification cards—a sequence of thought on the shape of justification in Paul, with the deck stacked under the controlling category of eschatology: (1) creational eschatology, (2) anthropological eschatology, (3) covenantal eschatology, (4) forensic eschatology, (5) final eschatology, (6) inaugurated forensic and covenantal eschatology, and (7) declaration in the present.[174] Briefly put, according to Wright: (1) the Creator's intention is, finally, to remake creation, which (2) means human beings themselves being set right. (3) This setting right of humans and remaking of creation God accomplishes through the establishment or giving of His covenant to Abraham. (4) To His covenant promises God

169 Wright himself gives reason to believe that he may have some understanding for this slight, but significant, redirection of category: see *Justification*, 193.

170 See above, p. 60 n. 23.

171 Insight into Luther's understanding of promise and its role in his theology has driven the most developed systematic interpretation of Luther's theology in the last generation, namely, that of Oswald Bayer.

172 See Rom. 1:17f. in view of 1:16; 1 Cor. 2:10 in the context of 1 Corinthians 2; Gal. 1:12, 16; Eph. 3:3, 5, where Paul associates this terminology with the work of his apostolic office; cf. 1 Cor. 3:13, where the topic is the character of that work itself.

173 Mumme, *Präsenz Christi*, chs. 3, 4, and 6.

174 See above, p. 84 n. 163.

is faithful; He shows Himself righteous and in the right. (5) God vindicates Himself by fully and finally vindicating His covenant people, who are marked as His people by faith, which locates them in this people, in Messiah. (6) Full and final justification is brought forward—the final eschatology is inaugurated—in Messiah; the intended goal of "the ultimate reconstruction" of human being and so of image-bearing humans[175] has come forward into the present. (7) This "bursting of the Creator's future purpose into the present time is matched exactly by the declaration, in the present and in advance, of the verdict on the last day."[176]

Clearly the greatest interest here lies in how Wright and Luther play that final card, but prior to it the pairing of play in the first six is noteworthy. The exposition of Luther above shows that, in articulating justification, he, too, does not stop short of renewed creation nor of human beings as renewed creatures in this creation. This renewal comes through the Creator's effective promises: He does what He says; He is faithful. And faith pairs with divine faithfulness and truthfulness in reckoning such faithfulness and truthfulness to God—in reckoning divinity to God. Thus in (justifying) faith God is God and man is man. Faith now entails and marks what the future renewal of the image of God in human beings will be. Christ Himself, the resurrected God-man, is this image, and He is renewing this image in believers, who likewise are in Him. Six cards, and Luther can play on them all.

When it comes to the decisive declaration in the present,[177] Wright plays directly into Luther's hand. According to Wright, the declaration of justified status in the Messiah is a status conferred by the declaration itself. To put this in systematic-theological terms, this forensic declaration is synthetic as opposed to analytic: it brings about the reality it declares by the declaring of it.[178] The declaration of the Creator in raising Jesus from the dead is repeated in the case of believers through the Spirit's work in the preaching of the Gospel. The declaration, which obtains in Christ, sets people into a status of being in the right, resulting in real and full assurance of justification in a justification scheme that holds participation and declaration together. Wright's exposition of faith in

175 See Wright, *Paul and Faithfulness*, 936, here discussed under the fifth point in the sequence, but inaugurated in the resurrection of Messiah, the sixth point.

176 Wright, *Paul and Faithfulness*, 944.

177 To this point and the substance of this paragraph in general, see Wright, *Paul and Faithfulness*, 944–64.

178 Wright, *Justification*, 206. Cf. Mark Mattes, "Luther on Justification as Forensic and Effective," in *The Oxford Handbook of Martin Luther's Theology*, ed. Robert Kolb, Irene Dingel, and L'ubomír Batka (Oxford: Oxford University Press, 2014), 264–73, who draws the conclusion that justification is effective *because it is forensic*.

relation to the declaration of justification in the present could hardly be more Luther-an: faith is not some lighter work or even God-pleasing attitude of which people are capable. As with Luther, faith is not a human ability,[179] nor is it valued as a quality possessed by the believer. Instead, "it is defined entirely by, and in terms of, its object," and thereby faith is "the sign of truly human life, giving glory to the powerful creator and believing that he does what he promises."[180] For both Luther and Wright faith has to do with being truly human.[181] The veracity and certainty of this verdict is not dependent on any subsequent work of the believer, such as efforts at personal renewal; rather, the future verdict spoken over the whole of life *will* correspond to the present verdict, which is spoken over nothing but faith.[182] For Christian life Wright's construal has the same explosive, game-changing potential that Luther's own theological program (if Luther was ever programmatic) did: it overturns the normal line of inquiry entirely. Human beings' ultimate status before their Creator is not dependent on renewal subsequent to their being declared in the right with God and members of His people; rather, subsequent renewal and transformation may actually look to the faithfulness of the God who declares the unjust just, who forgives sins, and may absolutely rely on the fact that what He has declared to be He will Himself bring to be, now in time and fully at the end of time. Thus the locuted status of righteousness becomes the point of departure for a theology of the Christian life that can hardly be brought under the heading of "ethics."[183] The verdict of non-imputation of sin ("not guilty") that is brought forward, into the present, in Jesus Christ is what frees people to resurrected human existence. As Wright himself recognizes, what he is saying actually affirms much of what the Old Perspective on Paul and the reformers' doctrine of justification were attempting to say, albeit set now in a larger framework. What may come as a surprise to Wright is that this overarching framework was already largely there with at least one of the reformers, who, at the end of the day, seems also to have been a rather attentive pupil of Paul even if he did toss about "justification" terminology rather loosely and read some medieval legalism onto Paul's Judaizers.

179 Luther, SC Creed 6.

180 Wright, *Paul and Faithfulness*, 952; cf. *Paul and Faithfulness*, 954f.

181 Luther, see above, p. 71 n. 92. Wright, *Justification*, 209: "Faith . . . indicates the presence of genuine, humble, trusting, and indeed we might say image-bearing humanity."

182 Wright, *Paul and Faithfulness*, 958. Note here the declaration of justification *by faith alone*.

183 Cf. Wright, *Paul and Faithfulness*, 1030, as well as *Paul: In Fresh Perspective*, 147, and *Justification*, 139.

Wright states very clearly that justification happens "by grace through faith in the present time on the basis of the work of the Messiah."[184]And he does get to the ever-important *solas* of justification in each instance: *sola gratia* (by grace alone), *sola fide* (by faith alone), *solus Christus* (Christ alone).[185] If readers familiar with the reach of Luther's terminology, the contours of his thinking, and the basic pattern of his soteriology read Wright without simply assuming, not least on the basis of Wright's own suggestion, that the two are at odds over soteriology, the overlap and similarity in these two students of Paul can be rather astounding. For both theologians as with their interlocutor Paul, the core problem of human beings is their failure to trust God as faithful and loving Creator, and the rectification of this problem comes solely from God's own faithfulness to His creation, toward which He acts generously, creatively, and healingly in mercy.[186]

Although the overlap between Luther's and Wright's readings of Paul and their given soteriologies is by no means full, there are hardly foes for the finding here. In fact, on a larger theological level there exists the possibility for a rather fast friendship between these two disciples of Paul. Friendship, of course, recognizes diversity and welcomes sharpening of thought, and here, too, there is potential, in both directions.

As indicated above, the New Perspective on Paul has identified a deficiency in a very standard interpretation of Second Temple Judaism, now being overcome in recent scholarship. Although some Jews of the period may have been impossibly seeking a status of righteousness according to the Torah, this does not mean that they were performing certain actions in the hope of meriting God's favor and thus getting to heaven, but it is not impossible that Luther read such medieval "legalism" back on Paul's antagonists. Similarly, Wright's emphasis on the need to evaluate what "righteousness" and related terminology denoted in their historical contexts is an important point that he brings to the table. One must also be impressed by the potential for an integrated biblical theology contained in Wright's ability to present Christian theology in a single, great narrative, and so avoid interpretation by way of disparity across God's covenantal dealings with human beings, and the world, in the Old and New Testaments. Frustration with Wright can sometimes come from his habit of painting with broad strokes; in regard to Luther, Wright's paint does not actually make it to the canvas. On the other hand, especially for persons first learning

184 Wright, *Paul and Faithfulness*, 926.

185 Wright, *Paul and Faithfulness*, 958—faith (see above, n. 184); *Justification*, 210—grace; *Justification*, 203—Christ.

186 See Wright, *Justification*, 89; cf. *Justification*, 70.

about the Christian faith, for novices in the discipline of academic theology, and even for the working preacher, simple, clear, and overarching structures—stories—that hang the whole message of the Sacred Scriptures clearly and succinctly together are absolutely necessary; and this exegete's story is both compelling and beautiful.

Luther first brings Wright some aid on an issue left open by and therefore somewhat bedeviling to the New Perspective in general, namely, whether the works or fidelity of Christians declared just in the present contribute to the final verdict of justification and thereby to salvation. As far as the multiple perspectives of this New Perspective on Paul go, some do see a requirement here,[187] which cannot be easily reconciled with the full assurance that Wright contends believers may have about their status with God, both now and in the future, nor with his assertion that the future verdict *will* correspond to the present verdict, and that the final verdict is not contingent on any subsequent moral work or personal renewal of the person-now-declared-justified.[188] How can people be sure of their standing with their Creator? Luther's way of dealing with this very pastoral question is not to answer it this way or that way in any abstract fashion, but through the full and polarizing application of a theology that affirms the final judgment being passed over the whole of life and thus over people's works while also maintaining that Christ alone saves and people stand just with God by faith in Him. The question of the verdict that lies behind a believer and the one that lies before presses precisely in the present. Luther's way of dealing with such questions is not an overarching answer but an ad hoc address responding to the question posed, grounded in core christological, sacramental, and ministerial convictions woven through his soteriology. Luther understands God to have a present-tense, mediate, and thereby certain way of dealing, on the one hand, with those whose status in Christ has become license to act and live as if outside of Christ. On the other hand, God has a way of gently handling those who are all too cognizant of the fact that they have thought about and acted toward others as though they were not in Christ, in contradiction of their own Christian identity. In the present contradiction of past verdict in view of future verdict, no detached treatment will do. Instead, what is needed is a present-tense, authoritative declaration that some are not in Christ and not justified and that others indeed are and so have no sins counted against them. The present and ongoing passing of verdict over the life of persons called as people of God is a *sine qua non* that holds the certainty of baptismal identity

187 See Yinger, *New Perspective on Paul*, 82 and 103f.

188 E.g., Wright, *Paul and Faithfulness*, 955.

and future, full salvation together. This polar application of what Luther knew as Law and Gospel under the Office of the Keys he saw operative in the apostle's ministry, and held that this apostolic authority belongs presently to the Church's ordained ministerium.[189]

Second, Luther's understanding of a present-tense, ministerially delivered declaration of justification is undergirded by a christological conviction that has the potential to strengthen Wright's eschatological insights. Christ, as both God and man, is He who perpetually comes. The apocalyptic element of salvation always hinges on His once coming as the crucified and risen one and on His coming again in glory, but this element of salvation is not thereby limited to these two temporal instances. The apocalyptic encounter with Christ at play in Paul's own ministry continues apostolic-ministerially, perpetually, and so presently veiled in humility until that glorious return. Discrepancies between present and future (and final) justification are thus answered not only eschatologically but christologically, by God who comes as man at every point that can be labeled "now."

This brings us to a third and final instance of Luther's whetting stone. I have already stated that elements of participation, indwelling, presence, and renewal, at least in Luther's later theology, point more in a direction of salvation as anthroposis than theosis, and humanization rather than divinization. To this the observation may be added that if the motion of Christ's salutary work takes its bearings from the incarnation, two things result. First, a good many questions regarding human agency anywhere in soteriology rather quickly dissolve: the object of faith has become man and having this object the believer becomes man. Second, the decisive and valuable bookends to Wright's grand narrative are not contradicted, namely, the restoration of *creation*—and with that man as proper and full creature—by the *Creator*. If things are in fact set to rights by a restoration of the Creator-creature relationship, how could this happen precisely through the removal of this distinction?

When Luther is examined directly, on the basis of his own work, and not simply dismissed by way of popular and generalized appropriations of his thinking, he hardly matches the target of N. T. Wright's criticisms for truncated misreading of Paul. In fact, a close look at Luther evidences overarching agreement between his and Wright's understanding of salvation and even of

189 See 1 Cor. 5:1–5 and 2 Cor. 2:5–11.

justification. On the basis of what can be shown from Luther's own writings, one may hope that scholars of the New Perspective, especially those of such eminence as Wright, would stop misusing Luther in glib and unscholarly fashion as part of what is a rhetorical foil, which in terms of the eminent reformer may be effective as a foil but is less than honest as scholarship. On the other hand, students of Luther, those who identify themselves as Lutheran, and even those with just an honest appreciation of Luther's theology should not hesitate to seriously consider and, where exegetically warranted, appropriate valuable insights of the New Perspective proponents such as Wright. Serious meditation on the writings of Paul resulting in "Ah ha!" moments of insight that enable Christians to run through the great and unified whole of their Scriptures with fresh wind in their sails to meet a faithful and promise-keeping God acting out of mercy for their salvation can hardly be considered non-*Luther*-an. This is, after all, exactly how the reflections of the aged preacher, professor, and reformer of Wittenberg describe that he was "altogether born again," and sent running "through the Scriptures."[190]

190 *Preface to Luther's Latin Writings*, AE 34:337, WA 54:186.8–11.

The Source of Biblical Authority: Gospel or God?

Cameron A. MacKenzie

WHAT DO WE DO WITH THE BIBLE? THAT QUESTION HAS bedeviled the institutional church ever since the Enlightenment, and answers have varied widely—everything from snipping away the miraculous, as Thomas Jefferson did with the Gospels,[1] to Rudolf Bultmann's "demythologizing" the Bible but "preaching the Word" anyway.[2] Of course, there are still some holdouts who accept the text as factually true—supernatural content and all—but their numbers are small, at least in mainstream academic circles such as the Society of Biblical Literature.[3] Accordingly, the degree to which the Bible

1 *Thomas Jefferson's Life of Jesus* (Springfield, IL: Templegate, 1975). For Jefferson's religion, see Alf J. Mapp Jr., *The Faiths of Our Fathers: What America's Founders* Really *Believed* (New York: Fall River Press, 2003), 3–21; and Peter S. Onuf, *The Mind of Thomas Jefferson* (Charlottesville: University of Virginia Press, 2007), 145–48.

2 Rudolf Bultmann, *Jesus Christ and Mythology* (New York: Charles Scribner's Sons, 1958), 78–83. For Bultmann's theology, see John Macquarrie, "Rudolf Bultmann," in Dean G. Peerman and Martin E. Marty, eds., *A Handbook of Christian Theologians*, enlarged ed. (Nashville, TN: Abingdon, 1984), 445–63; and Alisdair I. C. Heron, *A Century of Protestant Theology* (Philadelphia: Westminster Press, 1980), 99–118.

3 Of course, the SBL is not the only professional association for biblical scholars, but, founded in 1880 and with more than 8,000 members (as of 2015, https://www.sbl-site.org/SBLDashboard.aspx. Accessed 12/3/16), it is one of the oldest and most important. Nevertheless, in 1949, conservative scholars formed the Evangelical Theological Society

exercises any sort of authority in contemporary churches also varies widely and may explain why some churches found it relatively easy to accept social change in the form of women's ordination or homosexual unions while others did not, since the biblical text excludes both.[4]

For Lutheran churches, there is always an additional problem besides the Bible: just what do they do with *Luther* and the Scriptures. After all, when you name your church after a person, it is inevitable that for any doctrine or practice, someone is going to ask what so-and-so thought about it. That certainly is true for the Lutherans. Even Bultmann, for example, defended his demythologizing project as the extension of Luther's doctrine of justification by faith, from soteriology to epistemology. The first excluded security based on good works; the second, security based on knowledge of nature or history. Of course, Bultmann was not arguing that his position was the same as Luther's, but that demythologizing was a *Lutheran* way of handling the Scriptures in the modern world.[5]

Luther lived on the other side of the Enlightenment. His world was filled with the supernatural, and he had no trouble believing in either a God or a devil who makes his presence known in the affairs of men.[6] He believed in signs and

---

and restricted membership to those who affirmed the inerrancy of the Scriptures. Conservative scholars are also eligible to join the SBL, but from the beginning, advocates of higher critical approaches to the Scriptures have been more prominent in the leadership. See Ernest W. Saunders, *Searching the Scriptures: A History of the Society of Biblical Literature 1880–1980* (Chico, CA: Scholars Press, 1982), 31, 52–54, 68–71, 83. https://www.sbl-site.org/assets/pdfs/SearchingScriptures.pdf. Accessed 12/3/16. See also Adele Reinhartz, "Editor's Foreword: The *Journal of Biblical Literature* and the Critical Investigation of the Bible," *Journal of Biblical Literature* 134 (2015): 457–70. http://web.b.ebscohost.com/ehost/pdfviewer/pdfviewer?vid=3&sid=aaa59d11-97b1-4972-8566-eb9c34d252b1%40sessionmgr2. Accessed 12/3/16. Reinhartz points out that in the 1970s, SBL and its publications began promoting not just historical-critical approaches to the Bible but other forms of criticism as well, for instance, literary, linguistic, anthropological, and gender approaches.

4 See Matthew Harrison and John Pless, eds., *Women Pastors? The Ordination of Women in Biblical Lutheran Perspective* (St. Louis: Concordia, 2008); and The Lutheran Church—Missouri Synod, *A Plan for Ministry to Homosexuals and Their Families* (St. Louis: LCMS, 1999).

5 Bultmann, *Jesus Christ and Mythology*, 83–84.

6 Denis R. Janz, *The Westminster Handbook to Martin Luther* (Louisville: Westminster John Knox, 2010), s.v. "Devil"; and Heiko A. Oberman, *Luther: Man between God and the Devil*, trans. Eileen Walliser-Schwarzbart (New York: Image Books, 1989), 102–6. Hans-Martin Barth, *Der Teufel und Jesus Christ in der Theologie Martin Luthers* (Göttingen: Vandenhoeck & Ruprecht, 1967), 13, maintains that "Luther's idea of the devil follows directly from his understanding of Christ and his idea of God. Therefore, they must definitely be considered together."

portents (though not astrology) and the efficacy of curses and spells.[7] Therefore, a Bible that recorded divine interventions in human history from the flood to the exodus, from the virgin birth to the resurrection, and that promised still another and final such intervention with the second coming presented Luther with no intellectual problems.[8] The problems of faith were matters of human sin (people are proud and think they can save themselves) and human experience (people find it difficult to believe in a loving God when human existence is so miserable) but not skepticism about the facticity of biblical accounts.

So what the Bible recorded in its narratives—whether natural occurrences or supernatural—was factual and true. The reliability of biblical accounts was not an issue for the reformer nor for his contemporaries. What those narratives *meant* was the challenge, not what they reported. If, for example, we consider one of Luther's most famous disputes, that with Huldrych Zwingli over the presence of Christ's body and blood in the Lord's Supper, neither of the two combatants questioned the authenticity of our Lord's actually instituting the Sacrament on the eve of His crucifixion and of saying when He did, "This is My body." Luther and Zwingli argued over how to understand the words that Jesus had really spoken.[9]

But this is certainly not the case today. Many (most?) biblical scholars no longer accept the canonical Gospels as reliable accounts of the historical Jesus, of what He said and what He did. They may still study the Gospels as works of theological literature or as sources for understanding the communities that produced them but not for telling us about a first-century Jew named Jesus—or at least not much.[10] So, for example, in the 1990s the scholars of the Jesus Seminar assessed the reliability of Jesus' sayings that contain the words "This is My body."

7 For a brief description, see Martin Brecht, *Martin Luther: His Road to Reformation 1483–1521*, trans. James L. Schaaf (Philadelphia: Fortress, 1985), 11–12. Dated but still helpful is Robert Herndon Fife, *Young Luther: The Intellectual and Religious Development of Martin Luther to 1518* (New York: Macmillan, 1928), 24–31. For astrology, see Heinrich Bornkamm, *Luther's World of Thought*, trans. Martin H. Bertram (St. Louis: Concordia, 1958), 185–87.

8 "The problems of the relationship of the Bible to natural science, to history, to anthropology, and to philosophy, which have become such significant problems since the Enlightenment, did not exist for him" (Paul Althaus, *The Theology of Martin Luther*, trans. Robert C. Schultz [Philadelphia: Fortress, 1966], 86).

9 On this controversy, see the chapter by Roland Ziegler, below, pp. 217–49.

10 For varying degrees of skepticism regarding the historical character of the canonical Gospels since the Enlightenment, see *The Historical Jesus: Five Views*, ed. James K. Beilby and Paul Rhodes Eddy (Downers Grove, IL: IVP Academic, 2009), especially the introduction entitled "The Quest for the Historical Jesus" (9–54).

In Matthew and Luke they concluded that the sayings were totally inauthentic while in Mark they judged a similar saying also inauthentic but perhaps containing ideas close to Jesus' own.[11] But if Jesus never really said the words over which the sixteenth-century reformers argued so vehemently, it hardly seems worthwhile continuing that argument today, let alone permitting it to become church-dividing as it did in that earlier period. A commonly held view today is that the Bible itself presents differing theologies and varying doctrines.[12] If that's the case, why should the Church attempt to establish doctrinal unity among the churches?

Carl Braaten, a preeminent theologian of the Evangelical Lutheran Church in America (ELCA), stated as much more than thirty years ago when he wrote:

> Critical attention to what the texts [of the Bible] actually say has exploded the notion that one orthodox dogmatics can be mined out of Scripture. There are different theological tendencies and teachings in the various texts. Ecumenically this has led to the practical conclusion that the traditional demand for a complete consensus in doctrine may be wrongheaded, if even the Scriptures fail to contain such a consensus. Perhaps the unity of the church can be realized without the kind of doctrinal uniformity demanded by the sixteenth-century theologians.[13]

Given that kind of thinking about the Bible, it is hardly surprising that historically Lutheran churches, for example, Braaten's own ELCA, have been able to establish full communion fellowship with historically Reformed churches,

11 "Most Fellows [of the Jesus Seminar] were convinced that the [Lord's] supper tradition had been so overlaid with Christianizing elements and interpretation that it is impossible to recover anything of an original event, much less any of the original words spoken by Jesus" (Robert W. Funk, Roy W. Hoover, and Jesus Seminar, *The Five Gospels: The Search for the Authentic Words of Jesus. New Translation and Commentary* [New York: Macmillan, 1993], 117–18, 260, 387). The Seminar used color codes to summarize their judgment regarding the sayings of Jesus. "This is My body" was printed in black in Matthew and Luke but gray in Mark. See *The Five Gospels*, pp. 35–37, for the meaning of the colors.

12 For example, see Bart D. Ehrman, *The New Testament: A Historical Introduction to the Early Christian Writings*, 2nd ed. (New York: Oxford University Press, 2000), 12–13; James D. G. Dunn, *Unity and Diversity in the New Testament: An Inquiry into the Character of Earliest Christianity* (Philadelphia: Westminster Press, 1977), 372; Norman Perrin, *The New Testament, an Introduction: Proclamation and Parenesis, Myth and History* (New York: Harcourt Brace Jovanovich, 1974), 17–19; and Pheme Perkins, *Reading the New Testament: An Introduction*, 2nd ed. (New York: Paulist Press, 1988), 10, 18–20, 163–64.

13 Carl E. Braaten, "The Holy Scriptures," in *Christian Dogmatics*, ed. Carl E. Braaten and Robert W. Jenson (Philadelphia: Fortress, 1984), 1:77.

such as the Presbyterian Church (USA), the United Church of Christ, and the Reformed Church in America.[14]

Besides the certainty of doctrine, this new way of thinking about the Bible also calls into question *Lutheran* identity in other particulars. For example, is there still a Lutheran method of interpreting the Bible? Or, to put it another way, can a Lutheran today still identify with Luther's approach to the Scriptures when he no longer agrees with Luther on the origins of the Bible and the facticity of its narratives? Of course, he can try—and many do—but only by neglecting critical elements of Luther's thought. He may still sound like Luther, but he has lost the substance of Luther's thought regarding the Bible.

For some, one way to solve the dichotomy between Luther's viewpoint and that of modernizing Lutherans concerning the Scriptures is to conflate the authority of the Bible with that of the Gospel. In other words, to claim that the Bible exercises authority in the Church because of its central theme and not on account of its origins as a unique text inspired by the Holy Spirit.[15] In his *Christian Dogmatics*, Braaten summarized Luther's approach to the Scriptures this way: "Luther's departure [from Zwingli and Calvin as well as medieval tradition] consisted in deriving the authority of Scripture from its *gospel content*" (emphasis Braaten's), and then concluded as follows:

> Scripture's authority is not of a juridical kind; it is not essentially a book of legal doctrines, inerrant reports, or devotional materials. Scripture conveys the life-giving Word of salvation in Christ to those who accept it through faith. Authority in faith rests on the *gospel* of Scripture, not on the creeds and councils of the church or on the hierarchical offices, papacy and episcopacy. The Word of Scripture alone . . . is to be believed and accepted as finally valid *with respect to the concerns of faith and salvation*. [emphasis mine][16]

---

14 ELCA, "History" of Ecumenical and Inter-Religious Relations. http://www.elca.org/Faith/Ecumenical-and-Inter-Religious-Relations/Full-Communion/History?_ga=1.115529542.1993700260.1482247740. Accessed 12/20/16.

15 This approach has been around a long time. Robert Preus found it not only in twentieth-century theologians such as Emil Brunner (d. 1966) and Joseph Sittler (d. 1987) but also identified nineteenth-century theologians such as K. F. A. Kahnis (d. 1888) and C. E. Luthardt (d. 1902) as holding the same view. See Robert D. Preus, "Luther and Biblical Authority," in *Inerrancy and the Church*, ed. John D. Hannah (Chicago: Moody Press, 1984), 106, 108.

16 Braaten, "Holy Scriptures" (as in p. 96 n. 13), 64–65. Braaten was still saying the same thing in 2011. See Carl E. Braaten, *Principles of Lutheran Theology*, 2nd ed. (Minneapolis: Fortress, 2011), 12.

Braaten's conviction that Luther derived the authority of the Scriptures from the Gospel is similar to the position that one finds today on the website of the ELCA:

> Simply stated, the Scriptures tell about Jesus Christ. The Holy Spirit uses the Scriptures to present Jesus to all who listen to or read them. That is why Lutheran Christians say that the Scriptures are the "source and norm" of their teaching and practice.[17]

Because the Holy Spirit *uses* them to "present Jesus," the Scriptures are the standard for preaching and teaching.

In his *Reading the Bible with Martin Luther*,[18] Timothy J. Wengert develops this thesis at length: the authority of the Bible rests on the Gospel content that God uses to create and maintain faith. Wengert is, of course, one of the leading scholars in America today of the Lutheran Reformation. The Kolb-Wengert edition of *The Book of Concord* is a standard version of the Lutheran Confessions throughout the English-speaking world, so when someone like Wengert assures "today's Christians" that they can read the Bible with Martin Luther, we really ought to pay attention. Indeed, the rest of this essay will examine Wengert's contention that his approach to scriptural authority is really a Lutheran way to do so.[19]

In the first chapter of *Reading the Bible*, Wengert discusses the authority of Scripture and reduces it to the Gospel, indeed, though not even to the text of the Gospel but to its power: "For Luther, scriptural authority was not a precondition for faith but a result of it. . . . For Luther, Scripture is self-authenticating.

---

17 *ELCA Teaching: Scriptures, Creeds, Confessions: Scriptures*. https://www.elca.org/en/Faith/ELCA-Teaching/Scripture-Creeds-Confessions. Accessed 11/29/16. The Constitution of the ELCA is a little more ambiguous. While affirming both the Gospel purpose of the Scriptures and their authority, it does not link the two the way Braaten and the ELCA website do. See *Constitutions, Bylaws, and Continuing Resolutions of the Evangelical Lutheran Church in America*. November 2016 edition. http://download.elca.org/ELCA%20Resource%20Repository/Constitutions_Bylaws_and_Continuing_Resolutions_of_the_ELCA.pdf?_ga=1.78369364.1993700260.1482247740. Accessed 12/21/16.

18 Timothy J. Wengert, *Reading the Bible with Martin Luther* (Grand Rapids: Baker Academic, 2013).

19 Wengert is hardly alone today in maintaining that for Luther it was the Gospel that constituted the authority of Scripture. Besides Braaten, Oswald Bayer, in his *Martin Luther's Theology: A Contemporary Interpretation*, trans. Thomas H. Trapp (Grand Rapids: Eerdmans, 2008), 74–77, makes the same point.

The Bible is God's Word because it *does* God in Christ to me, killing the old and raising the new" (emphasis Wengert's).[20]

Wengert is on to something when he recognizes that Luther's appreciation for the Scriptures was on account of its Gospel content, theme, and power.[21] Right from the beginning of his career, Luther affirmed that the Bible was about Jesus Christ. In the preface he prepared for his students when he delivered his first lectures on the Psalms (1513), Luther wrote:

> Every prophecy and every prophet must be understood as referring to Christ the Lord, except where it is clear from plain words that someone else is spoken of. For thus He Himself says: "Search the Scriptures, . . . and it is they that bear witness to Me."[22]

In 1543, just a few years before his death, Luther published his exposition entitled *On the Last Words of David*, in which he was still contending for an exclusively christological interpretation of the Old Testament: "We Christians have the meaning and import of the Bible because we have the New Testament, that is, Jesus Christ, who was promised in the Old Testament and who later appeared and brought with Him the light and the true meaning of Scripture." Even though the Old Testament was written in their own language, without Christ the Jews remained ignorant of its meaning: "Since the Jews repudiate this Christ, they cannot know or understand what Moses, the prophets, and the psalms are saying, what true faith is, what the Ten Commandments purport, what tradition and story teach and prove."[23]

Furthermore, for Luther, a christological interpretation was always a soteriological one, since Jesus *is* the Savior and there is no other.[24] So the Gospel is first and foremost the message about Jesus and His saving work: "For at its

---

20 Wengert, *Reading the Bible with Martin Luther,* 10. In a note, Wengert acknowledges that he has taken the terminology "*does* God" to us from Gerhard Forde. It is not from Luther. Elsewhere Wengert reduces Scripture's "own provenance" to "justification by faith alone" (19).

21 This is virtually a commonplace in Luther studies. See, for example, Markus Wriedt, "Luther's Theology," in *The Cambridge Companion to Martin Luther*, ed. Donald K. McKim (Cambridge: Cambridge University Press, 2003), 90–91, 111–12; and Hans-Martin Barth, *The Theology of Martin Luther: A Critical Assessment* (Minneapolis: Fortress, 2013), 439–46.

22 *First Lectures on the Psalms* (1513–15), AE 10:7 (WA 3:13).

23 *Treatise on the Last Words of David* (1543), AE 15:268–69 (WA 54:29–30).

24 Bernhard Lohse, *Martin Luther's Theology: Its Historical and Systematic Development*, trans. Roy A. Harrisville (Minneapolis: Fortress, 1999), 223; and Althaus, *Theology of Martin Luther*, 181–82.

briefest, the gospel is a discourse about Christ, that he is the Son of God and became man *for us*, that he died and was raised, that he has been established as a Lord over all things."[25]

It is also true that Luther understood the Gospel message as the power of God to save people. He taught this in many places, for example, in the Large Catechism:

> Neither you nor I could ever know anything about Christ, or believe on Him, and have Him for our Lord, unless it were offered to us and granted to our hearts by the Holy Spirit through the preaching of the Gospel. The work of redemption is done and accomplished. Christ has acquired and gained the treasure for us . . . . So that this treasure might not stay buried, but be received and enjoyed, God has caused the Word to go forth and be proclaimed. In the Word He has the Holy Spirit bring this treasure home and make it our own.[26]

Again, this was a position that Luther maintained both early and late in his career as a theologian. So, for example, while explaining Gal. 3:2–3 in his early Galatians lectures (1516–17, published 1519), Luther said:

> If you want to obtain grace, then see to it that you hear the Word of God attentively or meditate on it diligently. The Word, I say, and only the Word, is the vehicle of God's grace. . . . The verdict that the Spirit is received from the hearing of faith stands firm. All those who have received the Spirit have received it in this way.[27]

Almost twenty years later, Luther was still making the same point. So in the Smalcald Articles (1537), Luther taught that it was the Gospel alone that brought "consolation and forgiveness" to sinners and that it did so through "the Word and the Sacraments and the like." Then in a later section, Luther insisted that "God grants His Spirit or grace to no one except through or with the preceding outward Word"; and again, "Whatever is praised as from the Spirit—without the Word and Sacraments—is the devil himself."[28]

Following the apostle (Rom. 1:16), Luther was committed to the Gospel as "the power of God unto salvation." Moreover, against Erasmus, he also insisted

25 *Brief Instruction on What to Look for and Expect in the Gospels* (1522), AE 35:118 (WA 10/1:9), emphasis added.

26 LC II III 38. Citations in English from the Book of Concord are from *Concordia: The Lutheran Confessions*, ed. Paul Timothy McCain, 2nd ed. (St. Louis: Concordia, 2006).

27 *Lectures on Galatians* (1519), AE 27:249 (WA 2:509).

28 SA III III 8 and III VIII 3, 10.

that the Christ-event was the key to *understanding* the Scriptures. "For what still sublimer thing," he asked,

> can remain hidden in the Scriptures, now that the seals have been broken, the stone rolled from the door of the sepulcher [Matt. 27:66; 28:2], and the supreme mystery brought to light, namely, that Christ the Son of God has been made man, that God is three and one, that Christ has suffered for us and is to reign eternally? . . . Take Christ out of the Scriptures, and what will you find in them?[29]

For Luther, therefore, not only is the Gospel the chief content of the Bible and the power of God to convert people but also the key to understanding everything else in the Scriptures, including and especially the Old Testament.[30]

That the Old Testament contains the *Gospel*, that is, the good news of Jesus Christ, is a prominent theme in Luther's work that again appeared early and late in the Reformation. For example, in his preface to the New Testament (1522), Luther maintained that God had promised to send the Savior already to Adam and Eve (Gen. 3:15), to Abraham (Gen. 22:18), and to David (2 Sam. 7:12–14), since "to strengthen this faith, God has promised this gospel and testament in many ways, by the prophets in the Old Testament."[31] Despite other changes, this passage remained in subsequent editions of Luther's New Testament and Bible.[32] Similarly, in his preface to the Old Testament, first published in 1523 but still present in the 1545 Bible, the reformer admonished Bible readers not to be offended by the language and stories of the Old Testament because they are "the swaddling cloths and the manger in which Christ lies, and to which the angel points the shepherds [Luke 2:12]. Simple and lowly are these swaddling cloths, but dear is *the treasure, Christ, who lies in them.*"[33] Clearly, for Luther, the Old Testament contains Christ.

---

29 *Bondage of the Will* (1525), AE 33:25–26 (WA 18:606).

30 See also the chapter by John A. Maxfield, below, pp. 123–53; Althaus, *Theology of Martin Luther*, 79–81, 86–89; and Eugene F. A. Klug, *From Luther to Chemnitz: On Scripture and the Word* (Kampen: J. H. Kok, 1971; repr., Fort Wayne, IN: Concordia Theological Seminary, 1981), 46–50.

31 *Preface to the New Testament*, AE 35:359–60 (WA DB 6:4–6). With slight modifications, the passage remained in the 1545 edition of Luther's Bible. See WA DB 6:5–7.

32 For change and continuity in Luther's *Preface to the New Testament*, see AE 35:357–62, especially the footnotes.

33 *Preface to the Old Testament*, AE 35:236 (WA DB 8:12), emphasis added. For the 1545 edition, see WA DB 8:13.

Significantly, Wengert praises Luther's interpretation of the Old Testament but ignores the fact that Luther finds explicit references to Christ in the text of the Old Testament. Instead, what impresses him about Luther's approach was his ability to find *believers* in the Old Testament, but are they believers *in Christ*? Once again, Wengert locates the authority of the Scriptures in their power, this time to support believers in their faith: "Luther and those who follow his approach prefer saying that the Hebrew Scriptures . . . gain authority when they too support Christians in their faith—that is their trust of God in Christ."[34] The Old Testament *supports* Christians, but are Christians present in these books? Christians believe in God's promises "in Christ," but did the people of the Old Testament do so? Wengert is simply not clear. While admitting that Luther found real Christians in the Old Testament, Wengert never quite says so himself.

Once again, it is a commonplace in Luther's writings that believers in the days before Christ came were believers *in the Christ* who was coming. In the later *Galatians Commentary* (1535), for example, Luther discussed Cornelius (Acts 10), prior to his hearing the Gospel from Peter, and compared his faith to that of the Old Testament believers:

> Cornelius was a righteous and holy man in accordance with the Old Testament on account of his faith *in the coming Christ*, just as all the patriarchs, prophets, and devout kings in the Old Testament were righteous, having received the Holy Spirit secretly on account of their faith *in the coming Christ*. . . . If Cornelius had died before Christ was revealed, he still would not have been damned, for he had the faith of the patriarchs, who were saved solely by faith *in the Christ to come*.[35]

But how did Cornelius and the rest learn of Christ and so believe in Him? Luther answered: from the Old Testament promises about Christ. Here's how Luther described the progress of faith prior to Jesus' coming:

> We have reason to regard the Holy Bible highly and to consider it a most precious treasure. This very chapter [Genesis 10] . . . has in it the thread that is drawn from the first world to the middle and to the end of all things. From Adam the *promise concerning Christ* is passed on to Seth; from Seth to Noah; from Noah to Shem; and from Shem to this Eber, from whom the Hebrew nation received its name as the heir for whom the *promise about the Christ* was intended in preference to all

34 Wengert, *Reading the Bible with Martin Luther*, 12.

35 *Lectures on Galatians* (1535), AE 26:210 (WA 40/1:338–39), emphasis added.

> other peoples of the whole world. This knowledge the Holy Scriptures reveal to us.[36]

For Luther, therefore, there was only one way of salvation—faith in Christ—for people both before and after His coming. Paul Althaus summarizes Luther's doctrine this way:

> [The] faith of the [Old Testament] fathers is not an essentially different or pre-Christian faith but, because Christ himself is already present in the Old Testament word of promise, genuine faith in Christ; it is one and the same faith which the church today has. . . . For the fathers it was faith in the promised Christ; for us it is faith in the Christ who has already appeared. . . . Faith in Christ is, however, justifying faith before as well as after Christ's historical appearance.[37]

Wengert's description of Luther's position is subtly different from that of Althaus. In concluding the section that analyzes Luther's understanding of the Old Testament, Wengert writes: "For Luther, the entire Old Testament was filled with believers and sinners, with commands and promises, with terror and comfort. In *this way*, it is simply filled to overflowing with Christ, the Savior of the world, because it is filled with believers clinging to God's promises."[38] If by "believers" Wengert means believers *in Christ* and by "promises" he means promises *of Christ*, then he is correct; but for some reason Wengert is reluctant to be so explicit. Perhaps this is on account of his dismissing Luther's presupposition regarding the Bible that there was "a single, divine author for both Testaments and therefore a logic that transcended both."[39] And we might add not only *logic* but also *content* that was common to both. As we have already seen, Luther maintained that the Old Testament included specific promises of a Savior, the Seed of Eve, Abraham, and David, who would deliver humanity from its sin. It is not clear at all that for Wengert, "reading the Bible with Martin Luther" means finding explicit promises of Christ in the Old Testament.

---

36 *Lectures on Genesis* (1535–45), AE 2:209 (WA 42:409), emphasis added, cited also in John A. Maxfield, *Luther's Lectures on Genesis and the Formation of Evangelical Identity*, Sixteenth Century Essays & Studies 80 (Kirksville, MO: Truman State University Press, 2008), 35.

37 Althaus, *Theology of Martin Luther*, 98–99. For a more thorough treatment of the Gospel in the Old Testament, see Heinrich Bornkamm, *Luther and the Old Testament*, trans. Eric W. and Ruth C. Gritsch, ed. Victor I. Gruhn, repr. ed. (Middletown, PA: Sigler Press, 1997).

38 Wengert, *Reading the Bible with Martin Luther*, 15–16, emphasis added.

39 Wengert, *Reading the Bible with Martin Luther*, 11.

But perhaps we are doing Wengert a disservice by criticizing him for what he does not say. After all, Luther himself has taught us "to put the best construction on everything"; and Wengert is clearly correct in recognizing that in Luther's theology the theme and power of the Bible are the Gospel. Nevertheless, Wengert is incorrect in locating the authority of the Bible in the Gospel. The Bible is powerful to save because of the Gospel. However, in Luther's thinking the authority of the Scriptures does not come from the Gospel but instead that authority *guarantees* the Gospel.[40] We know what the Gospel is because the Scriptures tell us.

Luther said this explicitly when comparing the Old and New Testaments in his *Church Postil*. As one might expect in a work devoted to supplying assistance to preachers of the Gospel, Luther strongly emphasizes the need to proclaim the Gospel aloud to people. In fact, Luther insists (and not only here) on the original *oral* character of the Gospel: "Christ himself did not write anything but only spoke. He called his teaching not Scripture but gospel, meaning good news or a proclamation that is spread not by pen but by word of mouth."[41] In fact, in one of his postils Luther called the Church "a mouth house, not a pen house, for since Christ's advent the Gospel is preached orally, while before it was hidden in written books."[42]

If, then, Christ expected His disciples to *preach* the Gospel (and they did), why did anyone write it down? Luther explained this in another of his postils as a measure taken to ensure the integrity of the Gospel message against errorists and heretics:

---

40 According to Eric W. Gritsch, *Martin—God's Court Jester: Luther in Retrospect* (Philadelphia: Fortress, 1983), 98, Luther insisted that "all preaching be normed by Holy Scripture . . . . His concern was to preserve Christian proclamation from error. . . . The church is therefore normed by Holy Scripture, the vessel of the Word of God." See also Jeffrey G. Silcock, "Luther on the Holy Spirit and His Use of God's Word," in *The Oxford Handbook of Martin Luther's Theology*, ed. Robert Kolb, Irene Dingel, and L'ubomir Batka (Oxford: Oxford University Press, 2014), 302; Klug, *From Luther to Chemnitz*, 54–66; and Preus, "Luther and Biblical Authority" (as in p. 97 n. 15), 102–3, 112–15, 123, 129, 131–33.

41 *Brief Instruction on What to Look for and Expect in the Gospels* (1522), AE 35:123. Luther published this work originally as an introduction to his *Wartburg Postil*. See the editor's introduction in AE 35:115–16.

42 Postil for Advent 1, Matt. 21:1–9, in *Church Postil I*, AE 75:51 n. 72. According to the note, Luther included these words in his 1522 edition of the *Church Postil*, but they did not recur after the 1532 edition. They are present in the Weimar edition's version of the 1522 *Advent Postil*. See WA 10/1.2:48.

> The need to write books was a serious decline and a lack of Spirit which necessity forced upon us . . . . For when heretics, false teachers, and all manner of errors arose in the place of pious preachers giving the flock poison as pasture, then every last thing that could and needed to be done, had to be attempted. So they began to write in order to lead the flock of Christ as much as possible by Scripture into Scripture. They wanted to ensure that the sheep could feed themselves and hence protect themselves against the wolves, if their shepherds failed to feed them or were in danger of becoming wolves too.

Luther then proceeded to cite as examples Luke, who wrote his Gospel because others did "not manage it too well"; and Paul, the purpose of whose writing was "to preserve what he first preached."[43] Although the writing of the New Testament followed the first preaching of the Gospel, the apostles and evangelists intended their written works as norms for subsequent preaching. In short, we know today what the Gospel is because we find it in the written Scriptures.

More than a decade later, Luther made a similar point in commenting on Paul's reference to the Scriptures in 1 Cor. 15:3–4. Luther maintained that "there is no other enduring way of preserving our doctrine and our faith than the physical or written Word . . . . Here we find it stated clearly: 'Scripture! Scripture!' " By "Scripture," Luther was not referring to the Old Testament only, for he immediately applied this principle specifically to the New Testament: "Nor must anyone seek or search for something else or learn or acquire something better or more sublime than what Scripture teaches of Jesus Christ, God's Son, our Savior, who died and rose for us."[44]

---

43 Postil for Epiphany, Matt. 2:1–12 (1522), in *Sermons II*, AE 52:206 (WA 10/1.1:627). See also *Theses Concerning Faith and Law* (1535): "57. Just as all the prophets and patriarchs spoke all things which are contained in the Scriptures by the Spirit of Christ. 58. Nevertheless, since in the meantime we are inconstant in spirit, and the flesh wars with the spirit, it is necessary, also on account of inconstant souls, to adhere to certain commands and writings of the apostles, lest the church be torn to pieces. 59. For we are not all apostles, who by a sure decree of God were sent to us as infallible teachers" (AE 34:113 [WA 39/1:47–48]).

44 *Commentary on 1 Corinthians 15* (1533), AE 28:76–77 (WA 36:500–501). Incidentally, Wengert lists the "bodily resurrection" along with other Christian fundamentals such as the Trinity and vicarious atonement as doctrines that "cannot be verified in any scientific or logical way . . . but must simply be asserted," in contrast to "scientific and historical facts" such as the flood and Jonah's being swallowed by a whale that can be verified (Wengert, *Reading the Bible with Martin Luther*, 9). However, in the passage just cited, Luther (and Paul!) maintain that our Lord's resurrection was indeed *historical* and was attested by "eyewitnesses [*die Zeugen*]," including Paul himself. Thus the resurrection is not a bare assertion but is God's action in human time and space—and verifiable.

In the Smalcald Articles, Luther provided precise evidence of what he meant by his Scripture principle. Realizing that he might die at any moment, the reformer offered his "testimony and confession" of what he truly taught and believed.[45] Not surprisingly, he identified the Gospel as "the first and chief article" of the Christian religion. But how did Luther define the Gospel? Basically by quoting Scripture passages:

> Jesus Christ, our God and Lord, "died for our sins and was raised again for our justification" (Romans 4:24–25).
>
> He alone is "the Lamb of God who takes away the sins of the world" (John 1:29), and God "has laid upon Him the iniquities of us all" (Isaiah 53:6).
>
> "All have sinned" and "are justified freely," without their own works or merits, "by His grace, through the redemption that is in Christ Jesus," "in His blood" (Romans 3:23–25).
>
> This is necessary to believe. This cannot be otherwise acquired or grasped by any work, law, or merit. Therefore, it is clear and certain that this faith alone justifies us. As St. Paul says:
>
> "For we hold that one is justified by faith apart from works of the law." (Romans 3:28)
>
> "That He might be just and the justifier of the one who has faith in Jesus." (Romans 3:26)[46]

In this critical passage, Luther relied on the Scriptures to define the Gospel and did so by means of particular passages or proof-texts, we might say. Clearly, the implication of this procedure was that a person should know that this is the Gospel *because* the Scriptures teach it concretely in specific places and with particular words.

---

45 Luther had done this once before, in the third part of his *Confession concerning Christ's Supper* (1528), in which he described his method in determining the articles of faith upon which he was willing to die: "I have most diligently traced all these articles *through the Scriptures*, have examined them again and again in the light thereof, and have wanted to defend all of them as certainly as I have now defended the sacrament of the altar" (AE 37:360 [WA 26:499–500], emphasis added).

46 SA Preface 3; II I 1–4. I have added the quotation marks in order to demonstrate the Bible passages; the editors of the McCain edition have added the verse numbers to Luther's citations of book and chapter.

Wengert doesn't like "proof texting,"[47] but Luther certainly did. Such a procedure was nothing new for the reformer in 1537. For years prior to the composition of these articles, Luther had been making this very point: an article of faith had to be based on clear teachings of Scripture. Luther developed this position in his debate with Rome. Already in his hearing before Cardinal Cajetan in October 1518, after quoting the Scriptures (Rom. 5:19) to show that one was saved by the obedience of Christ without indulgences, he said this: "I do not care whether this statement is contrary to an *Extravagante* or an *Intravagante* [terms from canon law].[48] The truth of Scripture comes first. After that is accepted, one may determine whether the words of men can be accepted as true."[49]

In 1519, the Leipzig Debate prompted further development of Luther's scriptural principle since his opponent, Johann Eck, employed canon law and conciliar decisions against Luther's positions. Luther responded to Eck with the Scriptures. Councils and canon law could err (and did), but not God's Word. Just a short time later Luther wrote against Eck and defended the proposition: "A simple layman armed with Scripture is to be believed above a pope or a council without it."[50]

---

47 Wengert, *Reading the Bible with Martin Luther*, 21. "Only when Scripture is approached . . . as God's Word that kills and makes alive . . . and thus as something that will not succumb to our categories, principles, or proof texting . . . will it drive us away from itself and toward faith in Christ."

48 *Extravagante* is a term "employed to designate some papal decretals not contained in certain canonical collections which possess a special authority," e.g., Gratian's decretals. An *Intravagante* would, of course, mean a decretal that was contained in one of the canonical collections. It is not clear to me whether anyone actually used the latter term or whether Luther was just poking a bit of fun at the canonists. See *Catholic Encyclopedia* s.v. "Extravagantes," available online at http://www.newadvent.org/cathen/05715a.htm. Accessed 12/29/16.

49 *Proceedings at Augsburg* (1518), AE 31:282 (WA 2:21). Luther published these proceedings shortly after his confrontation with the cardinal in order to set the record straight about what actually took place there. See the editor's introduction in AE 31:255–58.

50 WA 2:649.1–2. This particular proposition was not originally formulated by Luther. Thompson ascribes it to Nicoló de' Tudeschi (d. 1445), commonly known as Panormitanus. See Mark D. Thompson, *A Sure Ground on Which to Stand: The Relation of Authority and Interpretive Method in Luther's Approach to Scripture* (Carlisle, UK: Paternoster Press, 2004), 261. However, Luther defended the proposition against Eck in the aftermath of the Leipzig Debate in *Defense against the Malicious Judgment of Eck* in WA 2:625–54. See Brecht, *Luther: His Road to Reformation*, 327–30. It also appears twice in a letter from Luther and Karlstadt to Frederick the Wise, August 18, 1519, WA Br 1:468, 472. For the significance of the Leipzig Debate in the development of Luther's doctrine of Scripture, see Thompson, *Sure Ground,* 251, 254, and 261; and Lohse, *Martin Luther's Theology*, 118–26.

By 1520, therefore, Luther was using the Scriptures to test the medieval sacramental system. He did this thoroughly in his *Babylonian Captivity of the Church*. Once again, the Gospel was at stake, for Luther contended that the essence of a sacrament was the promise of the forgiveness of sins.[51] But how did one know if Christ had attached such a promise to any particular rite? Luther answered: from the Bible! "We ought to see," he wrote, "that every article of faith of which we boast is certain, pure, and based on clear passages of Scripture." So, for example, regarding ordination Luther maintained, "Not only is there nowhere any promise of grace attached to it, but there is not a single word said about it in the whole New Testament." He later added, "The church has no power to make new divine promises of grace." In other words, we know where to find forgiveness only because the Scriptures tell us. Even the Church must restrict itself to the Scriptures when it comes to the Gospel.[52]

Elsewhere in this treatise, Luther applied the Scripture principle and so rejected transubstantiation and monastic vows as well as the sacramental character of confirmation and marriage. He concluded that his papal opponents were "heretics and godless schismatics" because they "presume upon [their] figments alone against the clear Scriptures of God."[53] On the other hand, Luther found the Gospel in the Lord's Supper, Baptism, and penance *in particular Bible passages*, namely, the Words of Institution, Mark 16:16, and Matt. 16:19 (along with others).[54] Proof passages are a hallmark of Luther's method of demonstrating doctrine from the Scriptures.

Of course, the notion that Lutherans derive their doctrine from the Scriptures in this way is nothing new. From the sixteenth century to today, countless numbers of Luther's followers have experienced this approach in Luther's Small Catechism (1529), in which Luther directs the student to a Bible passage that proves the doctrine he is teaching: "Where is this written?" This is

---

51 "*Hence there are, strictly speaking, but two sacraments in the church of God—baptism and the bread.* For only in these two do we find both the divinely instituted sign and the promise of forgiveness of sins" (emphasis Luther's, *Babylonian Captivity of the Church* [1520], AE 36:124 [WA 6:572]).

52 *Babylonian Captivity of the Church* (1520), AE 36:106–7 (WA 6:560). For Luther's use of Scripture passages in his debates with his opponents, see Richard Bucher, *The Ecumenical Luther: The Development and Use of His Doctrinal Hermeneutic* (St. Louis: Concordia, 2003), 40–41, 45–48.

53 *Babylonian Captivity of the Church* (1520), AE 36:24, 29, 76–77, 91, 92 (WA 6:505, 508, 540, 549, 550).

54 In the case of the Lord's Supper, in a single word: "testament." See *Babylonian Captivity of the Church* (1520), AE 36:36, 37, 58–59, and 82 (WA 6:512, 513, 527–28, 543).

his approach in the Table of Duties in which Luther presents "certain passages of Scripture for various holy orders and positions, by which these people are to be admonished . . . about their office and service." Here Luther uses proof-texts, this time to apply the Law to specific vocations.[55] But this is also true—again—with respect to the Gospel particularly when he presents the evangelical character of the two sacraments: "Which are these words and promises of God [regarding Baptism]? Answer: Christ, our Lord, says in the last chapter of Mark . . ."; and "What is the benefit of such eating and drinking? Answer: That is shown us in these words, 'Given for you' and 'shed for you for the forgiveness of sins.' "[56]

For Luther, therefore, the Scriptures alone determine doctrine and define the Gospel. Wengert doesn't like the "alone" in this statement, so he shows that Luther used church history and the church fathers in his polemics and even recommended writings besides the Bible.[57] What Wengert does *not* show, however, is that Luther used nonbiblical authorities as anything but confirmations of what the Scriptures themselves taught, or commentaries as anything but guides to Scripture and responses to those who mishandled the biblical text. For the reformer, other sources, whether ancient or modern, added nothing to the Scriptures. Luther always gave the last word to the Bible.[58]

So, for example, in his *On the Councils and the Church* (1539) Luther maintained over and over again that on doctrinal matters or matters of conscience, a council must follow the Scriptures. So, too, the church fathers. Luther expressed his opinion this way:

> How much can one say about it? If you have all the councils you are still no Christian because of them; they give you too little. If you also have all the fathers, they too give you too little. You must still go to Holy Scripture, where you find everything in abundance, or to the catechism, where it is summarized, and where far more is found than in all the councils and fathers.[59]

55 SC "Table of Duties."

56 SC IV 2 and VI.

57 Wengert, *Reading the Bible with Martin Luther*, 16–21.

58 See Thompson, *Sure Ground*, 252–65, for an excellent treatment of the sufficiency of Scripture in relation to the church fathers and other theologians. See also Mark Thompson, "Luther on God and History," in *The Oxford Handbook of Martin Luther's Theology*, ed. Robert Kolb, Irene Dingel, and L'ubomir Batka (Oxford: Oxford University Press, 2014), 127–42; and Althaus, *Theology of Martin Luther*, 338–41.

59 *On the Councils and the Church*, AE 41:136 (WA 50:618). See also AE 41:58, 83, 86, 105, 119, 121, 123, 130–31 (WA 50:551, 572, 575, 591, 604, 605, 607, 613). Notice, too, that Luther recommends the catechism because it *summarizes* the Scriptures.

Luther took this position because *any* human authority, including the church fathers, had to pass a scriptural test:

> For their holiness does not make them infallible, and it does not imply that one must rely and depend on all the dicta of the fathers or approve and believe all their teachings. Rather take the touchstone of God's Word into your hands. Let this be your criterion for testing, trying, and judging all that the fathers have preached, written, and said, as well as all the precepts and human ordinances that have been promulgated. Otherwise one will be easily misled and deceived.[60]

Wengert points out that Luther recommended Melanchthon's annotations to Romans and 1 and 2 Corinthians, not however as another authority independent of the Bible but as a guide for reading Scripture and knowing Christ.[61] Regarding his own prefaces to his New Testament (1522), Luther argued that they were necessary to protect readers from all the false interpretations that were misleading people about the Bible:

> It would be right and proper for this book to go forth without any prefaces or extraneous names attached and simply have its own way under its own name. However[,] many unfounded [*wilde*] interpretations and prefaces have scattered the thought of Christians to a point where no one any longer knows what is gospel or law, New Testament or Old. Necessity demands, therefore, that there should be a notice or preface, by which the ordinary man can be rescued from his former delusions, set on the right track, and taught what he is to look for in this book.[62]

Thus Luther recommended and wrote books and treatises in order to promote biblical truth and not to provide additional authorities for doctrine and practice in the Church. In 1539, Luther wrote, "All other writing is to lead the way into

---

60 *Sermons on John 1–2*, AE 22:254 (WA 46:767), cited in Thompson, *Sure Ground*, 278.

61 Wengert, *Reading the Bible with Martin Luther*, 17. Besides the commentaries Wengert mentions, Luther also recommended Melanchthon's *Loci Communes* in his *Preface to the Complete Edition of Luther's Latin Writings* (1545) (AE 34:327; WA 54:179) and wrote numerous prefaces for the works of others. Concordia Publishing House has published such prefaces in volumes 59 and 60 of the American edition of Luther's Works.

62 AE 35:357 (WA DB 6:2). On more than one occasion Luther expressed dismay at the prospect that people might busy themselves with his works instead of the Bible. See Eike Wolgast, *Die Wittenberger Luther-Ausgabe: Zur Überlieferungsgeschichte der Werke Luther im 16. Jahrhundert* (Nieuwkoop: de Graaf, 1971), 14–15.

and point toward the Scriptures . . . in order that each person may drink of the fresh spring himself."[63]

But why did Luther take the approach of using the Scriptures as a *final* authority in the Church? Indeed, what kind of authority did the Scriptures have that made them a standard even for the Gospel? That Gospel was the scriptural center for sure, but the authority of the Bible came from its source, namely God. Wengert dismisses the idea of a "single, divine author" of the Bible,[64] but in so doing he is rejecting much more than an antiquated eccentricity in Luther.

As is the case with much of what Luther taught, he inherited his position on the authority of the Scriptures from his predecessors. According to Frans van Liere, "For medieval authors, the one thing that set the sacred scriptures apart from all other scriptures was that they all originated from one ultimate author, God. . . . Thus, everything that the text related was absolutely true, because God did not speak falsehood."[65] Thomas Aquinas thus exemplified the attitude of medieval theologians when he wrote at the beginning of the *Summa*, "God is the author of sacred Scripture."[66] Thomas also maintained the infallibility of the Scriptures: "It is unlawful to hold that any false assertion is contained either in the Gospel or in any canonical Scripture, or that the writers thereof have told untruths, because faith would be deprived of its certitude which is based on the authority of Holy Writ."[67] St. Augustine expressed the same confidence in a well-known comment that he included in a letter to St. Jerome:

> For I confess to your Charity that I have learned to yield this respect and honour only to the canonical books of Scripture: of these alone do I most firmly believe that the authors were completely free from error. And if in these writings I am perplexed by anything which appears to me opposed to truth, I do not hesitate to suppose that either the

63 *Preface to the Wittenberg Edition of Luther's German Writings* (1539), AE 34:284 (WA 50:657).

64 Wengert, *Reading the Bible with Martin Luther*, 11.

65 Frans van Liere, *An Introduction to the Medieval Bible* (New York: Cambridge University Press, 2014), 111. See also Henri de Lubac, *Medieval Exegesis: The Four Senses of Scripture*, trans. Mark Sebanc (Grand Rapids: Eerdmans, 1998), 1:24–28; and Jaroslav Pelikan, *The Christian Tradition: A History of the Development of Doctrine*, vol. 3: *The Growth of Medieval Theology (600–1300)* (Chicago: University of Chicago Press, 1978), 34–42.

66 "Auctor sacrae Scripturae est Deus" (*Summa Theologica*, I, q. 1, Art. 10. http://www.corpusthomisticum.org/sth1001.html. Accessed 10/19/16).

67 Thomas Aquinas, *Summa Theologica*, IIaIIae, q. 110 a.3 (http://www.sacred-texts.com/chr/aquinas/summa/sum366.htm. Accessed 8/2/16).

> manuscript is faulty, or the translator has not caught the meaning of what was said, or I myself have failed to understand it.[68]

We should not be surprised that Luther spoke the same way about the author and authority of the Scriptures, both early and late in his career, and so frequently that it is virtually a commonplace in his work. In the first Psalms lectures, for example, Luther called Scriptures "the tongue of God."[69] At the start of the Reformation, in a tract directed specifically against the papacy, Luther wrote of those who so misused the Scriptures that they were making "liars out of the Holy Spirit and my Lord Christ."[70] But then in 1545, Luther could still write, "He who wants to hear God speak should read Holy Scripture."[71]

The idea that God has spoken and still speaks when someone reads or hears the Scriptures is one that recurs often in Luther. In fact, he frequently referred to Scripture by saying "the Holy Spirit says."[72] Mark Thompson has shown that Luther used a variety of verbs but all with the same subject in references to the Scripture when commenting on a single chapter of Genesis: "The Holy Spirit," Thompson wrote, "provides instruction," "commands us," "impresses comfort on us," and even "points out the hypothetical assertion."[73]

In arguing for the clarity of Scripture, Luther maintained that "the Holy Spirit is the simplest writer and adviser in heaven and on earth. That is why his words [the words of Scripture] could have no more than the one simplest meaning which we call the written one, or the literal meaning of the tongue."[74] This means that a person does not even have to be a believer to understand the words. So, for example, in his debate with the Sacramentarians Luther insisted: "These words, 'This is my body,' etc. are clear and lucid. Whether a Christian or

---

68 Augustine to Jerome, Letter 82 (AD 405) (NPNF[1] 1:350).

69 *First Lectures on the Psalms* (1513–15), AE 11:50 (WA 3:569).

70 *On the Papacy in Rome against the Most Celebrated Romanist in Leipzig* (1520), AE 39:103 (WA 6:323).

71 *Against the Roman Papacy, an Institution of the Devil* (1545), AE 41:332 (WA 54.263). See Thompson, *Sure Ground*, 56.

72 Here are some examples: AE 12:340 (WA 40/2:370.18)—quoting Ps. 32:5 in 1532; AE 26:270 (WA 40/1:423)—quoting Gal. 3:12 in 1535; AE 22:473 (WA 47:184) in 1539; AE 26:264 (WA 40/1:414) and 266 (WA 40/1:417) in 1535; AE 37:210 (WA 26:320)—quoting John 3:16 and Rom. 8:32 in 1528; and AE 45: 208 (WA 11:321)—citing Matthew and Luke in 1523.

73 Thompson, *Sure Ground*, 59. See *Lectures on Genesis* (1535–45), AE 2:296, 308, 307 (WA 42:474, 482).

74 *Answer to the Hyperchristian Book*, AE 39:178 (WA 7:650).

a heathen, a Jew or a Turk hears them, he must acknowledge that they speak of the body of Christ which is in the bread."[75]

Luther did not ignore the human authors. In fact, he referred to them often, but he regarded them as instruments of the Holy Spirit who was speaking through their words.[76] "The Scriptures, although they too are written by men, are neither of men nor from men but [are] from God."[77] Armin Buchholz has identified a single paragraph in Luther's *Answer to the Hyperchristian Book* (1521) in which he uses "Scripture," "Holy Spirit," "St. Paul," and "God's Word" synonymously.[78]

Wengert never really denies that the Holy Spirit is the author of the Scriptures, and in one instance he suggests that maybe He is. While discussing Luther's meditating on the Scriptures, Wengert writes that "the biblical text drove one to consider why the Holy Spirit said this thing."[79] Clearly, however, Wengert is much more concerned with the power of the Spirit in the Bible and its message. For example, he cites 2 Tim. 3:16, "All Scripture is given by inspiration of God," but maintains that Luther was more interested in the next three words, "and is profitable."[80] Elsewhere, he writes of the Spirit as the power of the Scriptures,[81] especially to forgive sins and create faith,[82] and as a gift of the Gospel.[83] But for Luther the power and the Spirit were in the *words* of the biblical text.[84] God Himself speaks in the Bible.

---

75 *Confession concerning Christ's Supper* (1528), AE 37:272 (WA 26:406). According to Armin Buchholz, *Schrift Gottes im Lehrstreit: Luthers Schriftverständnis und Schriftauslegung in seinen drei grossen Lehrstreitigkeiten der Jahre 1521–1528* (Giessen: Brunnen Verlag, 2007), 212–16, 268, Luther could say that even children and fools, peasants, unbelievers, and heretics can understand the words of Scripture.

76 Buchholz, *Schrift Gottes im Lehrstreit*, 8 and 70; Thompson, *Sure Ground*, 61–67; and Preus, "Luther and Biblical Authority," 119.

77 *Avoiding the Doctrines of Men and A Reply to the Texts Cited in Defense of the Doctrines of Men* (1522) AE 35:153 (WA 10/2:92). See Thompson, *Sure Ground*, 68.

78 *Answer to the Hyperchristian Book* (1521) AE 39:160 (WA 7:635). See Buchholz, *Schrift Gottes im Lehrstreit*, 8.

79 Wengert, *Reading the Bible with Martin Luther*, 124.

80 Wengert, *Reading the Bible with Martin Luther*, 50.

81 Wengert, *Reading the Bible with Martin Luther*, 50.

82 Wengert, *Reading the Bible with Martin Luther*, 33, 84, 86, 90.

83 Wengert, *Reading the Bible with Martin Luther*, 65, 87.

84 Buchholz, *Schrift Gottes im Lehrstreit*, 274–75. On the Holy Spirit as author of the words of Scripture, see also Maxfield, *Luther's Lectures on Genesis*, 32–39.

Given Luther's conviction regarding the inspiration of the Scriptures, is it any wonder that he used the text of Scripture as his principal weapon in defending his doctrine not only against the papal church but also against the Sacramentarians, namely, Karlstadt, Zwingli, and Oecolampadius? After Pope Leo X issued his bull *Exsurge domine* that condemned Luther's teachings, the reformer defended himself by explicit references to the Bible: "I . . . have with a joyful heart undertaken to demonstrate *from Scripture* the truth of all the articles." He went on to explain his confidence: "Holy Scripture must necessarily be clearer, simpler, and more reliable than any other writings. Especially since all teachers verify their own statements through the Scriptures as clearer and more reliable writings, and desire their own writings to be confirmed and explained by them. . . . Scripture alone is the true lord and master of all writings and doctrine on earth."[85]

Luther took the same approach with his adversaries on the left during the eucharistic controversy. For the Wittenberg reformer, it all came down to the words of Christ, recorded in Scripture, that instituted the Sacrament. They are so clear that even an unbeliever would agree with Luther on what they mean about the real presence of the body and blood of Jesus in the Sacrament:

> We know . . . that these words, "This is my body," etc. are clear and lucid. Whether a Christian or a heathen, a Jew or a Turk hears them, he must acknowledge that they speak of the body of Christ which is in the bread. How otherwise could the heathen and Jews mock us, saying that the Christians eat their God, if they did not understand this text clearly and distinctly?[86]

Of course, through the several phases of that controversy many arguments arose in addition to strictly exegetical ones, for example, whether the bodily presence of Christ in the Sacrament is consistent with His being a true man. But clearly for Luther the words of Scripture were fundamental—and decisive—as he demonstrated in his dramatic gesture at the Marburg Colloquy (1529). According to observers, prior to the start of a session, Luther had written in chalk the words "This is My body" and covered them with a tablecloth. Then, during the course of the conversation with Zwingli, Luther uncovered them again and said, "Here

---

85 *Defense and Explanation of All the Articles* (1521), AE 32:8, 11–12 (emphasis added) (WA 7:311, 317).

86 *Confession concerning Christ's Supper*, AE 37:272 (WA 26:406). See Bucher, *Ecumenical Luther*, 100–101.

is our Scripture passage. You have not yet wrested it away from us . . . . We have no need of another passage."[87]

That was Luther's essential method. When it came to doctrinal controversy, Scripture—and more specifically a particular place or places in Scripture—remained the ultimate proof.

However, right alongside the Bible, Luther also used the Gospel as a standard for doctrine and practice. Because the Gospel is the theme and purpose of the Bible, it made good sense to consider the impact of various activities and teachings upon the Scriptures' chief doctrine. Moreover, given Luther's use of the Scriptures to define the Gospel, employing the latter as a tool for evaluating activities and truth claims in the Church hardly contradicted his insistence that the Scriptures alone are the final authority for the Church.

Once again, this use of the Gospel is something that we find early and late in Luther's career. An excellent example of this in the "later" Luther is the Smalcald Articles from 1537. We have already seen how Luther used the Scriptures to define the Gospel in these articles. At the conclusion to his exposition of the article on Christ and redemption through Christ, he then insisted: "Upon this article everything that we teach and practice depends."[88] Almost immediately thereafter, Luther began using this chief article as a measuring rod for other doctrines and practices. In the very next article, for example, in the very first words, Luther wrote: "The Mass in the papacy has to be the greatest and most horrible abomination, since *it directly and powerfully conflicts with the chief article*."[89] Subsequently, Luther used similar language both as a summary ("all these things . . . are against the chief article") and specifically in rejecting purgatory, monastic societies, invocation of saints, monastic chapters and cloisters, and the papacy.[90]

Employing the Gospel as a standard in the Smalcald Articles did not, however, preclude Luther's also using the Scriptures as his rule. For example, regarding the Mass, Luther cited Matt. 15:9 to prove his point: "Every human invention we may safely discard, as Christ declares, 'In vain do they worship Me, teaching as doctrines the commandments of men.'"[91] In rejecting patristic authority, Luther insisted, "The true rule is this: God's Word shall establish

87 This account is from Osiander's report on the proceedings at Marburg, AE 38:67 (WA 30/3:147).

88 SA II I 5.

89 SA II II 1, emphasis added.

90 SA II II 24, 12, 21, 25; II III 2.

91 SA II II 2.

articles of faith, and no one else, not even an angel can do so."[92] Frequently, therefore, Luther criticized Rome for instituting something without authorization by God's Word, such as the private Mass, Masses for the dead, pilgrimages, monastic societies that "assigned and transferred . . . all Masses, good works, and such, both for the living and the dead," relics, and indulgences.[93] Likewise, "the pope is not, according to divine law or God's Word, the head of all Christendom."[94] When compared with Holy Scripture, Luther wrote that the pope's teaching "at its best has been taken from the imperial and heathen law."[95] Sometimes Luther used both Scriptures and the Gospel, for example, regarding prayers to the saints: "The invocation of saints . . . conflicts with the chief article . . . . It is neither commanded nor counseled, nor has it any warrant in Scripture."[96]

For Luther, therefore, Gospel and Scripture were two different but completely complementary standards that he employed throughout his career. Wengert, of course, knows well how Luther did theology, but he wants to argue that the Gospel really was Luther's authority and not the text of Scripture. But it's difficult to find an example of Luther discarding a Bible passage because it contradicted the Gospel. On at least one occasion, Luther said something that sounds like that. This was in a set of theses that Luther prepared for a couple of doctoral students in the fall of 1535. Luther wrote: "Therefore, if the adversaries press the Scriptures against Christ, we urge Christ against the Scriptures."[97]

However it may sound, this statement is hardly remarkable, given that Luther's opponents, whether on the right or left, routinely used Scripture to make their argument, whatever else they might use. So Luther's point was simply the obvious one that the Scriptures, wrongly understood and applied, cannot negate Christ and His saving work.[98] So, for example, in his debate with Erasmus, Luther had to remind his opponent that citing the Law did not make

92 SA II II 15.

93 SA II II 8, 12, 18, 21, 22, 24.

94 SA II IV 1.

95 SA II IV 14.

96 SA II II 25.

97 *Theses Concerning Faith and Law*, AE 34:112 (WA 39/1:47).

98 There is an excellent example of how Luther proceeded when someone quoted Scripture in favor of works in his *Lectures on Galatians* (1535), AE 26:295 (WA 40/1:459): "You are stressing the servant, that is, Scripture—and not all of it at that or even its more powerful part, but only a few passages concerning works. I leave this servant to you. I for my part stress the Lord, who is the King of Scripture. He has become my merit and the price of my righteousness and salvation. I hold to Him, I cling to Him."

one capable of obeying it. Instead, it showed a person his inability to keep it.[99] Similarly, when the Sacramentarians wanted to use John 6 in order to prove the folly of Luther's position regarding the oral consumption of Christ's body and blood in the Sacrament, Luther responded with arguments showing that John 6 could not be referring to the Lord's Supper at all.[100] As Richard Bucher has demonstrated, Luther's rule for making use of Scripture in controversies meant citing the "*right* Scripture *rightly* interpreted."[101]

Perhaps Wengert's most persuasive argument on behalf of Gospel authority, not scriptural authority, is his contention that Luther used the Gospel in his discussion of whether the Epistle of James belongs in the canon of the New Testament and ended up relegating it to "an appendix of less important books," largely on account of its failure to emphasize Christ.[102] Wengert is correct to point out that Luther used the Gospel to rank the books of the New Testament in his original preface to that part of the Bible. For Luther, some books are more important than others, as he said regarding his favorite epistles: "You do not find many works and miracles of Christ described, but you do find depicted in masterly fashion how faith in Christ overcomes sin, death, and hell."[103]

In general, however, Luther did not use the Gospel as a canonical criterion. James ended up where it did in the Luther Bible, first of all, because "from ancient times [it] had a different reputation" from the other books of the New Testament. It belonged to the "antilegomena," books whose canonicity had been questioned in the early church. That was also true of Hebrews, Jude, and Revelation, so they, too, joined James at the end of the list.[104] The reformer's own analysis of the epistle confirmed the judgment of those "ancients" who had rejected it, although he did not insist that his own opinion must prevail over others.[105] Despite his failure to find the Gospel in James, Luther did not let the absence of the Gospel (in its strict sense) from shorter books, such as

99 When Erasmus raised the question about why the Bible contains so many laws, precepts, threats, and promises, Luther responded, "Paul here replies: 'Through the law comes knowledge of sin.' . . . It is the task, function, and effect of the law to be a light . . . but such a light as reveals sin, evil, death, hell, the wrath of God" (*Bondage of the Will*, AE 33:261 [WA 18:766]).

100 See, for example, Bucher, *Ecumenical Luther*, 85, 88–89, 101–6.

101 Bucher, *Ecumenical Luther*, 45.

102 Wengert, *Reading the Bible with Martin Luther*, 7.

103 AE 35:362 (WA DB 6:10).

104 AE 35:394, 395 (WA DB 7:344, 384).

105 AE 35:395–96, 397 (WA DB 7:384, 386).

Philemon and 1 and 2 John, deter him from retaining them in the canon. They had not been questioned by the early church. He even added favorable comments about them, such as "this epistle gives us a masterful and tender illustration of Christian love" and "the other two epistles [of John] are . . . examples of love and of faith."[106] So the Gospel may have been Luther's central concern in determining the value of a biblical book, but it was not determinative of whether a book was biblical in the first place.

It is one thing, however, to acknowledge Luther's use of the Gospel to decide the significance of individual books and quite another to launch an attack on those who hold to the infallibility and inerrancy of the Scriptures. But this is precisely what Wengert does. "Luther's decision to make the *evangel*—the good news—key in judging James calls into question all forms of biblical fundamentalism."[107] And what characterizes adherents of fundamentalism? "Fundamentalists," Wengert asserts,

> must start outside of Scripture to authenticate it. That is, they begin with a definition of truth that they then apply to the biblical text. . . . In order to be true the Bible must not have two things: it must *not* contain errors and it must *not* contain falsehoods; that is, it must be *in*-errant and *in*-fallible.[108]

Whether this is an adequate description of fundamentalism or not—and surprisingly, Wengert does not try to show that it is[109]—it raises questions about what he thinks of Luther's belief in the infallibility of the Bible. Was Luther also guilty of importing a definition of truth into Scripture when he said things such as "The saints could err in their writings . . . but the Scriptures cannot err" (1521) or "We are not all apostles, who by a sure decree of God were sent to us as infallible teachers" (1535)?[110] In his *Confession Concerning Christ's Supper* (1528), Luther wrote, "If the fanatics have been discovered in a single detail to be manifestly false, we would be sufficiently warned by God not to believe them,

---

106 AE 35:390, 393 (WA DB 7:292, 326).

107 Wengert, *Reading the Bible with Martin Luther*, 8.

108 Wengert, *Reading the Bible with Martin Luther*, 8, emphasis Wengert's.

109 Wengert (*Reading the Bible with Martin Luther*, 8 n. 17) does refer the reader to George Marsden, *Fundamentalism and American Culture*, 2nd ed. (New York: Oxford University Press, 2006), as "the best book" on the subject, but offers no specific references either to Marsden or to any fundamentalist writer.

110 *The Misuse of the Mass* (1521), AE 36:137 (WA 8:485); *Theses Concerning Faith and Law* (1535), AE 34:113 (WA 39/1:48).

but to cling to his [God's] words. For the Holy Spirit neither lies nor errs nor doubts."[111] Do statements like these display a "fundamentalist" attitude?

Furthermore, because of its divine origin, Luther also contended that Scripture could not contradict itself: "It is certain that the Scriptures cannot be at variance with themselves."[112] Similarly, "It is impossible for Scripture to contradict itself except at the hands of senseless and stubborn hypocrites."[113] As do many modern fundamentalists, Luther affirmed a six-day creation (in a sermon from 1523) and advised those who could not grasp that idea not to create a gloss to explain it away, but instead "[to] accord the Holy Ghost the honor that He is more erudite than you. When you read the words of Holy Scripture, you must realize that God is speaking them."[114]

Late in his life (1541 and again in 1545), Luther published a biblical chronology that illustrates his commitment to biblical infallibility. Luther prepared a listing of historical events in the order in which they had occurred. Because of his *a priori* commitment to the truth and accuracy of Scripture, Luther worked at harmonizing the various strands of chronology that existed in different books of the Bible, for example, the books of Kings and Chronicles. In his preface he admitted that some excellent historians had also written on the same topics, but, Luther said, "I preferred the Holy Scripture to them. I use them in such a way that I am not compelled to contradict the Scriptures. . . . I believe that in the Scriptures God speaks truthfully."[115]

James Barr has studied Luther's approach to biblical chronology in this work and demonstrates the various ways in which the reformer dealt with diverse data in the books of the Bible. Luther did not simply reject what the Bible said in a particular place. Instead, he explained how one could bring passages into harmony with others so that they did not contradict each other. So, for example, regarding the problem of whether Ahaziah was twenty-two years old (2 Kings 8:26) or forty-two (2 Chron. 22:2), Barr comments, "It hardly enters Luther's mind that one or other of these figures might simply be wrong. He

---

111 AE 37:278–79 (WA 26:418.17–20).

112 *That These Words of Christ, "This Is My Body," Still Stand Firm against the Fanatics* (1527), AE 37:50.

113 *Lectures on Galatians* (1535), AE 26:295 (WA 40/1:458).

114 Cited and translated in Francis Pieper, *Christian Dogmatics* (St. Louis: Concordia, 1950), 1:281. See also pp. 276–98 for Pieper's treatment of "Luther and the Inspiration of Holy Scripture." For the original text of the passage quoted, see WA 12:440.16–18. For Luther's belief in a six-day creation, see also his *Lectures on Genesis* (1535–45), AE 1:5, 121 (WA 42:5, 91).

115 WA 53:27.

thinks of far more complicated possibilities than that."[116] Luther was also very much aware of differences between the years mentioned in Genesis and those in Stephen's speech (Acts 7). Although Luther acknowledged that, technically speaking, Stephen was wrong, the reformer was *not* content to leave it at that but explained that it was a result of Stephen's speaking informally, that is, on the basis of common speech, which is often confused and unclear. In other words, it was not Stephen's *intent* to present an *assertio propria*, explained by Barr as "a formally correct statement," but just to tell the story. In order to show that by speaking this way Stephen was not unique, Luther compared the martyr's approach to the way that New Testament writers often used the Old Testament imprecisely. Thus rather than saying that the Holy Spirit got it wrong, Luther resorted to authorial intent. It is hardly a falsehood if an author intended merely to be approximate rather than exact.

But why would Luther go to the trouble of explaining all this if he had not already committed himself to the infallibility of the scriptural text? Although Barr is highly critical of Luther's various attempts to construct his chronology, he recognizes that Luther's activity revealed a theological commitment to the Bible that many—like Wengert—no longer share:

> The accuracy of the Bible in giving information about the numbers of years in distant times, to which no human memory or reason could have access, only went to prove that it was divinely inspired and equally infallible in matters of normal human history and in theological matters.[117]

Luther's approach to the historical content of the Bible was not the same as resting Scripture's authority on the Gospel, as Wengert insists. Does the story of Jesus really depend on Ahaziah's right age? Of course not, but it does depend on the facticity of the biblical account of our Lord's conception, birth, ministry, death, and resurrection, not to mention accounts of other divine interventions in human history such as the exodus. Luther's commitment to biblical authority included confidence in what God has done in history and what He has said about it in the Bible. Confidence in the Gospel promises, therefore, was a consequence of confidence in the God who speaks truthfully. It is not clear that Wengert's approach can make the same claim.

---

116 James Barr, "Luther and Biblical Chronology," *Bulletin of the John Rylands Library* 72 (1990): 55.

117 Barr, "Luther and Biblical Chronology," 65.

Besides the question of biblical authority, there is a great deal more in Timothy Wengert's *Reading the Bible with Martin Luther* that deserves attention. Some of it is likewise very questionable—indeed, objectionable—for example, Wengert's use of the pericope of the adulterous woman (John 8:1–11) to take a swipe at those who condemn people in "same-gendered, committed relationships."[118] Luther called homosexual relationships a "monstrous depravity [*portento*]" and credited them to "Satan, who, after people have once turned away from the fear of God, so powerfully suppresses nature that he blots out the natural desire and stirs up a desire that is contrary to nature." Luther was not at all shy about calling sin, sin. One wonders if a stronger commitment to the *biblical text* as itself authoritative might have kept Wengert on the same page as Luther when it came to this vice.[119]

But Wengert only promised to read the Bible *with* Martin Luther, and "with" is a slippery preposition. Reading and listening to the Scriptures "with" Martin Luther does not necessarily mean "in the same way" as Martin Luther. This is certainly the case when it comes to biblical authority. While Wengert wanted to identify scriptural authority with its Gospel content, Luther insisted that God the Holy Spirit inspired the biblical authors to write what they did—all of it. It was their word but it is also His. Therefore, it is absolutely reliable; and therefore, too, one can trust it absolutely. From the Scriptures, then, Christians can both know and proclaim the Gospel, confident that it really is "the power of God unto salvation" (Rom. 1:16).

118 Wengert, *Reading the Bible with Martin Luther*, 25.

119 *Lectures on Genesis* (1535–45), AE 3:251, 255 (WA 43:55, 57).

The Enduring Importance of Luther's Exposition of the Old Testament as Christian Revelation

John A. Maxfield

At its heart Martin Luther's Reformation was focused on bringing the Gospel of Jesus Christ to the center of the Church's proclamation so that Christian faith and life would be created and shaped by that Gospel. A strong argument can be made that Luther's Reformation was most successful in precisely this goal. For despite the failure of the Reformation to bring about a sweeping reform within the historic structure of the (Western) Catholic Church, with the result that the Reformation is often characterized as "the division of Christendom,"[1] Luther's goal of bringing the Gospel to the center of Christian faith and life not only was realized, if imperfectly, within Lutheranism but also had a significant influence on both Catholic reform and other forms of Protestant reform. This happened despite the important—and

1 Hans J. Hillerbrand, *The Division of Christendom: Christianity in the Sixteenth Century* (Louisville: Westminster John Knox Press, 2007). In his preface, Hillerbrand notes: "The alert reader will . . . have noticed that title and subtitle of this book blatantly omit any reference to the Reformation. This is altogether intentional and expresses my conviction that the most important feature of the story of sixteenth-century Christianity was that a fundamental and fateful division occurred" (p. x). Cf. also Diarmaid MacCallough, *The Reformation: Europe's House Divided, 1490–1700* (London: Allen Lane, 2003).

one must say critical and enduring—differences and disagreements that drove reformers of various convictions into different and competing agendas of reform in the sixteenth century. Indeed, although they sometimes have been used to paint over critical and persisting differences and disagreements, the "three solas" of the Reformation do summarize significant themes common to most forms of evangelical reform of the time: that salvation is a gift of God offered to sinners by grace alone (*sola gratia*); that salvation is received by sinners through faith in Christ alone (*sola fide*) and cannot be achieved through a life of good works; and that the teaching and the life of the Church must be guided, shaped, and normed by Scripture alone as the highest authority (*sola scriptura*), for Scripture alone gives infallible witness to Christ and the Gospel.[2] These convictions of Luther and other evangelical reformers were grounded in their understanding of the Bible and grew stronger rather than weaker as the papal church rejected evangelical reforms and condemned as heretical Martin Luther and all who followed his teaching. Thus in the sixteenth century and in the five centuries since, Luther's Reformation has stood on the foundation of the reformer's interpretation of Scripture, or it has foundered in the face of the papal church's authority over scriptural interpretation and competing Protestant interpretations.

Yet how well has Luther's interpretation of the Bible stood up in the face of criticism in his own day and since? While the many loyal disciples of Luther's Reformation treasured the reformer's biblical exposition as the most clear, the most faithful, the most convincing interpretation of the Bible since the days of the apostles,[3] the magisterium (teaching authority) of the Catholic Church condemned Luther's teaching as heresy—that is, as false in many of its core elements. And while many evangelical reformers who asserted their independence

2 While affirming that these three "sola" phrases can indeed be drawn from the Lutheran Reformation and its confessions, Jacob Corzine argues cogently that the grouping together of these three "solas" as slogans summarizing the thought of the reformers is a modern development, specifically from publications celebrating the four-hundredth anniversary of the Reformation by The Lutheran Church—Missouri Synod. See Jacob Corzine, "The Source of the Solas: On the Question of Which Are the Original Solas," in *Theology Is Eminently Practical: Essays in Honor of John T. Pless*, ed. Jacob Corzine and Bryan Wolfmueller (Fort Wayne, IN: Lutheran Legacy, 2012), 51–69.

3 Typical among Luther's disciples was the statement of Nicolaus Selnecker (1530–92): "We do not place our faith in Luther, as we place our faith in no other human being, but we love Luther because he leads us to Christ and because his writings are subject to the word of Christ. He instructs us out of this word" (Selnecker, *Recitationes aliqvot . . .* [Leipzig: Georg Defner, 1581], 268, quotation translated in Robert Kolb, *Martin Luther as Prophet, Teacher, and Hero: Images of the Reformer, 1520–1620* [Grand Rapids: Baker Books, 1999], 72).

of Luther and supported competing agendas of reform nevertheless praised Luther as a prophet of God, a third Elijah who was gifted by the Holy Spirit in his interpretation of the Gospel, many of these reformers still criticized Luther's Reformation as insufficient in its reform proposals and wrong in important—indeed, sweeping—areas of scriptural interpretation. Most important, Luther had to defend against other Protestants his central interpretive principle of the relationship between Law and Gospel (and thus between the Old and the New Testaments) as well as his convictions regarding the scriptural doctrine of the sacraments and their proper administration. In the centuries since the Reformation, especially since the eighteenth-century Enlightenment, an ideological revolution in the practice of scriptural interpretation has taken place through the development and use of historical-critical methods of biblical interpretation, leading to Luther's (and other "pre-critical") interpretation of the Bible being dismissed as unhistorical, unreasonable, unscientific, and just plain wrong. It is important to emphasize, however, that this judgment is not universal among Christians and is broadly rejected by many traditional Christians and Bible scholars today, both Catholic and Protestant.

The first task before us is briefly to examine modern evaluations of Luther's interpretation of the Bible, in particular his interpretation of the Old Testament, noting how such evaluations are often shaped by ideologies differing from convictions broadly shared in Luther's time, even among his opponents. Then I will evaluate Luther's biblical exposition in terms of the reformer's own convictions and goals, as these were shaped in the context of his time and especially in his vocation as a professor of theology and as a pastor. As shall be seen, Luther's exposition was significant in his day for the clarity and power of its proclamation of the Old Testament as a revelation of God intended to nurture Christian faith, thus significant also for viewing historic and contemporary Judaism in terms of its rejection of Jesus as the Christ. Finally, we will see that Martin Luther's exposition of the Old Testament is of enduring importance and remains relevant five hundred years after his time precisely because Luther interpreted the Old Testament as a Christian revelation, that is, as a revelation of the triune God and of the promise of salvation through Jesus Christ.

Modern Evaluations of Luther's Exposition of the Old Testament

Luther's understanding of the whole Bible as a revelation of the triune God and a proclamation of the Gospel of Jesus Christ is frequently disparaged in modern biblical studies, as well as in historical scholarship on the reformer's biblical interpretation. Precisely here is an ideological barrier between the modern interpreter and Luther's understanding. For example, in what still today, nearly seventy years after its original publication, remains the most comprehensive treatment of Luther's interpretation of the Old Testament, Heinrich Bornkamm develops an appreciative analysis of Luther's christocentric interpretation of the Hebrew Scriptures. Bornkamm distinguishes clearly this Christ-centered interpretation from patristic and medieval christological readings by way of allegories and extensive typology, as well as from Luther's own interpretation of various passages in the Psalms and prophets (including Moses) as prophecies of Jesus Christ and the Gospel. However, Bornkamm ends his analysis with a postscript in which he asserts categorically: "Recent Old Testament study has set us a world apart from Luther's point of view. We are unable to bridge this gap." In Bornkamm's view, Luther contributed significantly to unveiling the "real significance for faith" of the actual history of the Old Testament rather than exploring allegorical interpretations or typological relationships between that history and its fulfillment in Jesus. (Such interpretations were a common Christian inheritance from the early church and the Middle Ages.) Despite this contribution, however, historical-critical methods lead modern scholars to abandon the reformer's conviction regarding christological prophecy in the Old Testament, judging such views unscientific and contrary to modern historical interpretation of the biblical text. What remains for Bornkamm is Luther's engaging interpretation of the whole Bible in terms of God's address to human beings with the demands and accusations of the Law and the promises of the Gospel. The last words of Bornkamm's book convey both the problem for the modern reader of Luther's Old Testament interpretation and its opportunity:

> [Luther's] work has Christianized the Old Testament thoroughly, as we have seen. We cannot use it with a clear conscience much longer if we cannot give clear and new reasons to justify such an interpretation. If we take this task just as seriously as we take the inviolable truthfulness of historical research, then we can let go of the "swaddling clothes" of Luther's interpretation of the Old Testament and once again salvage the treasure in the manger.[4]

---

4 Heinrich Bornkamm, *Luther and the Old Testament*, trans. Eric W. and Ruth C. Gritsch, ed. Victor I. Gruhn (Philadelphia: Fortress, 1969 [German original 1948]), 261–66, quotes at 261 and 266. Paul Althaus, working in a similar context, came to the same view: "We, today, cannot simply repeat the actual details of Luther's interpretation of the Old Testament, any more than we can repeat the interpretation of the early church. The development of historical exegesis stands between us and Luther, and we cannot

It is important to consider the historical context in which Bornkamm worked and developed this analysis. As a student of Karl Holl, his scholarly work was the fruit of the "Luther Renaissance," a modern historical and theological approach to Luther's thought and work that was steeped in the discipline of historical scholarship with its goal of understanding the reformer and his reformation movement in their historical context: that of German history in the later Middle Ages, with the sixteenth-century Reformation viewed as a period of transition to the modern age. A major goal of the Holl School was to present Luther's theology as relevant for modern Christianity.[5] One of the ironies of modern historical research in the nineteenth and early twentieth century was the peculiar combination of a goal to perform an objective, scientific analysis of primary documents that would succeed in reconstructing history "as it essentially was,"[6] with a tendency among historians, especially in Germany, to view the past through the lens of more recent developments in German history, namely, the formation of a German national state. In terms of Reformation historiography, the theme of the great masterpiece of historicist analysis, Leopold von Ranke's *History of the Reformation in Germany*,[7] was the role that Luther and the German Reformation played in this shaping of a German cultural

---

simply go back to Luther as if it did not exist. This is what prevents us from interpreting the prophets christologically" (Althaus, *The Theology of Martin Luther*, trans. Robert C. Schultz [Philadelphia: Fortress, 1966 (German 2nd ed. 1963)], 102).

5 On the Holl School and developments in Luther studies between the world wars, see James M. Stayer, *Martin Luther, German Saviour: German Evangelical Theological Factions and the Interpretation of Luther, 1917–1933* (Montreal: McGill-Queen's University Press, 2000)

6 Here I am accepting as more accurate Richard J. Evans's translation of Leopold von Ranke's famous phrase "wie es eigentlich gewesen," which is frequently construed "as it actually happened." Evans explains, "Ranke meant not that he just wanted to collect facts, but that he sought to understand the inner being of the past" (*In Defence of History* [London: Granta Books, 1997], 17). The phrase comes from the preface to the original edition (1824) of Ranke's *Histories of the Latin and Germanic Peoples*: "Man hat der Historie das Amt, die Vergangenheit zu richten, die Mitwelt zum Nutzen zukünftiger Jahre zu belehren, beigemessen: so hoher Aemter unterwindet sich gegenwärtiger Versuch nicht: er will blos zeigen, wie es eigentlich gewesen" (Leopold von Ranke, *Geschichten der romanischen und germanischen Völker von 1494 bis 1514*, 3rd ed. [Leipzig: Duncker & Humblot, 1885], vii). For more extensive analysis of Ranke's understanding of history and its influence (often through misrepresentation) particularly in America, see Peter Novick, *That Noble Dream: The "Objectivity Question" and the American Historical Profession* (Cambridge: Cambridge University Press, 1988), 4, 26–31.

7 Trans. Sarah Austin, ed. Robert A. Johnson, 2 vols. (New York: F. Unger, 1966, reprinted from the 1905 edition). The English translation covers only the first three of Ranke's six volumes. A literal translation of the title of the original German edition, which was

identity, which in the sixteenth century resulted in German Protestantism and the separation of much of Germany from the ecclesiastical governance of the Roman papacy, and which finally in the later nineteenth century blossomed into a German national state and the German Empire (the "Second Reich").

Bornkamm lived and wrote in the period when this German national identity had been transformed into the engine for National Socialism and the travesty of Adolf Hitler's rise to power, his success in extinguishing political opposition to the Nazi Party soon after his election as German chancellor in 1933, the development of the Third Reich and the outbreak of World War II, and the aftermath of the war with its full exposure of the atrocities of total warfare and the Holocaust. The original German edition of Bornkamm's *Luther and the Old Testament* was published in 1948, but it had been completed much earlier, its publication prevented by censorship in Nazi Germany.[8] In this context Bornkamm's appreciation of Luther's lifelong engagement with the Old Testament was tempered by a sense of historical distance characteristic of modern historical methods: Luther lived and worked in one age with cultural attitudes, including the approach to the Bible, very different from Bornkamm's age, with the catastrophic view of the Jews and the "Jewish Problem" in the Nazi era looming in the foreground. Despite all the attractiveness of Luther's approach to the Old Testament as a "mirror of life,"[9] in the end Luther did not approach the Old Testament with the kind of historical distance or objectivity required in modern biblical studies. According to Bornkamm, such "swaddling clothes" as Luther's view of the Old Testament as a revelation of the triune God—indeed, of Christ and the Gospel—need to be outgrown.

Responding in a more recent generation to Bornkamm's analysis of Luther's interpretation and translation of the Old Testament as a "Christianization" of the Old Testament, Siegfried Raeder concedes that a christological or christocentric reading of the Hebrew Scripture is not the original historical and literal meaning. But he points to the ongoing use of biblical texts such as the Psalms—the prayer book of ancient Israel and of the Jews as well as of Christians—and questions "whether it is right . . . to lock up the message of the Old Testament in the limits of its original meaning, scrutinized by historians."

> The Old Testament is not a museum, but a living thing, going through centuries and winning new horizons of meaning and understanding.

published in 1839–47, better displays Ranke's focus on the relationship of the Reformation to the national aspirations of Germany: *German History in the Age of the Reformation*.

8 Bornkamm, *Luther and the Old Testament*, ix (author's preface).

9 See Bornkamm, *Luther and the Old Testament*, 11–44.

> For example, we do not know who was the first to pray: "My God, my God, why hast thou forsaken me?" (Ps 22:1). But there were many who followed in his footsteps, and the greatest of them was Jesus (if the critical historians would permit him to have prayed so).[10]

Raeder's concession to historical criticism of a very narrow, historical meaning of Psalm 22 certainly does not agree with Luther's understanding—as well as the tradition of interpreting the Law and the Prophets since the New Testament itself—that the Old Testament includes what can be called a literal-prophetic meaning, that is, divinely inspired prophecy of a person and event beyond the original historical context of the prophet and his original audience: the coming Messiah. But Raeder's point is an important one for understanding the Bible as a revelation of God, a point subsumed under a broader critique of modern historical positivism that has been called postmodernism. Postmodernist philosophy and study of language (linguistics) focuses on a much broader horizon: not merely the original author and audience in their historical context, but the context of any person or community that hears, reads, or otherwise encounters a text, in this case the text of the Bible. According to these broader horizons of inquiry, the Bible and its prophetic message is not exhausted in its original reception by the prophet or its proclamation to the people of his time. Rather, the Bible continues to convey the Word of God, both the Law and the Gospel—command and promise—to every person who hears the Word preached, speaks or sings the Word in Christian liturgy, and prays or reads the Word in personal devotion. So also for Luther, who in this respect anticipates some of the more interesting characteristics of postmodern hermeneutics. For Luther the whole Bible speaks of Christ and the Gospel of Christ in every age, from the age of the patriarchs to the present, for Christ and the Gospel are the culmination of God's revelation, beginning with the patriarchs of Genesis and continuing with the Law of Moses and the Prophets all the way through Malachi and even to John the Baptizer as the last of the prophets who prepared the way for the Lord (Luke 1:76; 7:24–35; Matt. 11:7–19).

To approach the subject of Martin Luther's exegesis of the Old Testament as Christian revelation is therefore at once to confront a conundrum of modern study of religion that is tied up in the very concept of "revelation." For the Bible is not merely a historical record of the religious experience and imagination of the ancient Israelites, the people of Judah returning to Jerusalem to build the second

---

10 Siegfried Raeder, "The Exegetical and Hermeneutical Work of Martin Luther," in *Hebrew Bible / Old Testament: The History of Its Interpretation*, vol. 2: *From the Renaissance to the Enlightenment*, ed. Magne Sæbø (Göttingen: Vandenhoeck & Ruprecht, 2008), 405.

temple, and the Jews and Christians of the first century. For Christians the Bible is the revelation of God come to its fulfillment and completion in Jesus Christ. Therefore at its heart, and one might say by its very definition, Christian interpretation of the Old Testament or Hebrew Scripture is interpretation grounded in the conviction that the one true God, the Creator of the universe, the God of Abraham, Isaac, and Jacob—that is, the God who established through Moses a covenant with the people of Israel through the revelation of Torah—has declared Jesus of Nazareth to be Lord and Christ through His resurrection from the dead (Acts 2:36; Rom. 1:4). This has been called the apostolic *kerygma* or preachment, and it pervades the New Testament and Christian theology.

But that characterization immediately brings us to this conundrum of modern scholarship of religion that I have mentioned. For to say that the Old Testament also teaches Christ and the Gospel of Christ is to assert that it is a prophetic revelation of God. This concept of prophetic revelation would not have been controversial to the Israelite under the Mosaic covenant as laid out in the Torah (the five books of Moses) and interpreted by the prophets, or to the Jews of the second temple awaiting the coming of Messiah as the fulfillment of God's promises to David and the kingdom of Judah. Nor would it have been controversial to the people first called Christians in the Syrian city of Antioch (Acts 11:26), who understood the Law and the Prophets to have been fulfilled in Jesus, as every book of the New Testament argues, if by each author in his own distinctive way. The problem of modern study of religion since the eighteenth-century Enlightenment[11] is the conviction espoused by many that such a concept of revelation is a violation of one of the essential principles of history, namely, that religious texts like any text are bound up in their peculiar historical context. According to this view, religious texts are human texts and not a revelation of God, except as a projection of human values into a humanly created or imagined divine realm (to cite the basic critique of all religion as expressed by Ludwig Feuerbach).[12] I have identified this modern position as a conundrum or problem because it blocks scholarly access to the past as experienced by Jews, Christians, and all religious communities espousing an origin from divine

11 Klaus Scholder demonstrates that the philosophical basis of critical theology was laid already in the seventeenth century, but its full effect in biblical studies is seen in the eighteenth-century Enlightenment. See Scholder, *The Birth of Modern Critical Theology: Origins and Problems of Biblical Criticism in the Seventeenth Century*, trans. John Bowden (London: SCM Press, 1990).

12 Ludwig Feuerbach, *The Essence of Christianity*, trans. George Eliot, introductory essay by Karl Barth, foreword by H. Richard Niebuhr (New York: Harper & Row, 1957 [German original 1841]).

revelation, except perhaps that of antiquarian interest alone, and with that a kind of despising of the past as primitive and unenlightened. It also blocks understanding of Luther's significance for biblical studies, as today Luther's practice of exposition is most often characterized as intellectually flawed by imposing a Christian interpretation on a Hebrew Scripture that is pre-Christian, and as morally tainted by intensifying a Christian anti-Judaism that has been characteristic of the Christian community since the New Testament.

Recent scholarship has wrestled with this problem largely by bringing Jewish and Christian scholars together in scholarly forums to discuss their ways of approaching the Hebrew Scriptures. One example is the publication of papers from a conference at the University of Notre Dame in 1990 entitled *Hebrew Bible or Old Testament? Studying the Bible in Judaism and Christianity*. In one of the chapters, Jewish scholar Jon D. Levenson explores the opportunity that modern historical criticism of the Hebrew Bible has provided to Christians and Jews to investigate the texts within a common scholarly community. He draws on a novel by Chaim Potok in which the character David Lurie tells his father, Max, about his biblical studies in a university, to which Max replies in the dialogue: "You will study Torah with *goyim* [i.e., Gentiles] and with Jews who are like *goyim*? What do they know of the Torah?"[13] Levenson rephrases Max's question for historical-critical biblical scholarship today: "*Is the price of this restoration of the past to the Bible not the relegation of the Bible to the past, so that the scholar's own practice or lack of it is of no relevance?*"[14] For Levenson, who practices the faith of Judaism, historical criticism as a method cannot comprehend or enlighten the relationship between the Jewish faith and the Hebrew Bible.[15]

---

13 Chaim Potok, *In the Beginning* (New York: Knopf, 1975), quoted in Jon D. Levenson, "Theological Consensus or Historicist Evasion? Jews and Christians in Biblical Studies," in *Hebrew Bible or Old Testament? Studying the Bible in Judaism and Christianity*, ed. Roger Brooks and John J. Collins (Notre Dame, IN: University of Notre Dame Press, 1990), 111.

14 Levenson, "Theological Consensus or Historicist Evasion?" 134, emphasis Levenson's. In this context Levenson raises an objection to the parasitical nature of modern biblical studies: "I am convinced that the restoration of historical context to the Bible can help bring it alive and add vast depth and meaning to our study of it. The problem to which I am pointing is that much biblical scholarship is not practicing any such hermeneutic of retrieval. Instead, its operative technique is too often a trivializing antiquarianism . . . and the enormous historical and philological labors are not justified by reference to any larger structure of meaning" ("Theological Consensus or Historicist Evasion?" 134).

15 See also Levenson's critique of biblical theology as practiced by critical scholars: Jonathan Levenson, "Why Jews Are Not Interested in Biblical Theology," in *Judaic Perspectives on Ancient Israel*, ed. J. Neusner, B. A. Levine, and E. S. Frerichs (Philadelphia: Fortress,

Recently in biblical studies, significant attention has been paid to the historical Christian (and Jewish) concept of the canon and "canonical interpretation," that is, interpreting the Old and New Testaments within their canonical and not only their original historical contexts.[16] For Luther the significance of the biblical canon, that is, the receiving of certain writings by Jews and Christians as the inspired Word of God, is that the New Testament must be the key to understanding the meaning of the Old Testament as prophetic of Christ. Interpreting Psalm 22, for example, Luther draws a general conclusion: "For us who believe in Christ, we hold by the authority of the Gospel that this entire psalm speaks of Christ. . . . For we do not explain the historical event [*rem gestam*] by the mysteries of the Scripture, but the mysteries of Scripture by the historical event; that is, we explain the Old Testament by the Gospel and not vice versa."[17]

This interpretation of the Old Testament, always in its relationship to the New Testament proclamation of Christ and the Gospel, has been characteristic of Christian biblical studies since the New Testament itself. Some recent scholars have labeled this approach as "supersessionism"—a term often used without clear definition and in fact having a broad range of meaning. Some would reject as supersessionist the central conviction expressed in the New Testament that Jesus is the Messiah, the fulfillment of God's unconditional promise to David of a dynastic line culminating in a "son of David" (2 Sam. 7:12–16; 23:1–5) who will possess an everlasting kingship over God's people and kingdom. Others object to a narrower supersessionism in which God's covenant with Abraham (Gen. 15:5, 12–21) is viewed as abrogated, with the result that the Christian Church has replaced Abraham's seed as the people of God (contrast Paul's understanding in Romans 9–11). In its various uses, however, the term supersessionism is used in a derogatory way to identify the imposition of Christian

---

1987), 281–307. Levenson does not reject historical criticism as a method, but he does deny its capacity to inform theology from the supposed objective and pluralistic framework of modern academia: "If it be admitted that biblical theology presumes existential commitment and that the commitment will necessarily include other sources of truth (the Talmud, the New Testament, etc.), then it becomes clear that biblical theology is different in kind from other branches of biblical studies and that, unlike them, it cannot so easily lend itself to ecumenical, pluralistic collaboration. One pursues either Jewish biblical theology or Christian biblical theology, but not both, for the term 'biblical' has a different reference for the Jew and the Christian" ("Why Jews Are Not Interested in Biblical Theology," 286).

16 See esp. Brevard S. Childs, *Old Testament Theology in a Canonical Context* (Philadelphia: Fortress, 1986); and James A. Sanders, *From Sacred Story to Sacred Text: Canon as Paradigm* (Philadelphia: Fortress, 1987).

17 *Operationes in Psalmos* (1519–21), WA 5:633.15–19 (my translation).

concepts on pre-Christian, Hebrew Scriptures. The term thus represents a historicist approach to the Old Testament that essentially denies the capacity of the prophet, through a revelation from God, to speak of future realities except by way of wishful (or hopeful) thinking.

The most sweeping rejection of any interpretation of the Old Testament in the light of the New Testament's witness to Jesus Christ, however, is grounded in the conviction that such interpretation imposes a Christian meaning on a text that is Jewish, not Christian. For example, Roger Brooks and John Collins write about "the Christian appropriation of the Hebrew Scriptures" and make the sweeping charge: "The traditional supersessionist claim that biblical religion finds its true fulfillment in Christianity has undeniably led to the denigration of Judaism, ancient, medieval, and modern, and cannot be held innocent of the outrage of anti-Semitism and Holocaust in our century."[18] Such a rejection of the central proclamation of the Christian Church since the Christian community was itself a Jewish community is likewise the essential supposition of James Carroll's popular "history" of anti-Judaism in Catholicism.[19]

This view of the relationship between the Old Testament Scripture and New Testament Christianity is merely to choose one side over the other in the decisive dispute about Jesus among the Jews in the apostolic era. It is prejudicial toward the development of rabbinic Judaism over against the Jewish and increasingly Gentile Christianity that ultimately experienced a great "parting of the ways"[20] as Christianity separated from Judaism during the course of the first and second (and later) centuries. However, as Jewish scholar Jacob Neusner has noted, it

18 Roger Brooks and John J. Collins, "Introduction," in *Hebrew Bible or Old Testament? Studying the Bible in Judaism and Christianity*, ed. Roger Brooks and John J. Collins (Notre Dame, IN: University of Notre Dame Press, 1990), 1. On the supposed "anti-Semitism" of Christian theology from its origins in the New Testament, see also Rosemary Radford Ruether, *Faith and Fratricide: The Theological Roots of Anti-Semitism* (New York: Seabury Press, 1974).

19 James Carroll, *Constantine's Sword: The Church and the Jews. A History* (Boston: Houghton Mifflin, 2002). For incisive critical reviews of Carroll's book as history, see Thomas F. X. Noble, "A Tendentious Telling," *First Things* 113 (May 2001): 59–63; and Robert Louis Wilken, "Dismantling the Cross," *Commonweal* 128, no. 2 (January 26, 2001): 22–28.

20 See, e.g., A. Cohen, *The Parting of the Ways: Judaism and the Rise of Christianity* (London: Lincolns-Prager, published for the World Jewish Congress, British Section, 1954); and Stephen Spence, *The Parting of the Ways: The Roman Church as a Case Study*, Interdisciplinary Studies in Ancient Culture and Religion 5 (Leuven: Peeters, 2004). For a recent challenge to this paradigm, see *The Ways That Never Parted: Jews and Christians in Late Antiquity and the Early Middle Ages*, ed. Adam H. Becker and Annette Yoshiko Reed (Minneapolis: Fortress, 2007).

is not the case that Judaism grew inevitably out of the Old Testament community of Israel by way of a more objective or historical approach to the Hebrew Scriptures. Rather, Christianity and Judaism were both developing at the same time but through very different ways of approaching and incorporating into their religious life the revelation of God through Moses and the Prophets. While first the apostles' oral preaching and teaching and then the written Gospels and other writings of the New Testament sought to relate how "the Law and the Prophets" were fulfilled in Jesus,[21] Judaism interpreted the Hebrew Scriptures in relationship to the oral traditions of the Jewish rabbis. In Neusner's important book on Judaism and Scripture, the third in a series on the development of Judaism in relationship to its authoritative texts, the opening lines state the situation in categorical terms:

> While the world at large treats Judaism as "the religion of the Old Testament," the fact is otherwise. Judaism inherits and makes the Hebrew Scriptures its own, just as does Christianity. But just as Christianity rereads the entire heritage of ancient Israel in [the] light of "the resurrection of Jesus Christ," so Judaism understands the Hebrew Scriptures as only one part, the written one, of "the one whole Torah of Moses, our rabbi." Ancient Israel no more testified to the oral Torah, now written down in the Mishnah and later rabbinic writings, than it did to Jesus as the Christ. . . . Since the Judaism at hand first reached literary expression in the Mishnah, a document in which Scripture plays a subordinate role, the founders of that Judaism clearly make no pretense at tying up to scriptural prooftexts or at expressing in the form of scriptural commentary the main ideas they wished to set out. Accordingly, Judaism only asymmetrically rests upon the foundations of the Hebrew Scriptures, and Judaism is not alone or mainly "the religion of the Old Testament."[22]

This way of approaching the Old Testament either from the perspective of rabbinic Judaism or of Christianity differs sharply from a historical, philological, and often literalistic analysis that limits the Hebrew texts of the Bible to the original contexts in the ancient Near East when they were spoken and recorded.

---

21 In addition to the entire Gospel of Matthew, which is shaped by its aim to demonstrate to Jewish readers that Jesus Christ is "the son of David, the son of Abraham" and the fulfillment of God's promise to be with His people as Immanuel, "God with us" (Matt. 1:1, 22–23; 28:20), consider the following among many New Testament passages: Luke 24:27; John 5:39, 46–47; Rom. 3:21.

22 Jacob Neusner, *Judaism and Scripture: The Evidence of Leviticus Rabah* (Chicago: University of Chicago Press, 1986), xi.

To return to our subject of Luther's approach to the Old Testament, we note a sharp contrast with modern historical studies of the Hebrew Scriptures. For despite the influence of humanist studies in his intellectual development, and his turn from the patristic and medieval focus on allegorical and other figural forms of spiritual interpretation to a more decisive focus on the literal and historical meaning of the text, Luther's exposition of the Old Testament is without question grounded in the conviction that God has spoken and continues to speak through the Old Testament, that the Bible as a whole is the revelation of God that has come to its completion in Jesus Christ, the Word of God made flesh (John 1:1, 14).

Luther's Approach to the Old Testament in Relation to His Views of Judaism

One of the most significant challenges to the relevance of Luther's exposition of the Old Testament, and the Bible as a whole, for Christians five hundred years after the beginning of Luther's Reformation is the charge that Luther's Old Testament interpretation is anti-Judaic and even anti-Semitic. As much of the expansive literature on Luther and the Jews has noted, Luther's response to rabbinic exegesis is a characteristic feature of his Old Testament exposition, but what especially pervades his so-called Jewish writings[23] is concern that through the influence of rabbinic interpretations of the Hebrew Bible Christians are losing the rich testimony of Christ that the Church had recognized in the Old Testament since the time of the apostles. Some would describe Luther's fear as a phobia, an irrational fear that had detrimental effects in his own day and catastrophic effects in later European history. But the history of biblical

23 Luther's writings that engage the Jewish people topically and extensively (not just theologically within texts on other subjects) are usually considered to be *That Jesus Christ Was Born a Jew* (1523), AE 45:195–229; *Against the Sabbatarians—Letter to a Good Friend* (1538), AE 47:57–98; *On the Jews and Their Lies* (1543), AE 47:121–306; *On the Ineffable Name* (1543), WA 53:579–648 (forthcoming in AE 61); and *The Last Words of David* (1543), AE 15:265–352. On the modern problem of categorizing certain of Luther's writings as "Jewish writings" (*Judenschriften*) and viewing them as directed against the Jews, see Kenneth Hagen, "Luther's So-Called *Judenschriften*: A Genre Approach," *Archive for Reformation History* 90 (1999): 130–58. For an accessible introduction to the broader topic of Luther and the Jews that places Luther's views in their historical context, see Thomas Kaufmann, "Luther and the Jews," trans. Stephen G. Burnett, in *Jews, Judaism, and the Reformation in Sixteenth-Century Germany*, ed. Stephen G. Burnett and Dean Phillip Bell (Leiden: Brill, 2006), 69–104.

interpretation since the sixteenth century has given ample evidence for the internal logic of Luther's response to rabbinic exegesis as well as to historical-critical exegesis of the Scripture that does not take into account, or even flatly rejects, its character as a revelation of the triune God, with the Gospel of Jesus Christ as its center and goal. In short, Luther himself developed early on a rich appreciation for the Hebrew language and used humanist philological studies in his academic lectures and in his translation of the Old Testament (with a team of scholars he called his "Sanhedrin"). Nevertheless, especially in his last decade of life, Luther viewed with suspicion and even fear the influence that Jewish Hebrew studies were having on Christian scholars in his time.[24]

From his earliest lectures as a professor of theology at the University of Wittenberg, his *Dictata super Psalterium* (1513–15), Luther raised the issue of Jewish interpretation of the Psalms. These lectures were not published, but preserved in Luther's own hand are the glosses (brief commentary notes) and scholia (more extensive lecture notes) that he prepared for his classroom lectures, as well as prefaces to his glosses and to the Latin texts of the psalms that were printed in Wittenberg for Luther and his students to use in the classroom. In his preface to the glosses Luther begins by quoting 1 Cor. 14:15, "I will sing with the spirit and I will sing with the mind also," and proceeds to contrast those who sing with the spirit and spiritual devotion to those who sing only with the flesh. The latter are further divided between "those who with an unsettled and weary heart sing only with the tongue and with the mouth," and "those who indeed sing with a cheerful and devout heart but are still enjoying it more in a carnal way." Finally, those who sing with the mind and with spiritual understanding are divided between those who do not understand what they sing and those who have a carnal understanding, "like the Jews, who always apply the Psalms to ancient history apart from Christ."[25] Luther instead taught his students to engage the Psalms as testimonies of Christ, as he made very clear in another preface that was printed at the top of the first page of the printed Psalms texts prepared for his students. This preface has the illuminating (indeed,

---

24 Particularly helpful for understanding Luther and the Wittenberg circle's approach to Hebraic studies is Stephen G. Burnett, "Reassessing the 'Basel-Wittenberg Conflict': Dimensions of the Reformation-Era Discussion of Hebrew Scholarship," in *"Hebraica Veritas?" Christian Hebraists and the Study of Judaism in Early Modern Europe*, ed. Allison P. Coudert and Jeffrey S. Shoulson (Philadelphia: University of Pennsylvania Press, 2004), 181–201. For evidence from Luther's lectures on Genesis, see John A. Maxfield, *Luther's Lectures on Genesis and the Formation of Evangelical Identity*, Sixteenth Century Essays & Studies 80 (Kirksville, MO: Truman State University Press, 2008), 48–59.

25 AE 10:3; WA 3:11.3–15.

agenda-setting) title "Preface of Jesus Christ, Son of God and Our Lord, to the Psalter of David." Here Luther opens with the words of Jesus: "I am the door; if anyone enters by Me, he will be saved, and will go in and out and find pasture. John 10:9." Citing Moses (Exod. 33:14–15), the prophet Zechariah (9:1), Peter (Acts 3:24), and Paul (1 Cor. 2:2) as witnesses of Jesus, the full revelation and presence of God among His people, Luther states his central principle and aim for interpreting the Psalms:

> From these we draw the following guideline for this dark, yet holy labyrinth:
>
> Every prophecy and every prophet must be understood as referring to Christ the Lord, except where it is clear from the plain words that someone else is spoken of. For thus He Himself says: "Search the Scriptures, . . . and it is they that bear witness to Me" (John 5:39). Otherwise it is most certain that the searchers will not find what they are searching for. For that reason some explain very many psalms not prophetically but historically, following certain Hebrew rabbis who are falsifiers and inventors of Jewish vanities. No wonder, because they are far away from Christ (that is, from the truth). "But we have the mind of Christ," says the apostle (1 Cor. 2:16).[26]

Throughout his lectures during his university career Luther continually weaves into his expositions of the biblical text the themes of faith versus unbelief; of spiritual knowledge of God and self versus spiritual darkness and ignorance of both God and self; of humble reliance on God versus self-sufficiency and reliance on works or one's station in life. Through each of these themes and many others Luther enacted in his vocational life the principle and witness he quoted from St. Paul: "For I decided to know nothing among you except Jesus Christ and Him crucified" (1 Cor. 2:2).

Analyzing Luther's anti-Judaism in the context of the cultural currents of his time, Heiko Oberman noted that "the basis of Luther's anti-Judaism was the conviction that ever since Christ's appearance on earth, the Jews have no future as Jews."[27] But for Luther this conviction cannot simply be understood in a broader context of the "Jewish problem" in a medieval (or Reformation) Christendom where the place and role of unbaptized, non-Christian Jews in society had been marginalized and even denied. For Luther the essential problem as he engaged the

---

26 AE 10:6–7; WA 3:12.11–13.13.

27 Heiko A. Oberman, *The Roots of Anti-Semitism in the Age of Renaissance and Reformation*, trans. James I. Porter (Philadelphia: Fortress, 1984), 46.

revelation of God in the Bible is that *no one* has a future apart from Jesus Christ and the righteousness before God that is given through faith in Christ; indeed, no one has a present existence except under the judgment of God that is death. Primarily through his engagement with Old Testament texts Luther came to an understanding that God had rejected His own people because of their ongoing unbelief. This is not the place to discuss Luther's inhumane recommendations for his society's treatment of the Jewish people especially in his 1543 treatise *On the Jews and Their Lies*—we can only state categorically that Luther's anti-Jewish mentality and prejudiced opinions must be rejected and left in the past where they unfortunately were more commonplace than unique. What is essential to our topic is to note that most of this treatise—indeed, its very title—is an expression of Luther's fear that *Christians* in his day were under an assault by Satan, who continuously attacked the very heart and lifeblood of Christian faith and life, namely, Christ and the Gospel as witnessed and proclaimed throughout the Bible, in both the Old and the New Testaments, and through Christian preaching. The "lies" of the Jews that Luther sought to refute were the rabbinic interpretations of various passages in the Old Testament that already before Luther's time as well as in his own exegesis were understood as prophetic of Christ and His kingdom. In Luther's understanding, these passages—Gen. 49:10; 2 Sam. 23:5 and 2 Sam. 7:12–16; Hag. 2:6–9; and Dan. 9:24–27—either were fulfilled in Christ or God is a liar who has failed to fulfill His promises.[28]

Were Luther's fears justified that Christians would lose this rich prophetic testimony of Christ in the Old Testament through the influence of rabbinic interpretations? There is no doubt that in Luther's time, through the influence of humanist biblical studies as well as Luther's (and other Protestant and

---

28 The central and longest portion of the treatise (AE 47:176–254) is devoted to Luther's interpretation of these passages. The theme of the Jews' interpretations of their history and God's faithfulness (or unfaithfulness) in keeping His promises is also the theme of the first writing in which Luther engages broadly the claim that the Jews remain God's faithful people but that they yet must await the fulfillment of His promises of a kingdom because of their sins: his 1538 open letter *Against the Sabbatarians: Letter to a Good Friend* (AE 47:65–98). In this letter Luther was responding to a report that some Christians in Bohemia were being convinced by Jews (though this was highly unlikely in reality) "to let themselves be circumcised and to believe that the Messiah or Christ has not yet appeared, that the law of the Jews must prevail forever, that it must also be adopted by all the Gentiles, etc." (AE 47:65). In the letter Luther encourages response to Jewish interpretations of their history and status by appeal to a broader selection of Old Testament passages, including Jer. 31:31–34 (which by no coincidence is the Old Testament reading now appointed in Lutheran lectionaries for the celebration of Reformation Day); Deut. 9:24–29; 2 Sam. 23:5–7 (also the basis for Luther's 1543 treatise *On the Last Words of David*, AE 15:267–352); and Psalm 89.

many Catholic interpreters') own emphasis on the historical and grammatical rather than allegorical interpretations, biblical studies was at a kind of crossroads. Frequently the charge was made that one or another theologian was "judaizing" the interpretation of the Old Testament, a charge Luther himself responded to in his first treatise dealing with the Jewish people and Judaism as such, his 1523 treatise *That Jesus Christ Was Born a Jew*.[29] Luther's fears of Jewish rabbis' influences on Christians, and especially on Christian interpretation of the Old Testament, increased in the late 1530s after he began using the Basel Hebraist Sebastian Münster's biblical annotations (published in 1534–35),[30] and especially in the early 1540s after he had read "a little book in which a Jew engages in a dialogue with a Christian. He dares to pervert the scriptural passages which we cite in testimony to our faith, concerning our Lord Jesus Christ and Mary his mother . . . ."[31] Such polemic against Jewish influence on Christian interpretation of the Old Testament persisted among Lutherans. Second-generation evangelical reformer John Calvin became the object of rigorous Lutheran critique for his typological interpretation of several psalms historically interpreted as messianic prophecies, as well as numerous other passages traditionally interpreted as revelatory of Christ and the triune God, in a 1593 treatise by the Wittenberg theologian Aegidius Hunnius titled *The Judaizing Calvin* (*Calvinus Judaizans*).[32] More important for assessing

---

29 AE 45:199–229.

30 See Burnett, "Reassessing the 'Basel-Wittenberg Conflict'" (as in p. 136 n. 24), 190 and passim; and Stephen G. Burnett, "Sebastian Münster and Jewish Interpretation of Genesis in His Hebraica Biblia (1534–35): Selection and Mediation of Jewish Insight for Christian Purposes," in *Auslegung und Hermeneutik der Bibel in der Reformationszeit*, ed. Christine Christ-von Wedel and Sven Grosse (Berlin: de Gruyter, 2017), 393–403.

31 WA 53:417.15–19 (*On the Jews and Their Lies*, 1543), quoted in Burnett, "Reassessing the 'Basel-Wittenberg Conflict,'" 193. Cf. AE 47:137. As Burnett notes perhaps too uncertainly: "Since Luther's description of the passage involves a Jew in dialogue with a Christian, discussing key prophetic passages in the Old Testament, he might well have seen a copy of Münster's *Messiahs of the Christians and the Jews* [published 1529/1539]. It contains Jewish interpretations of Dan. 9:24, Hag. 2:6–10, and Isa. 7:14, two of which Luther discussed at length in *On the Jews and Their Lies*" ("Reassessing the 'Basel-Wittenberg Conflict,'" 200–201 n. 84).

32 See the full title from a recent English translation: *The Judaizing Calvin: that is, Jewish interpretations and corruptions by which John Calvin has, in detestable fashion, shamelessly corrupted the clearest passages and testimonies of Holy Scripture regarding the glorious Trinity, the deity of Christ and of the Holy Spirit, and especially the prophecies of the Prophets regarding the coming Messiah—His birth, suffering, resurrection, ascension into heaven and session at the right hand of God.* The following confutation is offered by Aegidius Hunnius, Doctor of Sacred Theology and Professor at the Academy

Luther's fears in the wake of nearly five centuries of biblical interpretation, however, is to observe that modern biblical criticism has firmly established the historicist principle, mentioned above, that predictive prophecy is by definition excluded from philological analysis of the biblical text—Heinrich Bornkamm's "inviolable truthfulness of historical research." This can be confirmed by consulting any history of modern biblical interpretation[33] or any number of critical commentaries on the Old Testament passages that Luther promoted so rigorously as witnesses of Christ and the Gospel of salvation.

Luther's Exposition of the Old Testament in the Light of the History of Exegesis

Critical scholars of the Hebrew Scriptures today might be surprised by the many ways historical-critical analysis of the Old Testament is being knocked off its hegemonic pedestal, not only among Christian believers but also in the secular academy. In the burgeoning discipline of the history of biblical exegesis, a fascination has developed with "pre-critical" or premodern interpretation of the Bible, that is, interpretation before the Pyrrhic triumph of modern historical criticism in the eighteenth-century Enlightenment. For example, in a widely cited article that has functioned as a rhetorical manifesto for the discipline of the history of premodern biblical interpretation, David Steinmetz takes aim at the sufficiency of exegesis that focuses narrowly on the intended historical-literal sense of the human author of biblical texts, asserting boldly:

> The medieval theory of levels of meaning in the biblical text, with all its undoubted defects, flourished because it is true, while the modern theory of a single meaning, with all its demonstrable virtues, is false. Until the historical-critical method becomes critical of its own theoretical foundations and develops a hermeneutical theory adequate to the nature of the text it is interpreting, it will remain restricted—as it

---

of Wittenberg, trans. Paul A. Rydecki, foreword by James D. Heiser (Malone, TX: Repristination Press, 2012). For an analysis sympathetic to Calvin, see G. Sujin Pak, *The Judaizing Calvin: Sixteenth-Century Debates over the Messianic Psalms* (Oxford: Oxford University Press, 2010).

33 For example, see Henning Graf Reventlow, *History of Biblical Interpretation*, vol. 4: *From the Enlightenment to the Twentieth Century*, trans. Leo G. Perdue (Atlanta: Society of Biblical Literature, 2010).

deserves to be—to the guild and the academy, where the question of truth can endlessly be deferred.[34]

A whole genre of studies of biblical interpretation in the early church, the Middle Ages, and the Reformation has been the fruit of such appeals to dethrone the sole focus of biblical studies on "the inviolable truthfulness of historical research" as conceived in post-Enlightenment historical criticism. Roman Catholic scholars such as Henri de Lubac have explored the rich patristic and medieval tradition of spiritual interpretation of the Bible.[35] In similar if less exhaustive fashion, Robert Louis Wilken defends the use of allegory (among other meanings) in patristic and medieval spiritual interpretation, and overtly criticizes modern biblical studies as too narrowly focused on the historical context and the original intended message of the human author. He criticizes as well the attempt to reconstruct that context and meaning to the exclusion of any concept of divine revelation in the biblical text.[36]

Luther increasingly focused on the historical *and prophetic* meaning of biblical texts, emphasizing also that the sense intended by God as the ultimate author of inspired Scripture is singular rather than multiple in its meaning. But most important in its contrast to modern biblical criticism is Luther's consistent practice of interpreting the biblical text as a revelation of the triune God. Its content or subject matter—whether in historical narrative, reflective as well as

34 David Steinmetz, "The Superiority of Pre-Critical Exegesis," *Theology Today* 37 (1980): 38; see also David C. Steinmetz, "Theology and Exegesis: Ten Theses," quoted (and most easily accessible) in Richard A. Muller, "Biblical Interpretation in the Era of the Reformation: The View from the Middle Ages," in *Biblical Interpretation in the Era of the Reformation: Essays Presented to David C. Steinmetz in Honor of His Sixtieth Birthday*, ed. Richard A. Muller and John L. Thompson (Grand Rapids: Eerdmans, 1996), 7. Note especially the following theses: "The church which is restricted in its preaching to the original intention of the author is a church which must reject the Old Testament as an exclusively Jewish book" (Thesis 8); and "The church which is restricted in its preaching to the most primitive layer of biblical tradition as the most authoritative is a church which can no longer preach from the New Testament" (Thesis 9).

35 De Lubac's magisterial study is now available in an English translation: Henri de Lubac, S. J., *Medieval Exegesis: The Four Senses of Scripture*, trans. Mark Sebanc, 3 vols. (Grand Rapids & Edinburgh: Eerdmans & T&T Clark, 1998).

36 Robert Louis Wilken, "In Defense of Allegory," *Modern Theology* 14, no. 2 (April 1998): 197–212. Here Wilken echoes De Lubac's rich appreciation for patristic and medieval practices of interpretation, and opens his critique of the narrow, literalistic focus of modern historical criticism by stating, "If there is anything that is obvious, it is that the notion of a single sense [i.e., the narrowly historical sense] does not carry us very far in the interpretation of great works of literature, or of the Bible" ("In Defense of Allegory," 197).

messianic psalm, or the preaching of the prophets—conveys the promises of God that are fulfilled in Jesus Christ, and its narrative is about God creating faith in those promises, as well as God judging and condemning unbelief. In one respect Luther's exposition of the Old Testament is quite traditional, and therefore I will treat it only briefly. Luther carries on the patristic and medieval tradition of interpreting various Old Testament texts as revealing God's triune being; of understanding various psalms and passages in the prophets as oracles of Christ and His Church; in short, of understanding the New Testament as hidden within the Old, and the Old Testament fully revealed in the New, according to the oft-repeated dictum of St. Augustine.[37] Even when Luther began to separate himself from the traditional threefold spiritual interpretation of Old Testament texts (by way of allegory, tropology, and anagogy) and emphasized instead the literal meaning of the sacred text (which may include metaphor, typology, and prophecy),[38] he was continuing a pattern already established by the scholastic theologian St. Thomas Aquinas and others who insisted that all Christian doctrine must be established in the literal sense of the Bible and not in the creative application of spiritual exposition.[39]

---

37 Augustine *Quaestiones in Heptateuchum* 2, 73 (CCSL 33:106): "Multum et solide significatur ad uetus testamentum timorem potius pertinere sicut ad nouum dilectionem, quamquam et in uetere nouum lateat et in nouo uetus pateat." See also Augustine *On the Spirit and the Letter* 27 [xv], where Augustine applies this principle to the doctrine of grace: "This grace hid itself under a veil in the Old Testament, but it has been revealed in the New Testament according to the most perfectly ordered dispensation of the ages, forasmuch as God knew how to dispose all things" (NPNF[1] 5:95).

38 For a succinct analysis, see Scott H. Hendrix, "Luther against the Background of the History of Biblical Interpretation," in Scott H. Hendrix, *Tradition and Authority in the Reformation*, Collected Studies Series (Aldershot: Ashgate/Variorum, 1996), I (229–39).

39 Karlfried Froelich, "Christian Interpretation of the Old Testament in the High Middle Ages," in *Hebrew Bible / Old Testament: The History of Its Interpretation*, vol. 1: *From the Beginnings to the Middle Ages (Until 1300)*, part 2: *The Middle Ages*, ed. Magne Sæbø (Göttingen: Vandenhoeck & Ruprecht, 2000), 538–46. Froehlich notes three principles operative in Thomas: (1) "The literal sense is the only basis from which an argument over biblical interpretation can proceed"; (2) "The literal sense includes metaphor, parable, and intentional figuration"; and (3) "The literal sense is the only sense which any book other than the Bible can ever have. . . . Human books cannot have a spiritual sense." Yet despite these principles regarding the literal sense, Thomas continued to use the traditional spiritual senses of biblical texts. As Froehlich concludes, "Rather than fighting for the literal sense of Scripture, Thomas came to the defense of the spiritual senses, at a time when enthusiasm for the former seemed to sweep some colleagues off their feet. He was [quoting Beryl Smalley] 'the enlightened conservative on the four senses' " ("Christian Interpretation of the Old Testament in the High Middle Ages," 545–46).

What distinguished Luther's interpretation as a new and significant contribution to interpretation in his day was therefore not his christological interpretation of many Old Testament passages but rather his christocentric and Gospel-centric understanding of the Old Testament in its entirety. Thus Luther expounds important narratives in Genesis in relation to Christ and the Gospel. When God (*Elohim*) created the world, this was the triune God creating through His Word, that is, through His Son, the pre-incarnate Christ.[40] When Luther expounds the narrative of God calling Abram and making promises to him, the reformer interprets this as the creation *ex nihilo* of a believer in those promises, that is, of a believer from the unbelieving idolater of the house of Terah.[41] In Luther's understanding this was God creating faith—a believer who believes God and is thus credited with the righteousness of faith—and this is the same faith as Christian faith in the New Testament proclamation of the risen Christ. When Luther expounds the Joseph narrative (Genesis 37–50), he relates how Joseph tests and torments his brothers in Egypt, treating them as strangers as they bow before him as lord of the land. Luther's exposition details the "wonderful kind of game" that Joseph plays, a revelation of how God "plays" with his human creatures throughout history:

> Reducing man to nothing, giving him up to death, and afflicting him with disasters and troubles without number—this is not playing, is it? *It is a game of a cat with a mouse, and this is the death of the mouse.*[42]

But at the end of this and other such histories the narrative reveals that the drama has been a comedy (in the classic sense of a drama with a happy ending), and that "in the catastrophe [i.e., climax] of the comedy it appears that God has been playing with them in a most kindly manner and has not dealt otherwise with them than with dearly beloved sons."[43] When later in the story Joseph reveals himself to his brothers, Luther interprets the narrative as a description of how God deals with sinners whom He calls to be saints:

> Accordingly, this is a very beautiful example of how God deals with us. For when He afflicts the godly and conceals the fact that He is our

40 *Lectures on Genesis* (1535–45), AE 1:9–22. For a broader and more detailed analysis of Luther's exposition of Genesis, see Maxfield, *Luther's Lectures on Genesis and the Formation of Evangelical Identity*.

41 AE 2:245–51.

42 WA 44:466.27–30 (my translation; cf. AE 7:225), italics added to indicate German text in the midst of Luther's Latin exposition as recorded by his students.

43 AE 7:225; WA 44:466.39–40.

> God and Father and rather conducts Himself as a tyrant and judge who wants to torture and destroy us, He says at last in His own time and at a suitable hour: "I am the Lord your God. Hitherto I have treated you just as if I wanted to cast you off and hurl you into hell. But this is a game I am wont to play with My saints; for if I had not wished you well from My heart, I would never have played with you in this manner."[44]

To capture Luther's imagination here is to understand that the historical narrative of Genesis reveals profound spiritual truths regarding God and humanity, all interpreted through the lens of the Bible as a whole and therefore of the Christian faith. In Luther's understanding, through Moses the triune God is revealing His activity in the lives of human beings from the beginning of the world; through the historical narrative God interprets human existence in its relationship with the divine Majesty. From Genesis through Malachi as well as from Matthew through Revelation, this is a revelation of Christ and the Gospel of salvation for sinners through faith in Christ alone.

Why Luther's Exposition of the Old Testament Is Vital for Today

Wherever Luther saw an attempt to explain Scripture apart from this revelation of Christ and the Gospel, his critique was frequent and severe. In these contexts Luther consistently distinguishes the content or subject matter of a passage from the individual words and the grammar that convey this subject matter. He uses the Latin word *res* (generally meaning a "thing," "object," "matter," etc.), which in this context bears its most pregnant meaning of the reality of something as opposed to mere talk about its appearance, or naming of it; Luther distinguishes this *res* from the *verba,* that is, the words and grammar of the text. Such analysis pervades Luther's lectures on Genesis, which he delivered during the last decade of his life (from June 1535 to November 1545), where the object of critique as we shall see was frequently the influence of Jewish rabbis on Christian interpreters of the Book of Genesis. But the same analysis undergirds all of Luther's biblical exegesis since his first lectures on the Psalms between 1513 and 1515, from which we have already cited his principle that the Gospel illuminates the history of the Old Testament.[45]

---

44 AE 8:4–5; WA 44:582.29–36.

45 See above, pp. 136–37 nn. 25–26.

Similarly, when Luther dealt with the important topic of the Bible's clarity and unique authority to establish and inform Christian doctrine, the reformer carefully distinguished the overall saving message of the Bible, and the clarity and certainty of that message, from the difficult teachings and the inexhaustible character of the Bible as the revelation of God whose infinite nature is beyond human capacity fully to grasp. For example, in the masterpiece of humanist rhetoric that forms the opening salvo of his response to Desiderius Erasmus's assertion of the unclarity of the Bible on such lofty subjects as the powers of human free will, Luther centered his dialectic on a crucial distinction: There is God in Himself, which later in his book Luther develops and describes as the hidden God (*Deus absconditus*), and there is God as He has revealed Himself in Scripture. Luther went on to explain:

> That in God there are many things hidden, of which we are ignorant, no one doubts.... But that in Scripture there are some things abstruse, and everything is not plain—this is an idea put about by the ungodly Sophists [i.e., scholastic theologians], with whose lips you also speak here, Erasmus; but they have never produced, nor can they produce, a single article to prove this mad notion of theirs.[46]

By noting the echoes of scholastic theology in Erasmus's argument, Luther was purposely tying Erasmus's skepticism regarding assertions about Christian doctrine to the very kind of sophistry that both the humanist scholar and the evangelical reformer decried in the scholastic methods and inheritance of theology. But while for Erasmus the problem with scholasticism was its endless debates on trivialities, for Luther the problem was the *uncertainty* that scholasticism spreads regarding the meaning of Holy Scripture: "Satan has frightened men away from reading the sacred writings and has made Holy Scripture contemptible, in order to enable the plagues he has bred from philosophy to prevail in the Church."[47]

Luther continues in this tightly worded passage to acknowledge that there are many *passages* (*multa loca*) in the Bible that are obscure "because of our ignorance of their vocabulary and grammar." But these difficult or obscure texts "in no way hinder a knowledge of all the subject matter [*omnium rerum*] of Scripture." Then comes the reformer's clear description of the central hermeneutical principle that has informed and shaped his exposition of the Bible:

---

46 *Bondage of the Will* (1525), AE 33:25; Latin text in WA 18:606.10–19.

47 AE 33:25; WA 18:606.20–21.

> For what still sublimer thing can remain hidden in the Scriptures, now that the seals have been broken, the stone rolled from the door of the sepulcher, and that supreme mystery brought to light, namely, that Christ the Son of God has been made man, that God is three in one, that Christ has suffered for us and is to reign eternally? Are not these things known and sung even in the highways and byways? Take Christ out of the Scriptures, and what will you find left in them? The subject matter [*res*] contained in the Scriptures, therefore, is all quite accessible, even though certain passages might as yet be obscure since the words are unknown [*verbis incognitis*].[48]

Luther goes on to challenge both Erasmus and scholastic theologians to produce "any single mystery that is still abstruse in the Scriptures" now that Christ has come and the Gospel has been preached. He states, "It is true that for many people much remains abstruse; but this is not due to the obscurity of Scripture, but to the blindness or indolence of those who will not take the trouble to look at the very clearest truth." He cites Paul's criticism of unbelieving Jews in 2 Corinthians 4: "A veil remains upon their heart" and "If our Gospel is concealed, it is concealed in those who perish, whose heart the god of this age has blinded."[49]

Such criticism of scholastic theologians, and of Erasmus as the superlative example in Luther's mind of the humanist scholar who does not grasp the Gospel, pervades Luther's writings and lectures on the Bible. Already in his second series of lectures on the Psalms (*Operationes in Psalmos,* 1519–21), working with a difficult passage in the Hebrew text of Psalm 22, Luther had come to the conclusion: "Therefore grammar alone remains, which, as is proper, yields to theology, since meaning [*res*] is not subject to nor yields to words but words to meaning; and speech rightly follows feeling just as writing follows the spirit."[50] More than twenty years later, in the preface that he penned on Christmas Day 1543 for the first volume of his Genesis lectures, Luther mused about the richness of the biblical text and the role that love of the text and of meditating on the text must play in the practice of reading and understanding it. He notes that the commentaries of the church fathers demonstrate the will for such a spiritual understanding,

---

48 WA 18:606.22–31; translation slightly amended from that in AE 33:25–26. For further analysis of this passage, see Armin Buchholz, *Schrift Gottes im Lehrstreit: Luthers Schriftverständnis und Schriftauslegung in seinen drei großen Lehrstreitigkieten der Jahre 1521–28* (Frankfurt/Main: Peter Lang, 1993), 84–91.

49 WA 18:607.7–14; cf. AE 33:27.

50 WA 5:634.14–16; this passage is discussed briefly in Raeder, "Exegetical and Hermeneutical Work of Martin Luther" (as in p. 129 n. 10), 378.

though "they did not find perfection." But Luther sharply criticized contemporary humanist scholars such as Erasmus when they attempted to understand the biblical text through the science of philology and the goal of eloquence but without knowledge of Christ:

> How ridiculous [Luther wrote] are those today who with excellent (or, as they wish, with "pure") Latinity have attempted to grasp the meaning [*res*] of Scripture or have attempted paraphrases. These people are utterly inane in intellect and spirit, and they are, as it is said, "Asses listening to the lyre."[51]

The latter phrase is an ancient Greek proverb that, ironically, Luther probably took from Erasmus's *Adages*, where the humanist scholar explores the sources and meaning of the proverb and states that it "can be applied to people who make an unseemly attempt to follow a craft of which they have no experience, having rather a natural unfitness for it."[52] Just as Luther accused Erasmus of spiritual dullness and an unbelieving skepticism in the opening sections of his refutation of Erasmus's *Diatribe on Free Choice*, so here in this preface Luther derides the intellectual and spiritual vacuity of scholars who approach the biblical text without grasping its spiritual message. Similarly, in the Genesis lectures Luther once told the students in his University of Wittenberg classroom: "Every time Erasmus, a marvelously learned and eloquent man, begins to speak about justification and matters of faith, he stammers most wretchedly and talks like a fool. When he discusses other matters, he reveals a very high degree of ability."[53]

In a table talk from August 1537, Luther is reported to have written with chalk on the table: "Res et verba Philippus,/ verba sine re Erasmus,/ res sine verbis Lutherus,/ nec res nec verba Carolostadius." Here Luther was being self-critical as well as criticizing Erasmus and Andreas Karlstadt while exalting his younger colleague Philip Melanchthon. The ditty can be translated: "Substance and style, Philip; style without substance, Erasmus; substance without style, Luther; neither substance nor style, Karlstadt." One of the reporters of this table

---

51 WA 42:2.14–17. For an annotated English translation of this preface, see John A. Maxfield, "Martin Luther as Professor of Theology and Teacher of the Bible: The Preface to His Genesis Lectures (1543)," *Lutheran Theological Journal* 49, no. 2 (August 2015): 80–84. By "excellent (or pure) Latinity" Luther is denoting the humanist interest in a refined style in the scholarly language of the Renaissance.

52 Desiderius Erasmus, *The Adages of Erasmus*, selected by William Barker (Toronto: University of Toronto Press, 2001), 73–75.

53 AE 3:67; WA 42:596.21–23.

talk added, "When [Luther] had written this Master Philip [Melanchthon] and Master Basil [Monner] happened to come in, and the former said that this is true as far as Erasmus and Karlstadt are concerned, but too much is attributed to him [i.e., Melanchthon], and 'words' [cf. my translation as 'style' for *verba* in this context] must also be attributed to Luther."[54]

Luther frequently leveled such dismissive mockery against all those who tried to understand the text of the Bible, and especially the Old Testament, without faith in Christ guiding their understanding. The same view therefore characterizes Luther's response to Jewish rabbis, who according to their religion interpreted the Bible entirely without knowledge of Christ or reference to Christ. But it also included those Christian Hebraists of his day who leaned too heavily on the rabbis and their grammatical knowledge as they interpreted the sacred text.

This criticism was not limited to expositions of messianic psalms and other prophecies that had traditionally been interpreted as referring to Christ. An example of the broader range in the Old Testament's proclamation of the Christian Gospel comes from Luther's exposition of Genesis 4, the story of Cain's unaccepted offering and God's reproving of Cain. Here Luther notes that Augustine's interpretation of the passage was theologically sound even though he had not understood the Hebrew text accurately—in other words, Augustine got the *res* right even though he did not understand the *verba*. Luther translated the passage according to "the peculiar nature of the Hebrew" and then discusses his own approach to interpretation:

> In every exposition the subject should be considered first; that is, it must be determined what is under consideration. After this has been done, then the words should be adapted to the content [*res*] if the character of the language so permits, not the content to the words. Because the rabbis and those who follow them do not do this (for they have lost the content and adhere only to the words), they often arrive at the most absurd opinions. Since they do not have thoughts that are worthy of the spiritual things with which the sacred records deal, they digress from the content and drag the words into vain and carnal thoughts.[55]

What follows in Luther's exposition can be described as the Christian inversion of Max's question to his son in Chaim Potok's novel: "You will study Torah with

---

54 WA TR 3:460–61, no. 3619 (cf. AE 54:245). On this passage, see also Gerhard Hahn, "'Res sine verbis Lutherus': Konturen der Autorschaft Martin Luthers," in *Autorentypen*, ed. Walter Haug and Burghart Wachinger (Tübingen: Max Niemeyer, 1991), 130–43.

55 WA 42:194.30–195.2, 195.6–13 (my translation); cf. AE 1:263.

goyim and with Jews who are like *goyim*? What do they know of the Torah?"[56] Luther states:

> Since it is certain that the Jews have let go of Christ, how, then, can they correctly understand the things either of the Gospel or of the Law? They do not know what sin is, what grace is, what righteousness is. How, then, can they properly explain passages of this kind? Somewhat like them are our Sophists, for what do they have about such things that is sound? Therefore, the content not being understood, it is impossible for the words to be correctly understood. For even if knowledge of the words ordinarily comes first, nevertheless knowledge of the content is preferable. For when the content is changed, the words are also changed to another meaning, and an entirely new grammar comes into being.[57]

Luther then names and criticizes the interpretation of a thirteenth-century Jewish commentator from Catalonia (in modern Spain) named Gerondi (that is, Moses Nahmanides, 1194–1270), whose exposition he had evidently come across through the Christian Hebraist Sebastian Münster's Hebrew Bible.[58] Luther acknowledges that "Gerondi has the optimal knowledge of the words (just as today there are many who far surpass me in knowledge of Hebrew grammar)." But Gerondi distorts the meaning of the passage when he interprets the text as indicating that Cain's offering, because he was the firstborn, would have been more acceptable than Abel's had he only done well.[59] To this, Luther replied with his own conviction about the passage:

> In the first place, as I have said, it is necessary that we have the content. But the content that cannot escape notice—undoubtedly the basic issue—is that nothing is pleasing to God unless it is done out of faith. [Here Luther cites Romans and Proverbs.] . . . The second basic issue is

---

56 See above, p. 131 n. 13.

57 WA 42:195.14–21; cf. AE 1:264. For further analysis of the relationship between the "res" and "verba" and thus between theological meaning and grammar, and this "new grammar" that comes into play when the content is understood (or misunderstood), see Risto Saarinen, "The Word of God in Luther's Theology," *Lutheran Quarterly* 4, no. 1 (Spring 1990): 31–44; and Albrecht Beutel, *In dem Anfang war das Wort: Studien zu Luthers Sprachverständnis* (Tübingen: J. C. B. Mohr [Paul Siebeck], 1991), 196–205.

58 Hans-Ulrich Delius, *Die Quellen von Martin Luthers Genesisvorlesung*, Beiträge zur evangelischen Theologie 111 (Munich: Kaiser, 1991), 41–42; see also Burnett, "Reassessing the 'Basel-Wittenberg Conflict'" (as in p. 136 n. 24), 191; and Burnett, "Sebastian Münster and Jewish Interpretation of Genesis" (as in p. 139 n. 30), 399.

59 WA 42:195.22–29; cf. AE 1:264.

> that sin is something so enormous that it can be blotted out by no sacrifices or other works, but only by mercy, which must be accepted by faith. In like manner, the first promise of the woman's Seed [Gen. 3:15], without whom no one is redeemed, reveals and confirms this. The rabbis do not have these foundations. For this knowledge comes only from the spirit of Christ, who, like the noonday sun, illuminates darkness. Therefore whatever contends with these basic issues, let us repudiate as wicked and false.[60]

This one extended passage from Luther's Genesis lectures illustrates how Luther confronted rabbinic, scholastic, and humanist interpretations of scriptural passages when he discerned in them a lack of understanding of the content, meaning, or subject matter of the Scripture as a whole. For Luther, understanding the words of the Holy Scripture requires thoughts worthy of the spiritual things with which the Scripture deals, specifically Christ and the righteousness of faith in Christ. In Luther's understanding, all passages in Scripture must be interpreted in relation to this subject matter (*res*). But the rabbis reject this understanding of Hebrew Scripture. Likewise the Christian Hebraists in Luther's time who were looking to the rabbis for understanding of Hebrew language and literature: by focusing only on the Hebrew words and grammar they cannot comprehend the "new grammar" that exists within the passage. What he means by this is that the meaning of individual words and even grammatical constructions is determined by their context, and the context of each passage in the Bible is shaped by the Bible's content as a whole, and that content is the Gospel of Jesus Christ.

In his rejoinder to Erasmus on free choice, Luther concluded his rebuttal of Erasmus's assertion of the uncertainty of many theological and soteriological assertions in the Bible[61] by saying that both the clarity and the obscurity of Scripture are twofold: "one external and pertaining to the ministry of the Word, the other located in the understanding of the heart." Luther explains:

> If you speak of the internal clarity, no man perceives one iota of what is in the Scriptures unless he has the Spirit of God. All men have a

60 WA 42:195.38–196.9; cf. AE 1:264–65.

61 Earlier in his rejoinder Luther did not fail to point out the inconsistency as well as the ungodliness of Erasmus's skepticism: "Who among Christians would put up with the idea that assertions are to be despised? That would be nothing other than to deny at once all religion and piety, or to have *asserted* that there is no religion or piety or any dogma. Why, then, do you too *assert*, 'I do not delight in assertions,' and that you prefer this mode of thinking rather than its opposite?" (WA 18:604.2–5, emphasis added; cf. AE 33:21).

> darkened heart, so that even if they can recite everything in Scripture, and know how to quote it, yet they apprehend and truly understand nothing of it. . . . For the Spirit is required for the understanding of Scripture, both as a whole and in any part of it. If, on the other hand, you speak of the external clarity, nothing at all is left obscure or ambiguous, but everything there is in the Scriptures has been brought out by the Word into the most definite light, and published to all the world.[62]

For Luther, from the first Gospel (*protevangelium*) in Gen. 3:15 (the messianic promise of the woman's Seed who will crush the serpent's head) to the Book of Revelation, and everything in between, the Bible reveals a knowledge of Christ that is opened up to the reader or hearer only by the Holy Spirit. This knowledge is Christian faith, and from the earliest centuries the Christian Church has affirmed with various definitions that Scripture must be interpreted in conformity with itself, with its revelation of Christ, and therefore with one or another form of a rule of faith (*regula fidei*). In Luther's understanding Scripture is its own interpreter, and for this reason every passage must be interpreted in the light of other passages of the Bible, and thus in view of the content (*res*) of the Bible as a whole.[63]

This brings us back to the problem of modern historical-critical scholarship. As we have seen, in an important way Luther's fear of the influence of rabbinic interpretation of the Old Testament on the Hebraists of his day anticipated the development of biblical studies since the sixteenth century. In the same passage from his Genesis lectures where he responded to the interpretation of Rabbi Gerondi on Genesis 4, Luther expressed his fear as follows:

> The rabbis distort the meaning of Scripture almost everywhere. Therefore I am beginning to hate them and to advise that those who read them read with careful judgment. For even if they have possessed certain things, for example through tradition from the Fathers,

---

62 *Bondage of the Will* (1525), AE 33:28; WA 18:609.4–14.

63 In a study of Luther's trinitarian exegesis in the Large Catechism (1529) and *The Last Words of David* (1543), Mickey Mattox concludes that Luther's "distinctive 'rule of faith' consists not in an external list of theological truths on the basis of which one ought to interpret the Scriptures, but in the simultaneous realities of the God who is known and the act of faith in which God is known. This is the *res* that controls the understanding of the *verba*, for right interpretation depends on the right knowledge of the God revealed in the words of Scripture" (Mickey L. Mattox, "From Faith to the Text and Back Again: Martin Luther on the Trinity in the Old Testament," *Pro Ecclesia* 15, no. 3 [2006]: 281–303, quotation at 302).

> nevertheless they have distorted things in various ways. . . . Hence it causes us much work to maintain a pure text from their glosses.
>
> The reason for the error is that they are indeed philologians, but they have no knowledge of the content [*res*]; that is, they are not theologians. Therefore they are compelled to twaddle and to crucify both themselves and Scripture. For how is it possible for you to judge correctly about things that are unknown? . . .
>
> Thus we see that philologians who are nothing but philologians, and have no knowledge of theological matters, have their cruxes in such passages, and they crucify not only Scripture but also themselves and their hearers. First the meaning should be established in such a manner that it is everywhere in agreement; afterward philology should be applied. But the rabbis do the opposite. For this reason I regret that our teachers and holy fathers have, for the most part, followed them.[64]

Jewish scholars and modern secularized theologians will of course object to Luther's definition of "theologians" as limited to *Christian* theologians. But in Luther's understanding, as we have seen, true knowledge of God is found only in the revelation that has come to its completion in the New Testament, in Christ.

For Luther the problem of rabbinic interpretations of the Old Testament was not different in kind from that noted above regarding Erasmus and the scholastic theologians—namely, the rendering of Scripture's meaning as unclear since it was not being interpreted in view of the whole. For the scholastic theologians, the problem was that their interpretation was shaped by their reliance on Aristotle's philosophy, in particular his understanding of ethics, and from this developed the scholastic view that righteousness is achieved through the practice of performing good works. Similar was Erasmus. Because he believed in the natural capacity of human free will to turn (or refuse to turn) to the grace of God, and thus that a person can and must cooperate with God in the work of salvation, he like the scholastic theologians could not grasp the Bible's central theme of God alone working salvation by grace alone. So also for rabbinic interpretation of the Hebrew Bible: Luther's concern was that Christian scholars looking to the rabbis for understanding of the Hebrew texts of the Old Testament would render those texts void of their testimony of Christ, of the promise of salvation through faith in Christ, and of the testimony to the righteousness that God reckons to the sinner when that sinner believes God's promises. Thus to characterize Luther's interpretation of the Old Testament as "anti-Jewish" or even "anti-Semitic" is to

64 WA 42:218.19–30, 219.35–40; cf. AE 1:296, 298.

miss the point that Luther's criticism, and indeed his fear, was focused broadly on the problem of unbelief—whether the subject of that unbelief was the Jewish rabbis, scholastic theologians, or humanist scholars such as Erasmus.

Luther's interpretation of the Old Testament remains important today precisely because he interpreted the Old Testament as a Christian—that is, from the conviction of faith in Christ and in the promises of Christ conveyed by God through His revelation in both the Old and New Testaments. Throughout his life as an expositor of the Bible, the reformer opened up for his hearers the Bible's revelation of Jesus. For as Luther had preached on Christmas Day in 1522: "The [swaddling] cloths are nothing other than the Holy Scriptures, in which the Christian truth lies wrapped, in which *faith* is described. For the entire Old Testament contains nothing else than Christ as He is preached in the Gospel."[65]

---

65 AE 75:220–21, emphasis added. In the *Short Instruction: What Should Be Sought and Expected in the Gospels* that opens the *Church Postil*, Luther writes more extensively: "It is sin and a shame that we Christians have gotten to the point that we not only do not understand but also first need someone to show us with other books and explanations what is to be sought and expected in [the Bible]. The Gospels and the Epistles of the apostles were written so that they themselves would be such pointers and lead us into the writings of the prophets and of Moses, that is, the Old Testament, so that there we ourselves could read and see that Christ was wrapped in swaddling cloths and laid in the manger, that is, that He is contained in the writings of the prophets" (AE 75:10; see also the sermon for the Second Day of Christmas on Luke 2:15–20, AE 75:254).

Luther as Bible Teacher: The Biblical Prefaces and His View of the Canon

Jason D. Lane

THE INITIAL CHALLENGE TO A STUDY ON MARTIN LUTHER AND the Scriptures, especially one that seeks to demonstrate Luther's high view of Scripture and his lasting contributions to the exegetical tradition, is to make clear what Luther was not. He was neither a dogmatician of the seventeenth century with a developed doctrine of plenary inspiration and inerrancy of the biblical text, nor was he like modern biblical critics who deny the authority of Scripture as God's Word. Conservative scholars who look to Luther for support on the authority of the Bible are often disappointed by the reformer's heavy emphasis on the preached Word and seemingly critical statements of the written Word. While liberal theologians seem to find support in Luther for their biblical-critical agenda, conservative Lutherans have felt obliged either to excuse Luther and to favor the more developed views of verbal inspiration among the later dogmaticians, or to attempt a defense of Luther's views on inspiration.[1]

1 For a defense of Luther's view of inspiration against modern criticism, see Franz Pieper, *Christian Dogmatics*, trans. J. T. Mueller (St. Louis: Concordia, 1950), 1:276–98. For a corrective to some of Pieper's arguments and critique of his tendency toward Fundamentalism, see Hermann Sasse, *Sacra Scriptura: Studien zur Lehre von der Heiligen Schrift*, ed. Friedrich Wilhelm Hopf (Erlangen: Verlag der Ev.-Luth. Mission, 1981), 314–16. For a balanced analysis of Sasse's teaching concerning Holy Scripture,

Luther's well-known criticism of the Epistle of James, for example, has become a stumbling block to understanding Luther's view of Scripture. His assertion that James is an "epistle of straw"[2] and cannot be considered apostolic because it does not preach Christ only highlights what many have perceived in Luther to be a doctrine of inspiration and biblical authority governed by his own subjective whim.[3] The common perception that Luther had a subjective view of biblical authority also seems to have paved the way for biblical critics of the nineteenth century to advance their own dismantling of Scripture and, with support from the great reformer, to justify their own indifference toward biblical authority. In his book *Der Charakter und Ursprung des Briefes Jacobi* (1835), which Luke Timothy Johnson calls "literally epochal," F. H. Kern advanced his historical-critical reading of James using Luther's criticism for support.[4] Others followed suit, under the influence of the church historian F. C. Baur (1792–1860), applying Luther's candid criticisms and comments on the priority of particular New Testament books to advance their historical-critical program.[5] Although it is undeniable that later scholars used Luther to promote historical criticism, it is also undeniable that a serious reading of Luther's works and an account of

---

see John T. Pless, "Hermann Sasse (1895–1976)," in *Twentieth-Century Lutheran Theologians*, ed. Mark Mattes (Göttingen: Vandenhoeck & Ruprecht, 2013), 167–72.

2 WA DB 6:10.33–34: "Darumb ist sanct Jacobs Epistel eyn rechte stroern Epistel . . . denn sie doch keyn Euangelisch art an yhr hat." Cf. *Preface to the New Testament* (1522), AE 35:362.

3 Hermann Sasse, *Here We Stand* (Adelaide: Lutheran Publishing House, 1988), 125. Sasse writes: "Luther's celebrated dictum, from his 'Preface to the Epistles of St. James and St. Jude' (1522), that the 'true test' by which all Biblical books are to be judged is to 'see whether they deal with Christ or not, since all the Scriptures show us Christ,' can open the floodgates to a false, because altogether subjective, criticism of the Bible. No one can deny that Luther himself was occasionally a victim of this danger."

4 Luke Timothy Johnson, *The Letter of James: A New Translation with Introduction and Commentary*, The Anchor Bible 37A (New York: Doubleday Publishing, 1995), 147. Kern's criticism of James originally appeared in the *Theologische Zeitschrift* in 1835, but three years later he abandoned his radical criticism, reworking and republishing his research in the form of a commentary: Friedrich Heinrich Kern, *Der Brief Jacobi* (Tübingen: Ludwig Friedrich Fues, 1838). For an example of where Kern still follows the contours of Luther's criticism of the contradictions between James and Paul, see *Der Brief Jacobi*, 42–60.

5 Johnson, *Letter of James*, 148; Hans Schwarz, *Theology in a Global Context: The Last Two Hundred Years* (Grand Rapids: Eerdmans, 2005), 35–38.

his many comments on the divine authority of Scripture could never grant what biblical critics have claimed in his name.[6]

Spotty studies in the history of biblical interpretation have rarely concerned themselves with Luther's actual practice of biblical interpretation. The few comments that he made about the nature of particular books of Scripture have superseded his actual reading and use of the Bible. From these statements, some scholars note that historical critics have used Luther for their own purposes, but without questioning whether these historical critics have got Luther right. Modern scholars simply assume, for instance, that Luther's advocacy for particular books and passages over others created a "canon within a canon," resulting in tiers of authority in the Bible that invited biblical criticism to take shape as it did. Commentators on James argue as a matter of course that Luther and the Lutheran Reformation are ultimately responsible for the demise of the Epistle of James. In this vein, Johnson writes:

> The historical-critical model, despite its explicit break from dogma, continued to be shaped by the premises and perceptions of the Reformation. . . . Because of Luther's enormous influence on the form of scholarship that became the historical-critical paradigm, the same judgments on James have continued within a substantial portion of the discipline.[7]

Richard Bauckham also places the ill effects of historical-critical scholarship on Luther's shoulders:

> Luther's principle of canon within a canon, determined by discriminating among the New Testament books as to which of them clearly convey the Gospel of Christ, remained extremely influential in the German Lutheran tradition and therefore also in much of modern New Testament scholarship which is heavily indebted to the work of German Lutheran scholars.[8]

Bauckham then claims that any attempt to measure James or any book of the New Testament against the Pauline corpus, as Luther did, "is really Marcion in modern Lutheran dress."[9]

---

6 For an excellent survey of Luther's comments on the nature of Scripture, see Robert Kolb, *Martin Luther and the Enduring Word of God: The Wittenberg School and Its Scripture-Centered Proclamation* (Grand Rapids: Baker Academic, 2016), 75–97.

7 Johnson, *Letter of James*, 125.

8 Richard Bauckham, *James* (London: Routledge, 1999), 117.

9 Bauckham, *James*, 118.

But is the claim true? Does Luther's view of Scripture inevitably invite a subjective and critical view of Holy Scripture? How should one understand Luther's criticisms about particular books? How does Luther uphold the authority of the Word of God if certain books are open to criticism? Did he in fact urge a subjective reading of Scripture? And if so, what kind of "subjective" reading of Scripture would Luther authorize? Can we still follow Luther's way of reading and interpreting the Bible? Is his reading of Scripture so much different from that of later Lutherans? Is Luther's interpretation of Scripture so much different from ours today? Many of these questions can be answered by defining terms and reading Luther more carefully when he speaks about Scripture. Other questions, particularly the nature of Luther's "subjective" biblical interpretation, require a more intentional study of Luther's theology, his way of reading the Bible, and the way he taught others to interpret Scripture. This is the more pressing challenge facing any study on Luther and the Scriptures: *How did Luther read the Bible?* And what, if anything, can we learn from him?

The Doctrine of Scripture and the Canon of Scripture

Luther's view of Scripture is often scrutinized under the lens of later formulations concerning Holy Scripture. The doctrine of Holy Scripture that would be articulated after Luther's lifetime should first be understood for what it is. Scripture as a doctrine to be confessed falls under the discipline of dogmatic theology and is concerned with the Bible's inspiration, authority, author, purpose, and so on. It is important to note that the doctrine of Scripture belongs to theological *prolegomena*—the first things of theology without which there is no theology. Properly speaking, then, the doctrine of Scripture is not and never has been an isolated article of faith, since Scripture is the principle of theology and the basis of all articles of faith. Even Johann Gerhard, the great representative of the Lutheran dogmaticians of the seventeenth century who wrote so prolifically on the nature of Scripture, considered the doctrine of Scripture to be a preface—albeit a necessary preface—to theology. Gerhard writes: "Some people think we should begin our explanation of the theological commonplaces with the article on God because He is the principle of being and the author of Holy Scripture itself. In the treatment of disciplines, however, one has respect not so much for the principle of being as for the principle of knowing."[10]

The dogmatic locus of Scripture is a clarification of theological epistemology and a summary of what the Bible says concerning itself. The clarification may be helpful for the purposes of apologetics, but Christians do not require a defense of biblical authority; they presuppose it. St. Anselm's famous dictum "credo ut intelligam" (*Proslogion* I), "I believe in order to understand," applies here. Just as a discussion of God's nature presumes God's existence, so also a discussion of theology presumes the means by which we can know the subject. For this reason, neither Luther nor the Lutheran Confessions make the doctrine of Holy Scripture into an explicit article of faith. And since Scripture belongs to the preface of theology in the seventeenth century, one could argue that Scripture was also never an isolated article of faith in the age of Lutheran Orthodoxy. But regardless of its place in the seventeenth century, the authority of Holy Scripture in the sixteenth century was assumed without question. As Robert Kolb explains: "Luther did not treat the nature of Holy Scripture as a doctrinal topic in any of his writings; he simply used it, or, as he seems to have thought, it put him to work in bringing its message to hearers and readers. In doing so, he made it quite clear how he regarded the writings of the prophets and apostles."[11] Hermann Sasse has also observed that the Bible's divine authority, and from this its inerrancy, was presupposed in the sixteenth century. Yet he notes that in the seventeenth century, when accelerated developments in the study of the natural sciences and new views concerning world history emerged into a new Western worldview, the Church was forced to rethink the nature of Holy Scripture and to consider whether biblical inerrancy might be a root problem for contemporary theology.[12] Orthodox Lutherans along with orthodox Calvinists responded to these new challenges with a formidable teaching concerning the nature of Holy Scripture: its inspiration, authority, sufficiency, clarity, and power.[13] Later Lutherans addressed problems that never directly presented themselves to Luther, even while they upheld the substance of Luther's biblical theology.

---

10 Johann Gerhard, *Theological Commonplaces: On the Nature of Theology and On Holy Scripture*, trans. Richard J. Dinda, ed. Benjamin T. G. Mayes (St. Louis: Concordia, 2009), 35.

11 Kolb, *Luther and the Enduring Word of God*, 75.

12 Sasse, *Sacra Scriptura*, 291.

13 Heinrich Schmid and Horst Georg Pöhlmann, eds., *Die Dogmatik der Evangelisch-Lutherischen Kirche* (Gütersloh: Gütersloher Verlagshaus Mohn, 1979), 40–73.

The doctrine of Scripture, especially the doctrine of plenary inspiration in seventeenth-century Lutheran Orthodoxy, has been widely criticized by modern theologians because it is thought to set limits on biblical exegesis. It is believed that the doctrine demands uniformity in biblical interpretation that does not allow for careful exegesis of individual books.[14] For example, Lutheran Orthodoxy's doctrine of inspiration would supposedly force one to interpret James in a way that agrees with Paul concerning justification, not because the human authors teach the same thing about justification, but because the Holy Spirit who inspired both authors is consistent. Thus the apparent contradiction about faith and works in Rom. 3:28 and James 2:24 does not need to be resolved on the basis of careful exegesis but is already resolved by trusting that the Holy Spirit does not contradict Himself. As more careful research is being done on later Lutheranism, however, it is being demonstrated that the charge that Lutherans overlooked the nuances of individual writers has no support in the sources. As early as Matthias Flacius, who on the basis of 2 Tim. 3:16 clearly confessed that the Holy Spirit is the author of Scripture, Lutherans harmonized different books and passages of the Bible by giving attention to the uniqueness of each human author's vocabulary, grammar, and style.[15] Johann Anselm Steiger describes Flacius's teaching of coherence (*cohaerentia*) among the biblical writers as a harmony that "resembles musical polyphony, which thrives on the diversity of the individual voices."[16]

Luther's emphasis on the individual voices can at times lead one to question his understanding of the coherence and unity of Scripture. His comment that the Epistle of James is "flatly against St. Paul and all the rest of Scripture in ascribing justification to works"[17] puts into question the unity of Scripture. However, Luther's judgments concerning individual books are guided by the Church's reception of the New Testament canon. He never questions the authority of any book that the Church has received universally as Scripture. Historically, the Church has made the important distinction between the disputed and undisputed books of the Bible. The *homolegoumena*, the undisputed books, are the books of Holy Scripture that were read in the liturgy of the Church and accepted universally throughout the Church. The *antilegomena*, the disputed books, are those books that had not been

14 Johann Anselm Steiger, "Interpretation of the Sacred Scripture in the Age of Orthodoxy," in *Hebrew Bible / Old Testament: The History of Its Interpretation*, vol. 2: *From the Renaissance to the Enlightenment*, ed. Magne Sæbø (Göttingen: Vandenhoeck & Ruprecht, 2008), 691–757; here, 705–6.

15 Steiger, "Interpretation of the Sacred Scripture in the Age of Orthodoxy," 706.

16 Steiger, "Interpretation of the Sacred Scripture in the Age of Orthodoxy," 706.

17 *Preface to the Epistles of St. James and St. Jude* (1546, 1522), AE 35:396.

used in the Church at all times and in all places, and whose apostolic authority was for one reason or another questioned.[18] Lists of *antilegomena* typically include seven New Testament books: Hebrews, James, Jude, 2 Peter, 2 and 3 John, and Revelation. Luther, however, had doubts about only four of them. He concluded that the authority of Hebrews, James, Jude, and Revelation is doubtful, not only because the Church had doubted them in the past but also because they lack "a true apostolic spirit."[19] Thus his reason for doubting them did not rest solely on their origin and provenance but also on their content. The fact that Luther singles out only four of the seven disputed books indicates a general openness toward the *antilegomena*. His criticism of Hebrews, James, Jude, and Revelation should not be viewed as an attempt to discard or reject the books from the canon—since they all remained in his Bible—but rather to guard readers from potential confusion about the central and certain teachings of Holy Scripture.

Luther on Scripture and the New Testament Canon

To clarify which books are the chief, apostolic books and which seem to lack apostolic authority, Luther abandoned the usual arrangement of the New Testament books. After listing twenty-three books of the New Testament and giving each a number, Luther placed Hebrews, James, Jude, and Revelation at the very end of his Bible without numbers and indented the names from the left margin as a way to differentiate these books from the previous twenty-three.[20] In a similar way, Luther had separated the books of the Apocrypha from the canonical writings of the Old Testament.[21] In his preface to Hebrews, the first of the four dubious books, Luther writes: "Up to this point we have dealt with the true and certain chief books of the New Testament. The four which follow have from ancient times had a different reputation."[22] Luther is of course correct, but he is clearly not using history or tradition as the final judge of biblical authority, even though some of his contemporaries did. For instance, Andreas Bodenstein von Karlstadt suggested in his 1520 tract on the canon of Scripture that the seven disputed books belong to the last rank of Scripture strictly because they

18 Kolb, *Luther and the Enduring Word of God*, 95.

19 *Preface to the Three Epistles of St. John* (1546, 1522), AE 35:393.

20 WA DB 6:13.2–28.

21 AE 35:394 n. 43.

22 WA DB 7:344.2–4; cf. *Preface to the Epistle to the Hebrews* (1546, 1522), AE 35:394.

have been disputed in the Church.[23] Luther is much freer in his judgment, and he encouraged others to be free in their judgment about them. So rather than accept or doubt these books based on their historical reception in the Church, he judged their content against the undisputed, canonical books. Thus Luther stands in the great tradition that traces back to Augustine, as he states in his defense against Johann Eck (1519):

> Let us both, dear reader, consult that most faithful letter of Augustine [to Jerome], in which he says, "I have learned to ascribe the honor of infallibility only to those books that are accepted as canonical. I am profoundly convinced that none of these writers have erred. As for the other writings, no matter how much the authors outrank me in holiness and doctrine, I read them in this way: I evaluate what they say, not on the basis of their own argument but only insofar as they can convince me by the authority of the canonical books or by clear reason."[24]

Luther's commitment to Augustine's judgment concerning the *antilegomena* reveals how he allows the various books of the canonical Scriptures to interpret the disputed books. As will become apparent, each time Luther was unsure about the authority of a book, he gave his best evaluation of it, his reasons for questioning its apostolic character or for praising it, and finally insisted that others improve upon his work.

Luther's standard for apostolic authority in the New Testament is Christ and not some theory about which books are linked historically to the apostles. In his preface to James, one of Luther's reasons for questioning the apostolic character of the letter is that it does not teach Christ:

> Now it is the office of a true apostle to preach of the Passion and resurrection and office of Christ, and to lay the foundation for faith in him, as Christ himself says in John 15[:27], "You shall bear witness to me."

---

23 Andreas Karlstadt, *Weliche Biecher Biblisch Seind Dises Büchlin Lernet Underschaid Zwüschen Biblischen Büchern und Unbiblischen, Darinnen Vil Geirret Haben, und Noch Irren. Darzu Weißet das Büchlin, Welche Bücher, in der Biblien, Ernstlich Seind Zuleßen* (Augsburg, 1520), C1v.

24 Martin Luther, *Contra malignum Iohannis Eccii iudicium . . . Martini Lutheri defensio* (1519), WA 2:626.33–38: "Tu vero, lector, illud Augustini utrinque adhibeto fidelissimum documentum, quo dicit: Ego solis eis libris, qui Canonici appellantur, hunc honorem deferre didici, ut nullum scriptorem eorum errasse firmissime credam: caeteros vero, quantalibet sanctitate doctrinaque praepolleant, ita lego, ut non ideo verum existimem, quia ipsi sic senserunt, sed si canonicorum librorum autoritate vel probabili ratione mihi persuadere potuerunt." Cf. Augustine's Letter to Jerome, no. 82, § 3 (AD 405) (NPNF[1] 1:575).

> All the genuine sacred books agree in this, that all of them preach and inculcate [*treiben*] Christ. And that is the true test by which to judge all books, when we see whether or not they inculcate Christ. For all the Scriptures show us Christ, Romans 3[:21]; and St. Paul will know nothing but Christ, 1 Corinthians 2[:2]. What does not teach Christ is not yet apostolic, even though St. Peter or St. Paul does the teaching. Again, whatever preaches Christ would be apostolic, even if Judas, Annas, Pilate, and Herod were doing it.[25]

For Luther, this is the test that Christ Himself urges we use when we read Scripture. We should test each of these disputed books against Christ. Thus Luther suggests that if anyone should urge Scripture against Christ—that is, if someone interprets the Gospel of Christ as Law—Luther responds, "We urge Christ against the Scripture."[26] In Luther's estimation, this is a move from light to light. Some books and passages are brighter than others. New Testament books are brighter than Old Testament books. New Testament books that preach Christ are the brightest. Those that do not clearly preach Christ may be of value, but they do not shine with the apostolic brilliance that Christ says we should expect.

Luther was not timid about voicing his opinion on which books he thought are the brightest lights and which magnify Christ most intensely. In a minor addendum to his *Preface to the New Testament,* titled "Which are the true and noblest books of the New Testament,"[27] Luther suggests that John's Gospel, Paul's Epistles, and 1 Peter are

> the true kernel and marrow of all the books. They ought properly to be the foremost books, and it would be advisable for every Christian to read them first and most, and by daily reading to make them as much his own as his daily bread. For in them you do not find many works and miracles of Christ described, but you do find depicted in masterly fashion how faith in Christ overcomes sin, death, and hell, and gives life, righteousness, and salvation. This is the real nature of the gospel.[28]

---

25 *Preface to the Epistles of St. James and St. Jude* (1546, 1522), AE 35:396.

26 *Theses Concerning Faith and Law* (1535), Thesis 49, AE 34:112 (WA 39/1:47.19–21: "Quod si adversarii scripturam urserint contra Christum, urgemus Christum contra scripturam").

27 AE 35:361–62. Luther's addendum was left out of the complete edition of the Bible in 1534 and did not appear in any separate editions of the New Testament after 1537. Cf. AE 35:358 n. 5.

28 *Preface to the New Testament* (1522), AE 35:362. Luther's comments about which books are most noble were not printed after the complete printed Bible appeared in 1534.

Luther's recommendation is highly pedagogical. He believed that these books should be the daily bread of every Christian and should be learned by heart as one would learn the catechism. Luther knew that the study of Scripture can be overwhelming to inexperienced Christians and that guidance is needed. His practical advice leads readers to the preaching of Christ in John and to the clearest doctrine in the New Testament: Romans, Galatians, Ephesians, and 1 Peter. These "are the books that show you Christ and teach you all that is necessary and salvatory for you to know, even if you were never to see or hear any other book or doctrine."[29] It is in comparison with these books that James gets labeled "straw," because it is of a lighter building material than the rock-solid foundation laid by John, Paul, and Peter.[30]

It bears repeating that with regard to the *antilegomena* Luther was extremely free in his judgments. He felt no obligation to reconcile apparent contradictions, but neither did he deter anyone from trying his hand at difficult passages. In his prefaces to Hebrews, James, Jude, and Revelation, Luther does not suggest ways to look at the Bible from the outside in. Luther consistently urges readers to interpret from the inside out, as he did. That is, Luther was in the practice of reading and comparing these books with the ones that he suggests should be the Christian's daily bread. He saw no reason to defend these books from the reasonable and traditional critique that they may not be apostolic. However, he also wanted to leave open the possibility that others may see something he could not. Therefore, in each of his prefaces to these books he has the formula of praise and critique, and then offers a possible solution, even though he doubts its plausibility. In summary, he praises the same books that he deems non-apostolic and of lesser importance than the daily-bread books for every Christian, but then suggests that others may be able to do better with the difficulties each book presents.

Luther questioned the apostolic authority of Hebrews because it appears to be written by a disciple who heard of the teachings of the apostles and who lived "perhaps long after them."[31] He also had difficulty reconciling Hebrews with the rest of Scripture, because in 6:4–6 and 10:26–27 it "flatly denies and forbids to

29 AE 35:362.

30 AE 35:362: "Therefore St. James' epistle is really an epistle of straw, compared to these others, for it has nothing of the nature of the gospel about it." See also Jason D. Lane, "Luther's Criticism of James as a Key to His Biblical Hermeneutic," in *Auslegung und Hermeneutik der Bibel in der Reformationszeit*, ed. Christine Christ-von Wedel and Sven Grosse (Berlin: de Gruyter, 2016), 111–24.

31 *Preface to the Epistle to the Hebrews* (1546, 1522), AE 35:394.

sinners any repentance after baptism."[32] Although Luther does not see how the letter's teaching of repentance can be reconciled with the teaching of the Gospel accounts or Paul's letters, since the writer's words are so clear, he nevertheless admits that one could try to smooth it over with a gloss.[33] He leaves it to another to sort out the confusing bits. "My opinion is that this is an epistle put together of many pieces, which does not deal systematically with any one subject."[34] His criticism of Hebrews serves as an initial warning to readers not to become lost in the difficult passages of the letter. However, his praise of Hebrews sheds light on his criticism of James. Using the same building analogy as St. Paul does in 1 Cor. 3:12, Luther admits that the writer of Hebrews does not lay the foundation of Christ, yet he makes a fine construction with gold, silver, and precious stones. "Therefore we should not be deterred if wood, straw, or hay are perhaps mixed with them, but accept this fine teaching with all honor; though, to be sure, we cannot put it on the same level with the apostolic epistles."[35] For Luther, every writer in the New Testament is building on the foundation of Christ, but each one's work must be tested.[36]

The Epistle of James receives Luther's praise as "a good book, because it sets up no doctrines of men but vigorously promulgates the law of God."[37] But this is also one of the reasons why it is an epistle of straw. Luther cannot count James as apostolic because, in summary, James "wanted to guard against those who relied on faith without works, but was unequal to the task. He tries to accomplish by harping on the law what the apostles accomplish by stimulating people to love."[38] The Law itself is straw; that is, it is temporal. It passes away wherever and whenever Christ, who is the end or *telos* of the Law, appears. Yet Luther is quick, even in the midst of his most critical comments, to invite others to discover what is veiled to him. "I cannot include him among the chief books, though I would not thereby prevent anyone from including or extolling him as he pleases, for there are otherwise many good sayings in him."[39] In other words, Luther could understand if someone else included James among the chief books and praised it as something more than a Law book. Indeed, even Luther praises it for its

32 AE 35:394.

33 AE 35:394–95.

34 AE 35:395.

35 AE 35:395.

36 Lane, "Luther's Criticism of James," 118–23.

37 *Preface to the Epistles of St. James and St. Jude* (1522), AE 35:395.

38 AE 35:397.

39 AE 35:397.

Gospel message.[40] Similar to James, the Epistle of Jude is of value, but "it is an epistle that need not be counted among the chief books which are supposed to lay the foundations of faith."[41] Luther argues that Jude was copied from St. Peter's Second Epistle and that, like the writer of Hebrews, Jude speaks of the apostles as if he were a disciple who came after them.[42]

Luther's treatment of Revelation is unique, just as the book itself is unique in its style and content. His two prefaces to the book demonstrate clearly his ongoing humility as a biblical interpreter and his growth in the Scriptures from 1522 to the end of his life. In 1522, Luther wrote in his preface: "About this book of the Revelation of John, I leave everyone free to hold his own opinions. I would not have anyone bound to my opinion or judgment. I say what I feel. To me this book is lacking more than one thing, and it makes me consider it neither apostolic nor prophetic. . . . I can in no way detect that the Holy Spirit produced it."[43] Luther was hesitant to offer up an exposition because he was unsure of the book's meaning. In 1530, however, Luther published a second and altogether new preface to Revelation that remained in subsequent publications of his German Bible. Rather than offering a subjective opinion about the letter, Luther attempted an interpretation that reflected his careful study of Scripture and church history, his experience, and his many conversations with colleagues. Luther's concern was primarily with the clarity and certainty of the book's interpretation.

> Because its interpretation is uncertain and its meaning hidden, we have also let it alone until now, especially because some of the ancient fathers held that it was not the work of St. John, the Apostle . . . . For our part, we still share this doubt. By that, however, no one should be prevented from regarding this as the work of St. John the Apostle, or of whomever else he chooses. Since we would nonetheless like to be sure of its meaning or interpretation, we will give other and higher minds something to think about by stating our own views.[44]

Luther was unimpressed with other expositions on the market and accused interpreters of casting only more doubt on an already mysterious prophecy. "Many have tried their hands at it, but until this very last day they have attained

40 Johann Haar, *Initium Creaturae Dei: Eine Untersuchung über Luthers Begriff der "Neuen Creatur" im Zusammenhang mit Seinem Verständnis von Jakobus 1,18 und mit Seinem "Zeit"-Denken* (Gütersloh: C. Bertelsmann, 1939), 28–63.

41 *Preface to the Epistles of St. James and St. Jude* (1522), AE 35:398.

42 AE 35:397–98.

43 *Preface to the Revelation of St. John* (1522), WA DB 7:404.2–5, 13–14; cf. AE 35:398.

44 *Preface to the Revelation of St. John* (1546, 1530), AE 35:400.

no certainty. Some have even brewed it into many stupid things out of their own heads."[45] What is consistent in Luther's thought from 1522 to 1530–46 is his concern that Revelation would be interpreted by speculation rather than by faith in Christ. Therefore, until he had managed a more certain interpretation, Luther urged Christ not only for those who read Revelation but also for himself: "I stick to the books which present Christ to me clearly and purely."[46] In 1530, he thought that the lessons of church history shed light on the mysterious prophecy and that he could make an attempt at a faithful interpretation.

According to Luther, the Revelation has to do with future events, especially the tribulations that were to afflict the Christian Church. Therefore, in order to find sure footing, Luther suggested holding up the history of the Church against the book's prophecies. "If, then, the two perfectly coincided and squared with one another, we could build on that as a sure, or at least an unobjectionable, interpretation."[47] If Luther's reading of the heavenly angels as church fathers and the evil angels as heretics is misguided, it is due to his insistence on concrete details and not to his misreading of the book's major themes. His preface is pedagogical and deeply pastoral, teaching Christians that the Gospel of Christ has been under attack in every age and yet remains forever. To summarize his interpretation, Luther exclaims:

> With this kind of an interpretation we can profit by this book and make good use of it. First, for our comfort! We can rest assured that neither force nor lies, neither wisdom nor holiness, neither tribulation nor suffering shall suppress Christendom, but it will gain the victory and conquer at last. Second, for our warning! [We can be on guard] against the great, perilous, and manifold offense that inflicts itself upon Christendom.[48]

For Luther, the clarity and assurance found in the book is found in Christ. Without Christ, there is nothing sure. Luther's preface ends not in mystery and speculation, but in the sure promise of final victory and the assurance that Christ and His saints will remain forever:

> If only the word of the gospel remains pure among us, and we love and cherish it, we shall not doubt that Christ is with us, even when things are at their worst. As we see here in this book, that through and beyond

45 *Preface to the Revelation of St. John* (1546, 1530), AE 35:400.

46 *Preface to the Revelation of St. John* (1522), AE 35:399.

47 *Preface to the Revelation of St. John* (1546, 1530), AE 35:401.

48 *Preface to the Revelation of St. John* (1546, 1530), AE 35:409.

all plagues, beasts, and evil angels Christ is nonetheless with his saints, and wins the final victory.[49]

Luther's judgment over the chief and secondary books of the New Testament fits squarely with his insistence that "all the Scriptures show us Christ."[50] This is a far cry from exercising a subjective or biased critique on the Scriptures. Luther's comments about James illustrate again that Luther does not address the question of canonicity. Unlike his prefaces to the Old Testament Apocrypha (*The Apocrypha: Those books that are not of Holy Scripture and are nevertheless useful and good to read*),[51] Luther makes no mention of canonical and noncanonical books in his prefaces to New Testament books. Jörg Armbruster's excellent work on Luther's prefaces to the German Bible clarifies various misconceptions about Luther's view of the canon. He shows that instead of a canonical argument, Luther's critique of apostolicity was to reestablish a New Testament hermeneutic that had Christ at the center.[52] Luther can therefore praise James and deny its apostolic authority, not because James is outside the canon but because the Law is not the Gospel. The authority of Moses is not that of Christ. His lengthy critique of James is rather a reaction to the many misinterpretations of the letter among his Roman Catholic opponents.[53] The greatest cause of offense in the Church, according to Luther, is the confusion of Moses and Christ, or Law and

49 *Preface to the Revelation of St. John* (1546, 1530), AE 35:411.

50 *Preface to the Epistles of St. James and St. Jude* (1546, 1522), AE 35:396.

51 WA DB 12:2.1–4: "Apocrypha. Das sind Bücher: so nicht der heiligen Schrifft gleich gehalten: vnd doch nützlich vnd gut zu lesen sind."

52 " 'Apostolic' does not mean the same thing here as 'canonical,' since Luther never factually revised the canon. . . . The criterion 'what inculcates Christ' applies to 'all books,' but is only used by Luther in examining the disputed books. In this context the statement makes it clear that the historical questions, such as the question of author, are not deciding factors in what makes a book apostolic, but rather their agreement in content with the undisputed apostolic witness of Christ" (Jörg Armbruster, *Luthers Bibevorreden: Studien zu Ihrer Theologie* [Stuttgart: Deutsche Bibelgesellschaft, 2005], 144, my translation). See also David Lotz, "Sola Scriptura: Luther on Biblical Authority," *Interpretation* 35, no. 3 (1981): 273; and Derek Cooper, "Saving the Strawy Epistle: The Recovery of James after Martin Luther," *Haddington House Journal* 11 (2009): 143.

53 *Doctoral Disputation of Heinrich Schmedenstede* (1542), WA 39/2:199.19–25. "That Epistle of James causes us much trouble, since the Papists latch onto it alone and leave all the rest [of Scripture]. Thus far I have been accustomed to deal with and interpret it according to the sense of the rest of Scripture. For you will agree that from it nothing can be set forth against the revealed Holy Scripture. If, therefore, they will not accept my interpretations, I will lay waste to it. I'm just about ready to throw Jimmy in the oven like the priest in Kalenberg."

Gospel. This confusion was the reason that Luther published his prefaces in the first place. In his *Preface to the New Testament* Luther explains why he decided against his own wishes to write introductions to the Bible:

> It would be right and proper for this book to go forth without any prefaces or extraneous names attached and simply have its own say under its own name. However, many wild interpretations and prefaces have scattered the thought of Christians to a point where no one knows what is gospel or law, New Testament or Old. Necessity demands, therefore, that there should be a notice or preface, by which the ordinary man can be rescued from his former delusions, set on the right track, and taught what he is to look for in this book, so that he may not seek laws and commandments where we ought to be seeking the gospel and promises of God.[54]

Luther's prefaces, including his preface to James, are therefore intended to serve as a brief instruction for reading the Bible in order to warn Christians against becoming fixated on the Law without seeing that the Scriptures are ultimately a witness to Christ (Luke 24:27; John 5:39). Seen in this way, his preface to James is a warning not to turn Christ into Moses.[55]

It is noteworthy that though Luther considers Moses to have written books of Law, he does not mean this pejoratively, nor does he in any way deny that Christ and the Gospel are proclaimed in the Old Testament.[56] Luther's label of the Old Testament as Law and the New Testament as Gospel is a broad pedagogical distinction intended to assist students of the Bible. His label of James as a Law book rather than a Gospel book is a guide to help readers place James and the other *antilegomena* in their proper setting among the other biblical books. Thus Luther teaches Christians to read Scripture by distinguishing between Law and Gospel.

Perhaps at this point just a brief word about the reception of Luther's biblical criticism is in order. Luther's christological reading of Scripture that fills his biblical prefaces was received and amplified by later Lutherans. Steiger argues that Luther's unsystematized biblical hermeneutic, which he applied to his own reading of Scripture, was brought to completion in a newly established academic discipline of theology called *hermeneutica sacra* or sacred hermeneutics.

---

54 WA DB 6:3.2–11; cf. *Preface to the New Testament* (1522), AE 35:357.

55 *How Christians Should Regard Moses* (1525), AE 35:161–74, WA 16:363–93.

56 For instance, see Luther's *Preface to the Old Testament* (1545, 1523), WA DB 8:13.9–22; cf. AE 35:236–37.

Johann Gerhard,[57] Salomo Glassius,[58] Johann Conrad Dannhauer,[59] and others sought to advance Luther's biblical exegesis by teaching it in an organized way to the Church. These works on biblical hermeneutics are in need of further study and translation into English.[60] Luther's criticism of those books that did not inculcate Christ was generally shared by later Lutherans, even if they were more willing to defend their canonical status with historical evidence. J. A. O. Preus notes that the Lutheran dogmaticians were perhaps more prepared to research the Church's historical reception of certain books than Luther, but they read the Scriptures as they had learned them from him.

> The Lutheran dogmaticians liked to give answers which were as close to mathematically correct as they could make them; but a study of their writings on canon reveal that they faced the same problem we do today. Except in their well-founded objections to Rome's arrogation of authority to establish the canon, they were surprisingly undogmatic in regard to the canon. So was Luther. When one considers their absolutism in matters which were clearly stated in Scripture, and then compares their mildness and latitude with regard to canon, we can only conclude that they felt themselves on ground which was not entirely doctrinal, but rather historical. And it was an incomplete and uncertain history.[61]

Historical investigations can bring us only so far. We can prove only so much about the origins of the Bible. Luther and his theological heirs were aware of

---

57 Johann Gerhard, *Tractatus de Legitima Scripturae Sacrae Interpretatione (1610): Lateinisch-Deutsch*, vol. 13 of *Doctrina et Pietas. Abteilung I*, ed. Johann Anselm Steiger (Stuttgart-Bad Cannstatt: Frommann-Holzboog, 2007). For an English translation, see below, n. 60.

58 Salomo Glassius, *Christlicher Glauben=Grund. Das ist / Deutliche Ausführung / Daß Allein die H. Schrifft der Christilichen Lehr / Glaubens und Lebens / Waares Principium, Vester Grund / Sichere Regel / und Unbetriegliche Richtschnur; Hingegen Aber / Was Dißfals von Des Papsts und Desselben Kirchen Autorität / Item von Traditionen / Kirchenbräuchen / Vätern / Concilien Etc. von Alten und Neuen Päpstischen Scribenten / Vorgegeben Wird / Falsch / Irrig und Verführisch Sey* (Nürnberg: Wolfgang Endter, d.A., 1654).

59 Johann Konrad Dannhauer, *Hermeneutica Sacra Sive Methodus: Exponendarum S. Literarum Proposita et Vindicata* (Strassburg: Städel, 1654).

60 For those wanting to know more about sixteenth- and seventeenth-century biblical hermeneutics, a good place to start for English readers is Matthias Flacius Illyricus, *How to Understand the Sacred Scriptures*, trans. Wade R. Johnston (Saginaw, MI: Magdeburg Press, 2011); and Johann Gerhard, *On the Legitimate Interpretation of Scripture*, trans. Richard J. Dinda (Malone, TX: Repristination Press, 2015).

61 J. A. O Preus, "The New Testament Canon in the Lutheran Dogmaticians," *The Springfielder* 25, no. 1 (1961): 29.

their limitations and therefore urged people into the Scriptures to read, mark, learn, and inwardly digest for themselves what the Spirit of God says to the churches. Scripture was for them not merely a historical book to be studied and understood, but a heavenly message of Christ that, above all, is to be believed.

Experiencing Holy Scripture

John Maxfield has raised important questions for any historical investigation into Luther as Bible teacher. He suggests that we should study how Luther viewed the Bible, how he taught his students to view it, how he thought biblical interpretation should be handled in his day, and how he interacted with the exegetical tradition. We should discover what sources he used, how he used them, and how he taught others to use them. Finally, and most important, we should find out how Luther interpreted the text authoritatively to speak to the experiences of his students, hearers, and the society at large.[62] Luther's view of Scripture, its interpretation, and his way of applying Scripture to his students, hearers, and readers are important aspects of any historical investigation into his exegesis. However, such an approach runs the risk of isolating Luther in the past and often becomes distracted by how brilliantly Luther applies the Bible in sixteenth-century Wittenberg. Although Luther was certainly led, like any interpreter of Scripture, to address life as it happened in his own place and circumstance,[63] it would be misleading to think of Luther's interpretation of Scripture as merely a product of circumstance.

If Luther is to be a model for us on how to study and interpret Holy Scripture today, he must offer us a catholic interpretation that extends beyond the borders of sixteenth-century Saxony. It is necessary, then, to move beyond a historical appraisal of his exegesis that seeks to give historical context to his premodern interpretation of the Bible and to lay hold of that which Luther teaches is universal to any Christian who studies Sacred Scripture. There is a difference. Historians are typically interested in Luther's view of Scripture and his interpretation of it. Luther, however, is interested in Scripture's interpretation of us. Thus Luther writes in his first commentary on the Psalms: "Note that the strength of Scripture is this, that it is not changed into him who studies it, but

62 John A. Maxfield, *Luther's Lectures on Genesis and the Formation of Evangelical Identity*, Sixteenth Century Essays & Studies 80 (Kirksville, MO: Truman State University Press, 2008), 32.

63 Robert Kolb, *Luther and the Stories of God: Biblical Narratives as a Foundation for Christian Living* (Grand Rapids: Baker Academic, 2012), 1–2.

that it transforms its lover into itself and its strength. . . . Now put down the virtues of Scripture: It is light, and therefore the souls are enlightened; it is truth, and therefore they are truthful; it is wisdom, and therefore they are wise; it is discipline, and therefore they are disciplined."[64] As Oswald Bayer has suggested, Luther's foundational thesis for biblical interpretation is that Holy Scripture is its own interpreter. "This thesis," Bayer writes, "goes far beyond the concordance method where one Bible passage interprets the other and brings both into agreement. This has to do rather with the potency of the text in regards to its reader, hearer, and interpreter. . . . The text makes itself heard."[65] The text interprets us, and God, through Scripture, disarms our reason and makes us passive to receive its power.

A modern study of Luther's view of Scripture is, as the above suggests, already skewed by the presupposition that Luther had a "view" of Scripture in the modern sense of that word or that he sought to "interpret" the Bible in the modern sense of that word. Ever since the Enlightenment, a worldview, or what Immanuel Kant calls "Weltanschauung,"[66] describes the way that humans perceive reality. Kant's anthropocentric aesthetic and view of reality has deeply influenced biblical interpretation in Western Christianity and widened the gap between our way of reading Scripture and Luther's way. Kenneth Hagen has argued forcefully that Luther's interpretation of Scripture is incompatible with modern approaches to the Bible and with philosophical approaches to biblical interpretation or modern hermeneutics. "The presupposition of hermeneutics," he writes, "is that Scripture needs to be interpreted. The presupposition of interpretation (in the modern sense) is the distance between the ancient world and the Bible and the modern world. The presupposition of 'distance' is the sense of the superiority of modernity."[67] Bayer makes a similar point: "It is not the interpreter who gives the text meaning or makes the text understandable; rather, the text ought to speak for itself that which, of itself, it has to say."[68] In other words, to view Scripture as a text in need of interpretation is to make God's Word subject to human reason. "The posture of superiority," Hagen argues, "is one of judgment.

---

64 *First Lectures on the Psalms* (1513–16), Ps. 68:13, AE 10:332–33; WA 3:397.9–10, 12–14.

65 Oswald Bayer, *Martin Luthers Theologie* (Tübingen: Mohr Siebeck, 2007), 62.

66 David K. Naugle, *Worldview: The History of a Concept* (Grand Rapids: Eerdmans, 2002), 58–59. According to Naugle, Kant first coined the term in his book *Critique of Judgment*, 1790 (part I, book 2, section 26).

67 Kenneth Hagen, *Luther's Approach to Scripture as Seen in His "Commentaries" on Galatians, 1519–1538* (Tübingen: Mohr Siebeck, 1993), 38.

68 Bayer, *Martin Luthers Theologie*, 62–63.

The subject stands in judgment over the object. The subject uses philosophical techniques of interpretation to treat an object that not only is not philosophical but also is against the wisdom of men."[69] Modern studies of Luther's exegesis seem to assume that Luther looked at Scripture from a neutral position, outside looking in, in order to interpret it and use it for his purposes. Scholars may disagree whether his purposes were to reform the Church or the university or the society, to save souls or to smite his opponents, but all agree that Luther used Scripture to do it. A misguided study of Luther and Scripture will make Luther the subject and Scripture the object.

Luther learned the Scriptures at a young age as the living voice of God in the context of the Church's daily and weekly worship. His early piety had been nourished by the Word of God as it was communicated in the rituals and prayers of the Church, especially through the Psalms.[70] Scripture was by no means peripheral to Luther's early understanding of the faith. The traditions of the Church and his own professors of theology taught Luther that one should regard Scripture alone as the cause of faith and that apart from Scripture any discussion of faith is mere opinion.[71] This was part of the medieval tradition that Luther had inherited. However, it was not until Luther began his concentrated study of Sacred Scripture and its grammar as professor and preacher that he "broke through."[72] His experience of Scripture's power and clarity eventually caused all other ecclesiastical authorities to pale in comparison to the radiance of the Bible.[73]

Although the medieval age is commonly criticized for being "dark" and without the light of the Gospel, the Scriptures were in fact at the heart of all academic and ecclesial life. Luther benefited greatly from the labors of Augustine, Jerome, Gregory, Boethius, and the many others who brought together their

---

69 Hagen, *Luther's Approach to Scripture*, 38.

70 Robert Kolb, *Martin Luther: Confessor of the Faith* (Oxford: Oxford University Press, 2009), 131.

71 Bernhard Lohse, *Martin Luther's Theology: Its Historical and Systematic Development*, trans. Roy A. Harrisville (Minneapolis: Fortress, 1999), 26. See also Luther's letter to Truttfetter, May 9, 1518, WA Br 1:169–71.70–74, no. 74.

72 See Johann Michael Reu, *Luther's German Bible* (Columbus, OH: Lutheran Book Concern, 1934), 101–14, for a helpful summary of Luther's study of Scripture which led to his evangelical breakthrough. See also Uuras Saarnivaara, *Luther Discovers the Gospel: New Light upon Luther's Way from Medieval Catholicism to Evangelical Faith* (St. Louis: Concordia, 2005), 35–49.

73 Volker Leppin, ed., *Reformatorische Theologie und Autoritäten*, Spätmittelalter, Humanismus, Reformation 85 (Tübingen: Mohr Siebeck, 2015), 1–7.

works in the centuries that followed. One of the major characteristics of medieval theology was the attention given to the grammar of Scripture. G. R. Evans has noted that the study of Latin grammar, the language of the medieval Bible, became essential once Latin ceased to be the vernacular of the people. The lack of sound Latin caused people to misunderstand the syntax of the Bible and its basic vocabulary. Some medieval scholars attempted to resolve these problems by studying language at its core: the epistemology of language. They drew on the works of Aristotle and Boethius to teach the first principles of logic and the laws of grammar. However, they soon discovered the inadequacy of human language and therefore had to apply themselves to the nature of theological language by developing better tools to study Scripture. The result was a powerful philosophy of language.[74] Luther's own interest in the grammar of Scripture and the philosophy of language is therefore indebted not only to humanism but also to medieval theology.[75] His careful attention to the Holy Spirit's grammar is a hallmark of both his exegesis and his instruction to others on how to read Scripture.

Grammar, logic, and rhetoric (*trivium*) were the classical tools of Luther's early schooling, but they remained the tools of his lifelong study of the Bible. Often overlooked is that Luther's oft-repeated dictum "experience alone makes the theologian"[76] refers to the interpretation of Scripture by means of sacred grammar and logic. In that same discussion about experience at his kitchen table, Luther explains, "A doctor of the Scriptures ought to have a good knowledge of the Scriptures and ought to have grasped how the prophets run into one another. It isn't enough to know only one part—as a man might know Isaiah, for example."[77] Here Luther makes a distinction between knowledge of the Scripture in all of its parts and understanding how those parts fit together as a united whole. The experience that makes a theologian takes place first when he is engaged with the grammar of the Holy Scriptures and learns by heart the vocabulary of each writer. A second step takes place when he compares a book or passage of Scripture against others, testing each part against the greater witness of the whole, and then submitting his own reason to the logic of the Holy Spirit.

---

74 G. R. Evans, *The Language and Logic of the Bible: The Earlier Middle Ages* (Cambridge: Cambridge University Press, 1984), vii–viii.

75 See Dennis Bielfeldt, "Luther on Language," *Lutheran Quarterly* 16, no. 2 (Summer 2002): 195–220, who lays out the debate concerning Luther's indebtedness to the medieval philosophy of language.

76 *Table Talk* no. 46 (1531), AE 54:7; WA TR 1:16.13: "Sola autem experientia facit theologum."

77 *Table Talk* no. 46 (1531), AE 54:7.

Finally, once one has intimate knowledge of the grammar of Scripture and has followed the logic of the biblical writers, one is then prepared to confess the truth in accordance with the Scriptures in any situation, even in the midst of cross and suffering. Luther described this experience with the Word elsewhere as *oratio*, *meditatio*, and *tentatio* ("prayer, meditation, and affliction"),[78] but it also reflects his own classical education in the *trivium*: grammar, logic, and rhetoric.

Luther's study of the Bible was also shaped by his monastic training, which embodied the Latin proverb *repetitio est mater studiorum* ("repetition is the mother of all learning"). He learned the Scriptures by reading, rereading, and reciting out loud the vowels and the consonants of Scripture, just as he explains that a child should learn and pray the catechism by speaking the words out loud. In his recollection of his evangelical breakthrough in his *Preface to the Latin Writings* (1545), notice how Luther describes his experience of being moved by the grammar of Scripture to understand its sacred logic, and then finally to confess the Gospel of Christ's righteousness:

> At last, by the mercy of God, meditating day and night, I attended to the context of the words, namely, "In it the righteousness of God is revealed, as it is written, 'The righteous live from faith.'" There I began to understand that the righteousness of God is that by which the righteous lives by a gift of God, namely, by faith. And this is the meaning: the righteousness of God is revealed by the Gospel, that is, the passive righteousness with which merciful God justifies by faith, as it is written, "The righteous live from faith." Here I felt that I was altogether born again and had entered paradise itself through open gates. There a totally other face of the entire Scripture showed itself to me. Thereupon I ran through the Scriptures that I had learned by heart [*ut habebat memoria*], and I started to collect other analogous phrases, such as the work of God, that is, what God does in us; the power of God with which He makes us strong; the wisdom of God with which He makes us wise; the strength of God; the salvation of God; the glory of God. However much I despised that phrase "righteousness of God" with hatred before, so much more did I now magnify it with my love as the sweetest phrase of all. Thus that passage from St. Paul became for me truly the gate of paradise.[79]

This is nothing less than a Copernican revolution of theology in the West. Luther discovered that the center of theology does not revolve around man and

78 *Preface to the German Writings* (1539), AE 34:285–87.

79 WA 54:186.3–16; cf. *Preface to the Latin Writings* (1545), AE 34:337.

his works to please God, or in some ascent of man to God; rather, theology revolves around Christ and God's work in Him for us. For Luther, a theologian is one who experiences God's gracious and powerful work through the Word. Yet this experience of God's powerful Word is found in a study of the written text, as one commits it to heart, compares it with other texts, and attempts to pray it and confess it before God and men.

It was in this medieval milieu of reading, rereading, and learning by heart important texts that Luther became a theologian. He wrestled with God's revelation in Holy Scripture. He read it and demanded to understand it. And that struggle to know what the Holy Spirit says made him pray and call on God for understanding. In one of his talks over dinner, Luther recalls:

> I didn't learn my theology all at once. I had to ponder over it ever more deeply, and my *tentationes* [*Anfechtungen*, "spiritual trials, wrestlings"] were of help to me in this, for one does not learn anything without practice. This is what the spiritualists and sects lack. They don't have the right adversary, the devil. He would teach them well. None of the arts can be learned without practice. What kind of physician would that be who stayed in school all the time? When he finally puts his medicine to use and deals more and more with nature, he will come to see that he hasn't as yet mastered the art. Why shouldn't this be so in the case of the Holy Scriptures, too, where God has provided a different adversary? It is therefore the greatest gift [of God] to have a text and to be able to say, "This is right. I know it." People think that they can know everything by simply listening to a sermon. . . . But I know that I have yet to comprehend the Lord's Prayer. No one can be learned without practice. The peasant put it well: Armor is fine for a man who knows how to use it. To be sure, the Holy Scriptures are sufficient in themselves, but God grant that I find the right text. For when Satan disputes with me whether God is gracious to me, I dare not quote the passage, "He who loves God will inherit the kingdom of God" [1 Cor. 2:9], because Satan will at once object, "But you have not loved God!" Nor can I oppose this on the ground that I am a diligent reader [of the Scriptures] and a preacher. [That's no good.] I should say, rather, that Jesus Christ died for me and should cite the article [of the Creed] concerning forgiveness of sin. That will do it![80]

As modern Christians, with the benefits of interpretive tools and yet with the burden of postmodern thinking, we so often approach Scripture from a distance, acknowledging a gap, whether of time, culture, or grammar, and

80 *Table Talk* no. 352 (1532), AE 54:50–51.

we assume that Luther did too. For Luther, however, becoming a theologian happens in the context of one's experience under the Word, when one's reason, emotion, and will is held captive to what God says. As Luther once so vividly put it: "One becomes a theologian not by understanding, reading, or speculating, but by living—no, rather, by dying and by being damned."[81] The study of theology and therefore the study of Scripture is not about growing in stature, but in becoming weak and passive to the work of Christ. Luther explains his own experience: "I . . . have become proficient by writing and teaching. I was not one of those who from nothing suddenly become the topmost, though they are nothing, neither have they labored, nor been tempted, nor become experienced, but have with one look at the Scriptures exhausted their entire spirit."[82] Luther's interpretation of Scripture and his instruction to other readers of Scripture cannot be comprehended apart from his own experience of committing Scripture to memory, comparing its parts, and preaching or confessing its message. If we do not follow Luther this far in his study of Scripture, and apply ourselves to it as well, Luther will often sound subjective to us and unequal to the modern task of exegesis.

Luther urges us to read the Scriptures and taste the power of faith that he himself has tasted. In a famous passage from his 1520 tract *On Christian Liberty*, Luther testifies of his own experience:

> The Christian faith has appeared to many an easy thing, and they count it among the virtues. They do this because they have no experience to test whether it is something more and have never tasted of its power. For it is impossible for one to write well about faith, or to understand whether the writings about it are right, who has not at some point tasted of its spirit and been pressed hard by tribulation. However, he who has tasted of it, even just a little bit, can never write, speak, think, or hear about it enough. For it is a living fountain, springing up into eternal life, as Christ says of it in John 4.[83]

It would be a mistake to speak of faith here apart from the Word of God. Faith is tested when the promises of God appear to be lies. Faith clings to the promises of God counterfactually, not trusting in that which is seen—cross, suffering, and temptation—but hoping in that which is not seen: righteousness and eternal life. Faith hopes against hope and produces joy.

---

81 "Vivendo, immo moriendo et damnando fit theologus, non intelligendo, legendo aut speculando" (*Operationes in Psalmos* [1519–21], WA 5:163.28–29).

82 AE 34:338.

83 WA 7:49.7–15; cf. AE 31:343.

We find this joy in what can only be described as an experiential reading of Scripture throughout Luther's prefaces. In his *Preface to the New Testament* (1522), which we have touched on already, Luther begins—after a brief identification of the Old Testament as Law and the New Testament as Gospel—with a *laudatio* of the Gospel or *euangelium*: "For the Gospel is a Greek word that means [in German] a good message, a good story, good news, or a shout of joy about which one sings, speaks, and makes merry."[84] Luther taught that the story of Christ is creative. It is not a set of facts about Christ, though it is historical. It is not a change of mind, though it changes minds and hearts. Instead, the joyful message of Christ's victory is, as St. Paul says, "the power of God for salvation to everyone who believes" (Rom. 1:16). It is thus *experienced*. "A poor man," Luther declares, "dead in sin and consigned to hell, can hear nothing more comforting than this precious and tender message about Christ; from the bottom of his heart he must laugh and be glad over it, if he believes it true."[85] Luther's instruction takes the Gospel out of the world of ideas, intellect, and right understanding and places it into the realm of experience and faith. For Luther, no one can live by faith and remain a casual observer of theology or the Christian life. The Gospel tosses us into an apocalyptic fight against the devil, the world, and our own flesh. Luther could even say that the first thing we learn from the Gospel is not Christ but the devil.[86] He means that a Christian can sniff out the devil and know who belongs to him, because the Christian knows the truth in Christ. Further, those who believe the Gospel of Christ, who lay hold of the promises and taste the power of faith—even if only a little—will be able to recognize it whenever and wherever they encounter it, and they will want to taste it more and more.

The Epistle to the Romans as the Key to Scripture

Luther's *Preface to the Epistle of St. Paul to the Romans* is his most instructive preface concerning the interpretation of Scripture and is arguably the key to Luther's biblical exegesis.[87] The priority of Romans is due, according to Luther,

---

84 WA DB 6:4.23–24; cf. AE 35:358.

85 AE 35:359; cf. WA DB 6:5.20–23.

86 "We learn first from the Gospel to know rightly the devil . . . and all those who hold fast to him"(WA 41:3.26–27, *Sermon on New Year's Day*, 1535).

87 Armbruster, *Luthers Bibelvorreden*, 110–15.

to the letter's clarity. He writes: "In itself it is a bright light, almost sufficient to illuminate the entire holy Scriptures."[88] Yet his description of Romans as a bright light is already indicative of Luther's own exegesis. He had come to know Romans as "the chief part of the New Testament" and "the purest gospel"[89] only, as he recalls, "by the mercy of God, meditating day and night."[90] Bayer suggests that this is a tension in Luther's understanding of theology and the study of Scripture. On the one hand, there is the grammatical and philological labor of the theologian that takes place by patient meditating and careful interpreting. On the other hand, there is the gift of the Spirit that comes through the words of Scripture to open the door of paradise.[91] The gift of the Spirit cannot come without the grammatical and philological work, but philology by itself does not guarantee the Spirit. Luther, having experienced this deep struggle and joyful epiphany himself, hoped that his preface would lead others into the light. "Therefore I too will do my best, so far as God has given me power, to open the way into it through this preface, so that it may be the better understood by everyone."[92] His preface also summarizes so much of what has been said thus far and makes a fitting conclusion to this chapter on Luther as Bible teacher.

Luther begins his instruction for interpreting Romans, as he himself learned to interpret it, by learning the text by heart. The monastically trained, classically educated Luther begins with the text and instructs his readers to know the grammar, every last vowel and consonant. Memory, however, is not the final goal of one's study of Romans. Instead, Luther suggests that one should begin with memorization because memory is the foundation of knowing and from memory one can proceed to own the words. "It is worthy not only that every Christian should know it word for word, by heart, but also that he should occupy himself with it every day, as the daily bread of the soul."[93] The movement is organic, as if from knowing by heart to believing in the heart, from oral recitation to confession and proclamation. There is no real division between grammar and logic, even if there is a distinction and progression from one to the other. In his tract *On Christian Liberty*, recall that Luther used the language of taste to describe the power of faith: "He who has tasted of it, even just a little bit, can

88 *Preface to the Epistle of St. Paul to the Romans* (1546, 1522), AE 35:366.

89 AE 35:365.

90 *Preface to the Latin Writings* (1545), AE 34:337.

91 Bayer, *Martin Luthers Theologie*, 62.

92 *Preface to the Epistle of St. Paul to the Romans* (1546, 1522), AE 35:365–66.

93 AE 35:365.

never write, speak, think, or hear about it enough."[94] But here the experience of taste is tied to meditation on the text: "We can never read it or ponder over it [*betrachtet werden*] too much; for the more we deal with it, the more precious it becomes and the better it tastes."[95] In very practical terms, Luther is suggesting that a study of Holy Scripture starts with learning Romans by heart through daily reading and rereading, until the words are imprinted on the mind and can be recalled in any time of trouble.

As any Christian knows, however, reading Scripture can be daunting, especially if the grammar and vocabulary are difficult. One may commit the words to memory, but without a clear understanding of the terms, the meaning remains hidden, just as righteousness remained hidden to Luther even when he had committed the entire Scriptures to memory. Therefore, the first major portion of the preface is a clarification of the most important terms of the epistle. "To begin with we must have knowledge of its language and know what St. Paul means by the words: 'law,' 'sin,' 'grace,' 'faith,' 'righteousness,' 'flesh,' 'spirit,' and the like. Otherwise no reading of the book has any value."[96] Learning Romans by heart, therefore, means committing the definitions of these key terms to heart too.

Luther's definitions are incredibly precise, even dogmatic, and worthy of further study. For instance, Luther warns against blurring distinctions between God's grace and God's gift. "Grace," Luther explains, "actually means God's favor, or the good will which in himself he bears toward us, by which he is disposed to give us Christ and to pour into us the Holy Spirit with his gifts. This is clear from chapter 5[:15], where St. Paul speaks of 'the grace and gift in Christ,' etc. The gifts and the Spirit increase in us every day, but they are not yet perfect since there remain in us the evil desires and sins that war against the Spirit."[97] Luther saw these definitions coming from Scripture in order to interpret Scripture.

> Without such a grasp of these words, you will never understand this letter of St. Paul, nor any other book of Holy Scripture. Therefore beware of all teachers who use these words in a different sense, no matter who they are, even Origen, Ambrose, Augustine, Jerome, and others like them or even above them.[98]

---

94 *On Christian Liberty* (1520), WA 7:49.12–14; cf. AE 31:343.

95 *Preface to the Epistle of St. Paul to the Romans* (1546, 1522), AE 35:365.

96 AE 35:366.

97 AE 35:369.

98 AE 35:372.

Thus the proper definition of St. Paul's terminology is foundational to understanding Romans and all of Scripture, as well as judging its interpreters, such as the church fathers or modern preachers. Parishioners should therefore beware of those preachers who use these words—sin, grace, spirit, flesh, righteousness, faith, and so on—in a different sense than St. Paul. Once they have taken these to heart, they will recognize false doctrine and false interpretations because they will have the taste for the right interpretation of Scripture from St. Paul and want more of it.

Luther's insistence that Romans is the key to the rest of Scripture may seem to some an exaggeration. Could not one come to know the sense of Scripture by reading Moses and the Psalter, Isaiah, and the four Gospel accounts? One of course could, by God's grace. But Luther did not write his prefaces for those who had already become proficient in the Scriptures. They were written for those who needed guidance. They were written for the very many Christians in the Church who struggle to carry on a steady practice of reading Scripture or who have never really read it before. For these, and even for the experienced, Luther suggests that one start with Romans and from there move out into the rest of Scripture. He had many ways to explain how one should interpret Scripture, but none of them offer Luther's way of reading and interpreting Scripture as clearly as his final words from his preface to Romans.

> In this epistle we thus find most abundantly the things that a Christian ought to know, namely, what is law, gospel, sin, punishment, grace, faith, righteousness, Christ, God, good works, love, hope, and the cross; and also how we are to conduct ourselves toward everyone, be he righteous or sinner, strong or weak, friend or foe—and even toward our own selves. Moreover this is all ably supported with Scripture and proved by St. Paul's own example and that of the prophets, so that one could not wish for anything more. Therefore it appears that he wanted in this one epistle to sum up briefly the whole Christian and evangelical doctrine, and to prepare an introduction to the entire Old Testament. For, without doubt, whoever has this epistle well in his heart, has with him the light and power of the Old Testament. Therefore let every Christian be familiar with it and exercise himself in it continually. To this end may God give his grace. Amen.[99]

99 AE 35:380.

LUTHER AND THE REFORM OF MARRIAGE AND SEXUALITY

Benjamin T. G. Mayes

ON JULY 17, 1505, ST. ALEXIUS'S DAY, MARTIN LUTHER ENTERED a monastery in Erfurt, intending to live in perpetual celibacy as part of his new, monastic life. Nearly twenty years later, on June 13, 1525, he engaged Katharina von Bora to marry in front of witnesses. The marriage was performed right there immediately afterward by Johannes Bugenhagen, the parish pastor.[1] Luther married Katie not because he passionately loved her, though he did cherish her.[2] This marriage was a demonstration of what Luther's Reformation of the Church stood for. Church life had to be brought back to the standards of the Holy Scriptures. Man-made prohibitions of marriage—snares to consciences—were to be disregarded.

Luther's teachings on marriage and sexuality constituted a central component of the Reformation. To this day perhaps the most well-known difference between Protestants and Roman Catholics is that Protestant pastors may marry, and Catholic priests may not. Yet Luther's reformation of marriage and sexuality has been attacked not just by Roman Catholics, but more recently by

1 Martin Brecht, *Martin Luther: His Road to Reformation 1483–1521*, trans. James L. Schaaf (Minneapolis: Fortress, 1985), 50; Martin Brecht, *Martin Luther: Shaping and Defining the Reformation 1521–1532*, trans. James L. Schaaf (Minneapolis: Fortress, 1990), 198.

2 As Luther wrote (soon after his wedding) to his friend Nicholas von Amsdorf (WA Br 3:541.4–8; AE 49:117), cited by Scott H. Hendrix, "Luther on Marriage," *Lutheran Quarterly* 14, no. 3 (2000): 343.

various Protestants. Some of the new Protestant anti-Luther sentiment is based on estrangement from Luther's view of biblical authority, creation, and natural law; and then some is based on misunderstandings of what Luther really taught. As an example of the former, Elisabeth Gerle says that Luther is in error when he supposed that sex is meant to occur only between a man and a woman in marriage. For Gerle, Luther's views on marriage and sexuality are irrelevant for modern people.[3] As an example of the latter, Kirsi Stjerna has recently argued that for Luther, sexual desire as it is experienced by both heterosexual and homosexual people is part of God's good creation, and as a result, marriage should be granted to everyone, heterosexual or not. She labels those who would oppose her views "diabolical." For Stjerna, Luther's views on marriage and sexuality are relevant for modern people, because if one reads Luther selectively (a reading she explicitly admits) one finds ways of thinking that, she says, affirm gay marriage.[4] Essentially Stjerna is arguing that Luther was inconsistent in his teaching on sexual desire and marriage. Here she follows a line of thought that is to be found even in older Missouri Synod Lutheran scholarship,[5] a line of thought that demands an answer.

Is Marriage Worldly?

In 1530, Luther stated that "marriage is an external, worldly matter, like clothing and food, house and property, subject to temporal authority, as the many imperial laws enacted on the subject prove. Neither do I find any example in the New Testament where Christ or the apostles concerned themselves with such matters, except where they touched upon consciences, as did St. Paul in 1 Corinthians 7 [:1–24]."[6] Luther's statement here, that marriage is "worldly,"

---

3 Elisabeth Gerle, "Luther and the Erotic," *Currents in Theology and Mission* 37, no. 3 (2010): 198–208, here at 200. A similar view of Luther's irrelevance for modern sexuality is presented by Volker Leppin, "Ehe bei Martin Luther: Stiftung Gottes und 'weltlich ding,'" *Evangelische Theologie* 75, no. 1 (2015): 22–33, here at 32–33. See also the literature reviewed by Charles L. Cortright, "Luther, the Body, and Sexuality: 'Es Ist Nicht Gut Das Der Mensch Alleyn Sey,'" *Logia* 25, no. 2 (Eastertide 2016): 6.

4 Kirsi I. Stjerna, "Luther on Marriage, for Gay and Straight," in *Encounters with Luther: New Directions for Critical Studies*, ed. Kirsi I. Stjerna and Brooks Schramm (Louisville: Westminster/John Knox Press, 2016), 126–43.

5 Oscar E. Feucht et al., *Sex and the Church: A Sociological, Historical, and Theological Investigation of Sex Attitudes* (St. Louis: Concordia, 1961), 75.

6 *On Marriage Matters* (1530), AE 46:265, cf. WA 30/3:205. Similar statements are found in *The Estate of Marriage* (1522), AE 45:25, WA 10/2:283; and *Order of Marriage* (1529), AE 53:111, WA 30/3:74.

is not categorical. There are aspects of marriage that Christ and the apostles addressed and that the Church must address: namely, wherever marriage is a matter of conscience. Luther gives the example of Paul in 1 Corinthians 7, where Paul dealt with numerous marriage topics. One might even say that to the extent marriage is a moral issue, governed by divine laws, then the Church must speak and ensure that the divine Law is upheld.

Nevertheless, some have asserted that what Luther means is that the Church should abandon all attempts to define marriage or advocate for any particular laws regarding it, but should instead leave it all to the state. (Here "worldly" is understood in a modern Western sense as being categorically separate from religious norms and churchly influence.) Also, since Luther denied that marriage is a sacrament, it is thought by some that the Church makes no decisions about it.[7] Yet such an argument, based on Luther's definition of marriage as a "worldly matter," overlooks his many claims that marriage is not human-made, but established by God. When Luther speaks of marriage as worldly, he does not remove it from divine institution and norms, but places it outside the category of redemption through Christ.[8]

This can be seen throughout Luther's marriage writings. In 1520, right after arguing that marriage is not a sacrament, Luther makes clear that (whether "worldly" or not) marriage is a *divine* institution, unchangeable by any human law. "Therefore, if a marriage has been contracted outside of these degrees, which are the only ones which have been prohibited by God's appointment, it should by no means be annulled on account of the laws of men. For marriage itself, being a divine institution, is incomparably superior to any laws, so that marriage should not be annulled for the sake of the law, rather the laws should be broken for the sake of marriage."[9]

According to Luther, engagement—that is, the agreement of the two parties to marry—is what puts them into the marriage bond. One might think that since the agreement comes from individuals, marriage may be defined by those individuals; it is a "worldly matter." But according to Luther, this is not what has established and defined marriage. The engaging must be done in accordance

7 Stjerna, "Luther on Marriage," 130–31.

8 Thomas A. Fudge, "Incest and Lust in Luther's Marriage: Theology and Morality in Reformation Polemics," *Sixteenth Century Journal* 34, no. 2 (2003): 322–26; Paul Althaus, *The Ethics of Martin Luther*, trans. Robert C. Schultz (Philadelphia: Fortress, 1972), 83–97; Hendrix, "Luther on Marriage," 340–41; Leppin, "Ehe bei Martin Luther," 30–32.

9 *Babylonian Captivity of the Church* (1520), AE 36:99, cf. WA 6:555.

with God's Word and command as recorded in Holy Scripture, as Luther explains in his tract *On Marriage Matters*:

> The verse itself [Matt. 19:6] clearly indicates that two kinds of joining take place, one by God, the other without God. Joining by God means that which is done by us according to his word and commandment; joining without God means that which is done by ourselves alone without his word and commandment. Now we have taught so often that we should do nothing unless we have the express approval of God's word; God himself has nothing to do with us, nor we with him, except through his word, which is the only means by which we recognize his will, and according to which we have to govern our actions.[10]

This falsifies the hypothesis that Luther saw marriage as "worldly" in the modern sense of being void of biblical norms. It also shows that in Luther's understanding not just any promise between two persons constitutes marriage but only that promise which conforms to God's Word.

Luther's definition of marriage as worldly may in part have been motivated by his desire to deflect the duty of giving judgment in marriage cases to the civil authorities. Again in *On Marriage Matters*, he wrote:

> Therefore I simply do not wish to become involved in such matters at all and beg everyone not to bother me with them. If you do not have sovereigns, then you have officials. If they do not render just decisions, what concern is it of mine? . . . As soon as we begin to act as judges in marriage matters, the teeth of the millwheel will have snatched us by the sleeve and will carry us away to the point where we must decide the penalty. Once we have to decide the penalty, then we must also render judgment about the body and goods, and by this time we are down under the wheel and drowned in the water of worldly affairs.[11]

That is, it is not the moral issues and principles that Luther deflects away from himself (for why then would he write this treatise?) but rather the judging of civil suits and criminal cases related to marriage, which often involved applying civil punishments and resolving truly worldly matters such as disputes about property.[12]

Defining marriage as "worldly" also acknowledges that marriage is not only for Christians or something that pertains to salvation (this is why Luther and

---

10 *On Marriage Matters* (1530), AE 46:276, cf. WA 30/3:213.

11 *On Marriage Matters* (1530), AE 46:265–66, cf. WA 30/3:205–6.

12 Scott Hendrix came to the same conclusion: "Luther on Marriage" (as in p. 183 n. 2), 345.

other Protestants denied that marriage is a sacrament). But it did not remove the divine norms that apply to marriage as instituted by God. Luther lived in a Christian society, not a modern, secular society. For Luther, God rules not just the right-hand kingdom, but the left-hand as well. God has established both the spiritual government and the temporal government, and He is at work in both of them. But they have different tasks. God's will is authoritative, or should be authoritative, for both.[13] Therefore despite his statement that marriage is a worldly matter, Luther continued to give advice on marriage questions throughout his career, basing his advice on Holy Scripture. As priests married beginning in the early 1520s, and as other marriages encountered difficulties, Luther was often requested to act as an arbiter and unofficial judge in marriage cases.[14] Yet in April or May 1524 he complained to Martin Bucer of the number of questions about marriage he had to answer, a statement he repeated in his pamphlet *That Parents Should Neither Compel Nor Hinder the Marriage of Their Children*, which was published in April.[15]

Not only did Luther advise marriage matters, he also judged them when he saw the civil government neglecting them or giving wrong judgments. For example, in May 1524 Luther became involved in a difficult marriage case involving the tailor Michael Hanck and his wife, Margareta Mollwitz. Luther assembled his own adjudications panel, consisting of himself, Johannes Bugenhagen, a civil judge, and eight witnesses. Under questioning it was found that the husband had been physically abusive toward his wife for years and did not provide a living for her but took and squandered whatever he found in their home. Luther recommended allowing Margareta to separate from him. The husband was left to the magistrates for punishment. She consented to return to him if after a period of three to six months he would be tested as to whether he wanted to change or was able to change. At first the Wittenberg city council did not accept the verdict, but

13 Bernhard Lohse, *Martin Luther's Theology: Its Historical and Systematic Development*, trans. Roy A. Harrisville (Minneapolis: Fortress, 1999), 319–20.

14 See Brecht, *Luther: Shaping and Defining the Reformation*, 93; WA Br 3:230–34, 257, nos. 702–4, 722; J. Löbe, "Merkwürdige Ehegeschichte eines Geistlichen in der ersten Zeit der Reformation, nebst Nachträgen zur Geschichte der Stadt Lucka in der Kirchen-Gallerie," *Mittheilungen der Geschichts- und Alterthumsforschenden Gesellschaft des Osterlandes* 9 (1887): 177–94.

15 Brecht, *Luther: Shaping and Defining the Reformation*, 90, 92; WA Br 12:60.5–7, no. 4225a.

later it agreed with Luther.[16] In the conflict with the council, Luther established himself as an authority on marriage matters. The important thing to see here is not the details of the case but the fact that Luther would not stand by and let marriage be handled in ways he viewed as wrong. This must factor into how we understand his declarations in various writings that marriage is a worldly matter. Here it is clear that Luther did not view marriage as something the civil government was permitted either to change or to ignore.

The hypothesis that Luther relinquished to the state the Church's right and duty to define marriage is untenable in view also of admonitions against the Wittenberg jurists that he delivered at the end of several sermons in 1544.[17] In these sermons Luther publicly denounced the Wittenberg jurists on a marriage issue. They were supporting the validity of secret engagements, that is, promises to marry contracted between two persons without parental consent. These admonitions show that Luther was not content to let civil government define marriage contrary to Scripture (even though, in this case, their view was in accord with papal canon law): "I am angry and intend to be so, for they are intruding on my jurisdiction. I cannot and will not endure it that the pope and [the archbishop of] Mainz with their filthy jurists should govern our church in Wittenberg. I would rather be torn apart with red-hot tongs."[18] "No secret engagements are to be instigated or recognized as valid in my church, no matter how it might happen. I will not have it, I will not endure it, and I will not take responsibility for it. Therefore, let all theologians, jurists, and judges refrain from sanctioning such vows. If I cannot be granted this, then I will abandon this pulpit and take my leave."[19] A wrongful practice of marriage (and specifically engagement) makes it into a case of conscience. In this way, marriage does not lose its normative foundation in Scripture, nor does the Church lose its responsibility to ensure that scriptural norms are upheld.

---

16 Brecht, *Luther: Shaping and Defining the Reformation*, 93; WA Br 3:288–90, 301.3–302.5. The marriage case against Michael Hanck, judged by Luther, is printed in WA Br 3:290 as an appendix to Luther's letter (possibly on May 10, 1524) to the Saxon court chaplain Georg Spalatin. Later, in a letter to Spalatin dated June 2, 1524 (WA Br 3:301–2), Luther complained that the Wittenberg city council had told the elector that Luther had not informed him of the details of the case correctly. Perhaps they were unaware of the examination that Luther had conducted in the presence of witnesses. He convinced them that his information was correct, and they promised to agree to his judgment.

17 Sermons of January 6, 13, and 20, 1544, AE 58:53–87.

18 Sermon for Epiphany, Matt. 2:1–12 (January 6, 1544), AE 58:70.

19 Sermon for the Second Sunday after Epiphany (January 20, 1544), AE 58:82.

> I shall give an example. Philip's son, etc., who has been inveigled into agreeing to [a secret engagement], now wants his father's consent to the marriage. But I do not permit this in my church. If this is done, conscience comes and says: "What have I done? I have consented to what my son has contracted, and I have set an example that sons can do as they please without [their parents'] consent," etc. And after three years [the couple] want to separate. These are the fruits of clandestine betrothals: namely, that they deprive God and parents of the obedience due them, etc.[20]

So the situations in which marriage becomes a case of conscience are indeed related to wrongful practices related to marriage. This gives Luther's statement that the Church and her pastors speak whenever marriage affects consciences a rather broad range of opportunities in which to speak.

Having seen that Luther often took measures to correct the practice of marriage, how should his claim be understood that what he wrote in 1530 on marriage should be considered only advice?[21] This is Luther's characteristic published modesty about his own authority. Yet in this same tract, *On Marriage Matters*, Luther often casts off this modesty and makes arguments from Holy Scripture that are applicable to all people.

To many people today, marriage seems to be a private affair, constituted by the promise that two people make to each other. In this case the Church's role would be simply to celebrate the love of the two people, after they have promised this love. To such people it must seem strange that anything or anyone would come between these two people and their love. Can Luther, who rejected many of the impediments to marriage established in canon law, be seen as removing all impediments to marriage?[22] Is it valid to appreciate the way that Luther attacked some impediments to marriage while setting aside his understanding that marriage is exclusively between a man and woman?[23] Rather than simply appreciating Luther's attack on impediments to marriage, one should really ask *why* Luther attacked certain impediments.

In 1519, Luther was not yet sure about engagement. He was beginning to suspect that secret engagements (that is, engagement without parental consent) were wrong and that parents ought to be involved.[24] By 1530, Luther was sure

---

20 Sermon for the Second Sunday after Epiphany (January 20, 1544), AE 58:83.

21 *On Marriage Matters* (1530), AE 46:266–67, WA 30/3:206.

22 See, e.g., Stjerna, "Luther on Marriage" (as in p. 184 n. 4), 131–32.

23 Stjerna, "Luther on Marriage," 135.

24 *Sermon on the Estate of Marriage* (1519), AE 44:11, WA 2:169.

that parental consent was required. Without this, an engagement and marriage were not binding.[25]

In *The Babylonian Captivity of the Church* (1520), Luther complained about various impediments to marriage established by the papal church, which the Church's prelates would dispense with in exchange for money. Yet Luther did not disapprove of all impediments. He distinguished the man-made ones from the scriptural, divinely established impediments such as those listed in Leviticus 18.[26] He speaks of "any impediment to marriage from which the pope can grant dispensation but which is not stated in the Scriptures."[27] Luther was not granting carte blanche freedom; he was granting freedom from man-made rules while calling people to obedience toward divine precepts.

> Here, therefore, those inflexible impediments derived from affinity, by spiritual or legal relationship, and from blood relationship must give way, so far as the Scriptures permit, in which the second degree of consanguinity alone is prohibited. Thus it is written in Lev. 18 [:6–18], where there are twelve persons a man is prohibited from marrying: his mother, stepmother, full sister, half-sister by either parent, granddaughter, father's or mother's sister, daughter-in-law, brother's wife, wife's sister, stepdaughter, and his uncle's wife. Here only the first degree of affinity and the second degree of consanguinity are forbidden; yet not without exception, as will appear on closer examination, for the brother's or sister's daughter—the niece—is not included in the prohibition, although she is in the second degree.[28]

Not only was incest an impediment to marriage. In 1520 Luther considered three situations as impeding engagement and marriage: (1) sexual impotence, (2) ignorance of a previous marriage, (3) a vow of chastity.[29] By the next year he had changed his position on the vow of perpetual celibacy. Vows of perpetual celibacy were no longer seen as binding on those who could not keep them, and marriage was a divine remedy for such situations. Yet at the very time (1521–23) when Luther was attacking monastic vows, including the vow of perpetual celibacy, he published a tract teaching that incestuous marriages are prohibited by

25 *On Marriage Matters* (1530), AE 46:267–77, WA 30/2:207. See also Jane E. Strohl, "Luther's New View on Marriage, Sexuality and the Family," *Lutherjahrbuch* 76 (2009): 159–92.

26 Hendrix, "Luther on Marriage" (as in p. 183 n. 2), 339.

27 *Babylonian Captivity of the Church* (1520), AE 36:98, WA 6:554–55.

28 *Babylonian Captivity of the Church* (1520), AE 36:99, cf. WA 6:555.

29 *Babylonian Captivity of the Church* (1520), AE 36:102, WA 6:557.

divine Law.[30] In 1522, despite rejecting papal impediments that were added to the divine definition of incest in Leviticus 18, Luther maintains the biblical definition.[31] Therefore one should not take Luther's rather flippant comments out of context: "So away with this foolishness; take as your spouse whomsoever you please . . . . Therefore, if you desire, go ahead and marry anyway."[32] These rhetorical flourishes do not cancel out Luther's clear position on genuine impediments to marriage.

So while Luther removed certain traditional Catholic impediments to marriage, he added another requirement that he found in Holy Scripture, parental consent, and he maintained other impediments such as forbidden degrees of relationship. The reason *why* he did this is because his goal was not to free people to follow their hearts but to call people to conform their lives to God's will as revealed in Holy Scripture. Why is Luther's teaching on impediments to marriage important? Among other things, if one ignores Luther's teaching on the forbidden grades of relationship in marriage,[33] the door is left open to incest.

Human Sexuality: Corrupted by Sin?

Should one follow his or her sexual desires or try to restrain them? The answer to this question will depend on whether sexual desire, after the fall, is something basically good, though perhaps tainted with sin, or thoroughly corrupted by sin but nevertheless blessed by God in the case of husband and wife. Several scholars have argued for the former position.[34] If sexual desires as we now experience them are created by God, and if a homosexual orientation is likewise created by God, then one necessarily concludes that homosexual practice and homosexual marriage are good.[35] This argument, directly from sexual desire to a right to marry, depends on the idea that the sexual urges we feel now are part of God's original creation. Can this argument be traced to Martin Luther? If God created

30 *Persons Related* (1522), AE 45:3–9, WA 10/2:265–66. The same thing is handled in *Estate of Marriage* (1522), AE 45:18–24, WA 10/2:277–81; and *On Marriage Matters* (1530), AE 46:315–17, WA 30/2:244–46.

31 *Estate of Marriage* (1522), AE 45:22, WA 10/2:280.

32 *Estate of Marriage* (1522), AE 45:24–25, WA 10/2:281–83.

33 As does Stjerna, "Luther on Marriage" (as in p. 184 n. 4), 141.

34 E.g., Feucht et al., *Sex and the Church*, 3–37; Stjerna, "Luther on Marriage."

35 Stjerna, "Luther on Marriage," 133–35.

the sexual urge, and our current sexual desires are the way that God created us,[36] is there any reason to resist such urges? Did not the fall into sin change the way that the human race experiences sex?

Scholars have noted that Luther and St. Augustine had the same teaching on these questions. This is not to say that Luther adopted all of Augustine's teaching on marriage. In particular, he rejected the view that a "sacramental bond" was one of the goods of marriage, that procreation is no longer necessary, and that celibacy is spiritually superior to marriage.[37] Yet when speaking of the corruption of sexual desires after the fall into sin, Luther and Augustine are on the same page. According to Augustine, before the fall into sin sex would have been subject to reason, an act of obedience without lust. In *The City of God*, he explained that sexual lust, even within marriage, is sinful,[38] though marital intercourse itself is "lawful and honourable."[39] There is a distinction between the sexual act itself, which within marriage is "by nature decent," and the way sexual desire operates in the human being corrupted by sin.[40] Luther makes exactly this distinction.

Sexual Procreation Is a Created Good

Luther frequently says that procreation within marriage is good, something created by God and preserved in goodness even after the fall into sin. In *The Estate of Marriage,* Luther affirms the goodness of sexual procreation on the basis of the creation account in Genesis 1–2. "After God had made man and woman he blessed them and said to them, 'Be fruitful and multiply' [Gen. 1:28]. From this passage we may be assured that man and woman should and must come together in order to multiply."[41] What makes this natural and necessary is

36 As is argued by Feucht et al., *Sex and the Church*, 78; Fudge, "Incest and Lust in Luther's Marriage" (as in p. 185 n. 8), 344. Cf. Cortright, "Luther, the Body, and Sexuality" (as in p. 184 n. 3), 5–10.

37 E.g., see Hendrix, "Luther on Marriage," 336; Althaus, *Ethics of Martin Luther*, 84–85. See also David G. Hunter, "Marriage," in *Augustine through the Ages: An Encyclopedia*, ed. Allan D. Fitzgerald (Grand Rapids: Eerdmans, 1999), 535–36; Augustine, *On the Good of Marriage* 3, 4–5, 17 (NPNF[1] 3:400–401, 406–7); Augustine, *On Marriage and Concupiscence* 1.13, 1.19 (NPNF[1] 5:269, 271).

38 Augustine, *The City of God against the Pagans* 14.16, 14.20, 14.2i (trans. R. W. Dyson, Cambridge Texts in the History of Political Thought [Cambridge: Cambridge University Press, 1998], 614–15, 620–21).

39 Augustine, *City of God* 14.18 (Dyson, p. 617).

40 Augustine, *City of God* 14.18 (Dyson, p. 618).

41 *The Estate of Marriage* (1522), AE 45:17–18, WA 10/2:275–76.

specifically God's binary creation of humanity as male and female and His specific command to procreate (Gen. 1:28). Luther also takes the need to procreate through sex as a natural need of the body.

> For this word which God speaks, "Be fruitful and multiply," is not a command. It is more than a command, namely, a divine [working][42] which it is not our prerogative to hinder or ignore. Rather, it is just as necessary as the fact that I am a man, and more necessary than sleeping and waking, eating and drinking, and emptying the bowels and bladder. It is a nature and disposition just as innate as the organs involved in it. Therefore, just as God does not command anyone to be a man or a woman but creates them the way they have to be, so he does not command them to multiply but creates them so that they have to multiply. And wherever men try to resist this, it remains irresistible nonetheless and goes its way through fornication, adultery, and [mute][43] sins, for this is a matter of nature and not of choice.[44]

Here Luther seems to leave no room for having self-control over one's sexual life and urges. The bachelor Luther perhaps did not think to emphasize sufficiently the need for self-control also within marriage. Nevertheless, the specifics of his argument cannot be discarded. He is arguing for marriage as a remedy against unchastity: fornication, adultery, homosexuality, auto-eroticism, and bestiality (the latter three being the unmentionable "mute sins").[45] The argument is not that all people should have the right to sexual release with whomever they want, but just the opposite: heterosexual marriage is the only legitimate setting for sex, and this is rooted in creation and nature.

When Luther speaks of sex after the fall as good, he always does so while speaking of it as procreation.

> In the second place, after God had made man and woman he blessed them and said to them, "Be fruitful and multiply" [Gen. 1:28]. From this passage we may be assured that man and woman should and must

42 AE 45:18 reads "ordinance [*werck*]."

43 Instead of "secret sins" (AE 45:18) Luther's German *stummen sund* requires the translation "mute sins."

44 *The Estate of Marriage* (1522), AE 45:18, WA 10/2:275–76.

45 On the definition of "mute sins," see Johann Gerhard, *Loci Theologici Cum Pro Adstruenda Veritate Tum Pro Destruenda Quorumvis Contradicentium Falsitate Per Theses Nervose Solide Et Copiose Explicati*, ed. Ed. Preuss, vol. 7 (Berolini: Gust. Schlawitz, 1868), 298, "De Conjugio," § 487. See also Benjamin T. G. Mayes, "Self-Pollution: Its Definition and Cure," in *From Taboo to Delight: Ethics of Sex*, ed. Gifford Grobien (St. Louis: Concordia, 2017), 141–53.

> come together in order to multiply. Now this [ordinance] is just as inflexible as the first, and no more to be despised and made fun of than the other, since God gives it his blessing and does something over and above the act of creation. Hence, as it is not within my power not to be a man, so it is not my prerogative to be without a woman. Again, as it is not in your power not to be a woman, so it is not your prerogative to be without a man. For it is not a matter of free choice or decision but a natural and necessary thing, that whatever is a man must have a woman and whatever is a woman must have a man.[46]

Luther refers here to the specific divine command to procreate. This is what is divinely commanded. He does not address the subject of sexual pleasure here.

The same can be seen in Luther's 1523 Genesis sermons, published in 1527 as *In Genesin Declamationes*. "But if we had remained spiritual in uncorrupted nature as Adam was at the first, then everyone would recognize a man as a man, and again then it would have been full of good and no displeasure would have followed. Thus man and woman, child-bearing, and bearing fruit is certainly God's work."[47] Here again procreation is viewed as God's good creation.

Writing in 1525, Luther emphasized marriage and procreation as a part of God's creation, like eating and drinking. It is where all human beings come from. Therefore marriage should not be disparaged.[48] In a sermon on January 15 of that year, Luther emphasized that if one feels an inclination toward the opposite sex, this is the work of God. That person should marry.[49]

In 1541, he wrote: "Eighth, nobody can deny that we praise and honor marriage as a divine, blessed, and well-pleasing ordinance of God's creation for the procreation of children and the prevention of carnal unchastity."[50]

Many more testimonies could be cited. In short, since God created humanity as male and female, joining Adam and Eve together in marriage and commanding them to multiply, sex (considered as procreation) is God's good creation. Marriage is the licit place for this to occur.

---

46 *The Estate of Marriage* (1522), AE 45:18, WA 10/2:275–76.

47 *In Genesin Declamationes* (1523/1527), WA 24:56, my translation.

48 *Christliche Schrift an W. Reißenbusch* (1525), WA 18:277.

49 Sermon of January 15, 1525, WA 17/1:9 (AE 56, forthcoming).

50 *Against Hanswurst* (1541), AE 41:197.

But Lust Is Sinful

Ever since the fall into sin, sexual love between man and woman is no longer pure. Now it is filled with lust. Yet this sinful aspect of sex is pardoned by God when it occurs within the marriage of a man and a woman.[51] Luther is remarkably consistent on this throughout his career.

In 1519, Luther distinguished sex before and after the fall. "Since the fall marriage has been mixed[52] with wicked lust. And now [i.e., after the fall] the desire of the man for the woman, and vice versa, is sought after not only for companionship and children, for which purposes alone marriage was instituted, but also for the pursuance of wicked lust, which is almost as strong a motive."[53] Lust is viewed by Luther as evil, in itself "wicked," though it is not regarded by God as sin within marriage. "The wicked lust of the flesh, which nobody is without, is a conjugal obligation and is not reprehensible when expressed within marriage, but in all other cases outside the bond of marriage, it is mortal sin."[54] That is to say, there is no qualitative difference between the lust felt toward one's legitimate spouse and that felt toward someone else. What makes one acceptable and the other not is that one is simply regarded by God as "not reprehensible" within the context of marriage.

In 1521, Luther again distinguished between sex as it was established by God in marriage and as it exists now, filled with lust. "In no sense does God attribute sin to the conjugal rights of married people, which is due solely to his mercy, although Psalm 51 [:5] refers to it as sin and iniquity in no way differing from adultery and whoredom, because it springs from passion and impure lust."[55] In and of itself the sexual lust experienced within and without marriage are the same. What makes one acceptable and the other not is God's mercy.

In 1522, Luther wrote *The Estate of Marriage* to encourage people to marry. He praised marriage and procreation as God's good creation. Yet at the very end Luther clarified his earlier statements. Sex as we now experience it in marriage is corrupted with sin.

---

51 Althaus, *Ethics of Martin Luther*, 84–86; Leppin, "Ehe bei Martin Luther" (as in p. 184 n. 3), 24; Strohl, "Luther's New View" (as in p. 190 n. 25), 162–69; Fudge, "Incest and Lust in Luther's Marriage" (as in p. 185 n. 8), 326.

52 *Sermon on the Estate of Marriage* (1519), AE 44:8 reads "adulterated" here, but the sin of adultery is not being discussed. WA 2:167 reads *vormischt.*

53 *Sermon on the Estate of Marriage* (1519), AE 44:8, WA 2:167.

54 *Sermon on the Estate of Marriage* (1519), AE 44:10, WA 2:168.

55 *On Monastic Vows* (1521), AE 44:376–77, cf. WA 8:654.

> With all this extolling of married life, however, I have not meant to ascribe to nature a condition of sinlessness. On the contrary, I say that flesh and blood, corrupted through Adam, is conceived and born in sin, as Psalm 51 [:5] says. Intercourse is never without sin; but God excuses it by his grace because the estate of marriage is his work, and he preserves in and through the sin all that good which he has implanted and blessed in marriage.[56]

In 1523, Luther preached a series of sermons on Genesis and had the opportunity to treat this same theme. On Gen. 1:28, he proclaimed: "Now if Adam had remained as he had been created, birth would also have proceeded just fine; they would have been conceived with full joy and without any evil lust, so that one would not be aware of any evil inclination."[57] That is, lust would not have been present before the fall into sin; lust is not God's good creation, but a now-inescapable corruption of it. Preaching on Gen. 3:7, he made it clear that lust is a result of the fall. "First their eyes became watchful, as the devil had said; they see and perceive that they are naked. From that time it was impossible to restrain all the body parts that they had, nor to curb the evil lust. They both looked at each other with evil lust and unchaste desires, since they were naked, which previously was unknown to them."[58]

In a sermon of January 8, 1531, Luther preached:

> If we take Adam's fall and our own nature into account, it is not pure or honorable in God's sight, for this carnal lust and other sinful inclination would not have existed in Paradise, nor would any man need to be shy or ashamed before another, nor to cover or dress himself, but husband and wife would have held fast to each other without wicked passion and lust, and begotten and borne children easily without toil or care, just as an apple is plucked from a tree. But now it is the case that no man or woman meets another without shameful desires. Hence Psalm 51 [:5] says, "Behold, I was begotten from sinful seed, and my mother conceived me in sin." All the saints, moreover, who were in the estate of marriage must confess that they could not overcome the sense of aversion. Thus Christ Himself willed not to be born of a man and woman in the natural manner, but selected a virgin for His mother

---

56 *The Estate of Marriage* (1522), AE 45:49, WA 10/2:304.

57 *In Genesin Declamationes* (1523/1527), WA 24:51, my translation.

58 *In Genesin Declamationes* (1523/1527), WA 24:90, my translation.

> and sanctified her flesh and blood, so that His birth would be a pure, holy birth.[59]

Before the fall into sin, sex would have been different, according to Luther. It would have lacked "wicked passion and lust." While Luther may not be denying the presence of some kind of sexual desire before the fall into sin, it certainly would have been different than now. Now no man or woman is without "wicked passion" and "shameful desires," not even within marriage. When the lust and impurity that is present in sex after the fall has been pardoned by God, only then is marriage a pure and holy estate.

> But now he says here that God wishes to have this estate so endowed with grace that, although it is impure by nature, it will not be impure for those who are Christians and have faith, but will henceforth be called "a pure marriage bed," not of itself or from our nature, but from the fact that God covers with His grace the natural sin or impurity implanted in us by the devil and will not impute it to us. Thus He sets to work and purifies this estate with His Word so that it consequently becomes a divine, holy estate—not that He takes away the passion or bridal love, or forbids this marital work, even though these cannot be done without sin (for the pope's doctrine treated this estate as impure and taught that one could not both serve God and be married). Rather, He calls it purified in the sense that God declares it pure by grace and does not impute the sin that is in its nature.[60]

The marital act, sex, cannot be performed without sin, but God pardons and covers this sinful aspect of sex and so regards marriage as pure and holy. In this sense, sex in marriage (though not the lust that attends it) is part of God's plan and is pleasing to Him.

> Second, He not only wants the marriage bed made pure but also marriage held in honor. Sinful desire and other fault is thus more firmly covered over, being called not simply pure but even honorable and precious by God's Word and command . . . . This, then, means that

---

59 Sermon of January 8, 1531, WA 34/1:73 (AE 56, forthcoming), trans. James L. Langebartels. The same description of sex before the fall as lacking erotic desire is found in *Lectures on Genesis* (1535–45/1544–54), AE 1:168: "And so, as often as they would have wanted to beget children, they would have come together, not urged on by that passion which is now in our leprous flesh but admiring God's dispensation and obeying Him with the utmost restraint, just as we now come together to hear the Word of God and to worship Him." Cf. WA 42:126.

60 Sermon of January 8, 1531, WA 34/1:73 (AE 56, forthcoming), trans. James L. Langebartels.

> bride and groom are not only put to bed and under the covers but also adorned with all beauty and carried into church with utmost honor.[61]

What is good and God-pleasing is God's institution of marriage and sexual procreation within marriage, not the sin that always attends it.

> For that reason there is no embellishment beyond this in marriage; it is when you look at the Word that you can have a good conscience to live with her, sleep together, and produce children. It is true that this certainly does not happen without sin, but give me one part of life which happens without sin! If this were to be calculated in that way, then I would never again preach, and no one could carry out his office. The article must remain: "I believe in the forgiveness of sins."[62]

Thus sex, even in marriage, is made impure by sin. Luther sets up a parallel here with the way that sin (for example, sinful thoughts and motives) attends and corrupts even good works, such as preaching. Marriage and sex after the fall are good, however, if they are regarded according to the divine institution of this estate, and according to divine forgiveness of the sin that attends them.[63]

The same distinction comes up repeatedly in Luther's extensive lectures on Genesis (1535–45, published 1544–54). Luther distinguishes between sex as God originally created man and woman without sin and as it is experienced now, after the fall into sin.

> But, good God, what has been lost for us here through sin! How blessed was that state of man in which the begetting of offspring was linked with the highest respect and wisdom, indeed with the knowledge of God! Now the flesh is so overwhelmed by the leprosy of lust that in the act of procreation the body becomes downright brutish and cannot beget in the knowledge of God. Thus the power of procreation remained in the human race, but very much debased and even completely overwhelmed by the leprosy of lust, so that procreation is only slightly more moderate than that of the brutes. . . . Therefore the blessing, which remains till now in nature, is, as it were, a cursed and debased blessing if you compare it with that first one; nevertheless,

61 Sermon of January 8, 1531, WA 34/1:74 (AE 56, forthcoming), trans. James L. Langebartels.

62 Sermon of January 8, 1531, WA 34/1:77–78 (AE 56, forthcoming), trans. James L. Langebartels.

63 See also sermons of January 7, 1532 (AE 57:80, WA 36:82–83) and February 27, 1536 (AE 57:220–28, WA 41:516–20); and a table talk from between December 16 and 18, 1536, no. 3508 (AE 54:218, WA TR 3:367–68).

> God established it and preserves it. So let us gratefully acknowledge this "marred blessing." And let us keep in mind that the unavoidable leprosy of the flesh, which is nothing but disobedience and loathsomeness attached to bodies and minds, is the punishment of sin.[64]

That is, the blessing of procreation has been preserved, though it is now marred and debased by lust, as a punishment of sin. The same distinction is seen when Luther discusses Gen. 2:25: "And, even better in many ways, Eve, our mother, would have sat among us naked; and no one would have been offended by the nakedness of her breasts and the other parts of the body, of which we must now be ashamed and which, because of sin, kindle lust."[65] That is, lust was not present before the fall into sin. Now it is. This is an indication of the sinful corruption of human nature through original sin. Another example:

> Moreover, although in the innocent nature the entire work of procreation would have been most holy and most pure, after sin the leprosy of lust has made its way into this part of the body. Hence those who live outside the married state burn most shamefully. And unless those who live in the married state restrain their passions and carefully guard their relations with each other, they encounter all sorts of temptations.[66]

All of this leads necessarily to the conclusion that our desires now are no indicator of what is good and right. Against the scholastic theologians, Luther taught: "Therefore they maintain about man and about demons that although they have lost their original righteousness, their natural endowments have nevertheless remained pure, just as they were created in the beginning. But this idea must be shunned like poison, for it minimizes original sin."[67] That is, the fallen condition of humanity must be taken seriously. One must not imagine that the way people find themselves in the world now is the way God created them. Luther sees this in the reaction of Adam and Eve to seeing each other after falling into sin (Gen. 3:7): "Now, after sin, when Adam and Eve see that they are naked, they are made ashamed, and they look for girdles with which to cover their disgrace. Yet how much greater disgrace is there in this, that the will is impaired, the intellect depraved, and the reason entirely corrupt and altogether changed! Is this what they mean when they say that our natural endowments are

---

64 *Lectures on Genesis* (1535–45/1544–54), AE 1:71, WA 42:53–54.

65 *Lectures on Genesis* (1535–45/1544–54), AE 1:140, WA 42:105.

66 *Lectures on Genesis* (1535–45/1544–54), AE 1:168, WA 42:126.

67 *Lectures on Genesis* (1535–45/1544–54), AE 1:165, WA 42:123–24.

perfect?"[68] Anyone who claims that human nature after the fall is just the way that God created it—if, for example, a man thinks that if he experiences sexual desire for many different women, or homosexual desires, then God must have created him that way—is ignoring the effect of original sin and even undermining the Gospel. "Then there was no purpose in sending Christ, the Redeemer, if the original righteousness, like something foreign to our nature, has been taken away and the natural endowments remain perfect. What can be said that is more unworthy of a theologian?"[69]

These many examples from early to late in his career as a theologian demonstrate that, according to Luther, one's sexual urges do not show us what is good and right. The original function of procreation would have lacked the corruption of lust, which is the only way we now experience it. This is important because Luther's arguments from sexual urges to the necessity of marriage rest *not* upon lust as a created good, but upon the belief that marriage is a divinely appointed remedy *against* those lusts. To deny marriage as remedy while keeping the necessity of marriage for those who feel the burning of lust is to take out the cornerstone of Luther's argument and to turn what he considers evil into something good, all the while appealing to his authority! Luther is remarkably consistent throughout his career in teaching the ongoing goodness of marriage and of sexual procreation within marriage while distinguishing this from the intrinsic badness of lust which always attends sex, even in marriage.

Apparent Contradictions with Responses

Despite these many testimonies, Luther's position on sexual desire being sinful after the fall has been misunderstood, in some cases by scholars who are relying on the translations in the American edition of *Luther's Works*.[70] In a number of places, Luther seems to say that sex as it is now experienced after the fall, and particularly our present experience of sexual desire, is a good creation of God. A closer examination of Luther's Latin and German, however, will show that these passages have been mistranslated. They actually support our thesis, that Luther consistently distinguished married love and procreation (as God's

68 *Lectures on Genesis* (1535–45/1544–54), AE 1:166, WA 42:124.

69 *Lectures on Genesis* (1535–45/1544–54), AE 1:166, WA 42:124. See also AE 1:168, WA 42:126.

70 For example, Cortright, "Luther, the Body, and Sexuality" (as in p. 184 n. 3), 5–10; Stjerna, "Luther on Marriage" (as in p. 184 n. 4), 126–43; Fudge, "Incest and Lust in Luther's Marriage" (as in p. 185 n. 8), 344.

creation) from lust (the sinful corruption of sexual desire, both within and especially outside of marriage).

In 1519, Luther praised married love as distinct from other kinds of love. This statement is rightly seen as part of Luther's affirmation of marriage as God's good creation.

> Now there are three kinds of love: false love, natural love, and married love. False love is that which seeks its own, as a man loves money, possessions, honor, and women taken outside of marriage and against God's command. Natural love is that between father and child, brother and sister, friend and relative, and similar relationships. But over and above all these is married love, that is, a bride's love, which glows like a fire and desires nothing but the husband. She says, "It is you I want, not what is yours: I want neither your silver nor your gold; I want neither. I want only you. I want you in your entirety, or not at all." All other kinds of love seek something other than the loved one: this kind wants only to have the beloved's own self completely.[71]

Because of Luther's description of this love as that "which glows like a fire," it may seem a sexual love and desire. Yet the "bride's love" mentioned here is *not* specifically sexual love, but love for the whole person, one that is, admittedly, ardent and that seeks intimacy. But Luther continues by distinguishing this kind of love from the lust-filled experience of sex, even within marriage. According to him, lust and seeking to satisfy one's own desires is what has corrupted this love after the fall. Luther adds his now-familiar distinction between married love before and after the fall:

> If Adam had not fallen, the love of bride and groom would have been the loveliest thing. Now this love is not pure either, for admittedly a married partner desires to have the other, yet each seeks to satisfy his desire with the other, and it is this desire which corrupts this kind of love. Therefore, the married state is now no longer pure and free from sin. The temptation of the flesh has become so strong and consuming that marriage may be likened to a hospital for incurables which prevents inmates from falling into graver sin.[72]

In 1525, Luther encouraged a former student, Wolfgang Reissenbusch, to marry, and stated that men and women have been created to bear fruit and multiply. Here Luther states that the continuing urge to procreate is part of God's

71 *Sermon on the Estate of Marriage* (1519), AE 44:9, WA 2:167.

72 *Sermon on the Estate of Marriage* (1519), AE 44:9, WA 2:167–68.

good creation. "And this is the word of God, by virtue of which in man's body seed for fruit, and the ardent, natural inclination toward the woman, was created and is preserved. This may be hindered neither with vows nor with laws, for it is God's word and work."[73] This is one of the places where Luther seems to state that the ongoing sex drive after the fall is God's good creation. Statements such as this have led interpreters to posit a tension or conflict in Luther's thought on the goodness or sinfulness of sexual urges after the fall.[74] These two ideas seem contrary to each other: First, that "be fruitful and multiply" (Gen. 1:28) is built into human nature by God in such a way that sexual urges are a normal part of human life experienced by most people; second, that lust in sex is sinful, a corruption of the inclination to "be fruitful and multiply." Yet Luther teaches both of these. But if one keeps in mind that, according to Luther, lust has marred the good creation of procreation, yet God still preserves it after the fall,[75] the apparent contradiction falls away. The necessity to engage in sexual relations for the union of husband and wife and for procreation was present in human nature before the fall, and would have expressed itself without lust, within heterosexual marriage. Now, however, it has been corrupted so that the necessity to procreate is still present but is linked with lust, which God did not create. When Luther wrote to his student in 1525, he did not ascribe goodness to the post-fall experience of sexual passion (self-gratifying desire, lust) in itself, but spoke instead of mankind having been created to procreate and that man was created with an "inclination" toward the woman.

In 1527, Luther lectured on the Epistle to Titus and spoke of the duty of women toward their husbands. The American edition of Luther's Works renders the fragmentary notes as follows: "*To love* [*their husbands and children*]. Is this not superfluous, since young women are the ones who love the most? This is directed against those who say that it is pagan to love in a physical way. People who say such things are rebuking, not teaching. These words mean that they should enjoy their husbands' bodies and provide for them."[76] Here Luther clearly defends the right of husbands and wives to love each other in a bodily, physical way, that is, to have marital intercourse. But does he indeed say that women are commanded to "enjoy their husbands' bodies"? Here the passage is mistranslated. The Latin text should instead be rendered: "Let them [the wives] treat

73 *Schrift an W. Reißenbusch* (1525), WA 18:275, my translation.

74 E.g., Cortright, "Luther, the Body, and Sexuality" (as in p. 184 n. 3), 6–7.

75 *Lectures on Genesis* (1535–45/1544–54), AE 1:71, WA 42:53–54.

76 *Lectures on Titus* (1527), AE 29:54, cf. WA 25:44.

the bodies of them [the husbands] well, care for them."[77] In any case, the notes are too fragmentary and disjointed to build on them alone an argument that husband and wife are commanded to enjoy the other's body, and to conclude from this that Luther thought sexual passion as experienced after the fall is good, contrary to his clear statements elsewhere.

It has been asserted that Luther spoke of the naturalness of the post-fall sexual urge in the *Large Catechism* of 1529.[78] There, preaching on the Sixth Commandment (Exod. 20:14), he does not, however, say that sexual urges as people now experience them after the fall are good and created so by God. Rather, he says that God instituted marriage and that He wants husbands and wives to be fruitful and beget children.[79] Here one must keep in mind that Luther distinguishes procreation as God's good ordinance from the way that fallen human beings engage in sex and experience sexual urges.

In his series of sermons published as the *Sermon on the Mount* (1530–32), Luther, commenting on Matt. 5:30, seems to say that God is pleased by sex. "He shows that the sexual union of husband and wife is also most pleasing to Him."[80] But Luther does not mean this. An accurate translation of the German is, instead: "He shows that He is greatly pleased when husband and wife live together well."[81] He is not saying that God is pleased by the sex act, even though in other places he makes clear that procreation is a good creation of God, though now corrupted by sin.

---

77 "Ut bene habeant eorum corpora, curant" (WA 25:44). As the amanuensis punctuated it, the expression "Ut bene habeant eorum corpora" belongs with what follows, "curant," not with what came before. The translation of "enjoy" for "bene habeant" is misleading, because it neglects the word "bene" and ignores the grammatical constructions required to mean "enjoy." See Charlton Thomas Lewis and Charles Short, eds., *A Latin Dictionary, Founded on Andrews' Ed. of Freund's Latin Dictionary* (Oxford: Clarendon Press, 1962), s.v. "habeo" II.N, "bene" I.A.2.e. A more natural reading of this expression is given in P. G. W. Glare, ed., *Oxford Latin Dictionary* (Oxford: Clarendon Press, 1982), s.v. "habeo" 22.a: "(w. adv., etc.) To treat (in a particular way)."

78 Strohl, "Luther's New View" (as in p. 190 n. 25), 174.

79 LC I 207–8, in W. H. T. Dau and F. Bente, eds., *Triglot Concordia: The Symbolical Books of the Ev. Lutheran Church, German-Latin-English* (St. Louis: Concordia, 1921), 639.

80 *Sermon on the Mount* (1530–32), AE 21:89, cf. WA 32:372.

81 ". . . und zeigt das er grossen gefallen daran habe, wenn sich man und weib wol begehen" (WA 32:373). The key phrase is "sich begehen." While in certain contexts this can mean "copulate," more commonly it means "live together." See *DWB*, s.v. "begehen" 10.b. Here Luther is using the exact same wording as in his translation of Sirach 25:2: "Wenn Brüder eins sind, und die Nachbar sich liebhaben, und Man und Weib sich miteinander wol begehen" (WA DB 12:215).

In a table talk from November 25, 1538, Luther refuted a Roman Catholic argument about the sinfulness of sex in marriage. "Another example: Every act of concupiscence is illicit; the marital act is an act of concupiscence; therefore [marriage is illicit]. I reply to the minor premise: The marital act is not an act of concupiscence. Rather, the act which attracts sex to sex is a divine ordinance. Even if by mischance the act is impure on account of original sin, in itself it's still licit and pure."[82] The American edition translation adds a faulty conclusion in brackets: "marriage is illicit." Luther simply says, "Therefore." This requires the understood conclusion: "the marital act is illicit." Roman Catholics, after all, did not disapprove of marriage; for them it was a sacrament. Next, Luther's Latin makes the distinction between married procreation as created, and lustful sex after the fall. An improved translation is: "I respond to the minor premise: It is not an act of concupiscence, but that act, sex [male] to sex [female], is a divine ordinance; although according to accident it is impure because of the sin of origin, nevertheless of itself it is licit and pure."[83] The Aristotelian expression "according to accident" shows that Luther is making the same distinction he makes elsewhere. The marital act is created. The attendant lust (concupiscence) is not. But the attendant defect must not be allowed to denigrate God's ordinance of procreation.

We have now seen that some English translations were made without keeping in mind Luther's distinction between sexual procreation as created by God and the lust that corrupts this good even within marriage, but especially when sexual desire seeks an outlet apart from the bond of marriage. Luther is consistent in maintaining this distinction. It undergirds his frequent admonitions to chastity, self-control, and even sexual moderation within marriage. It also plays a key role in his argument for the permissibility of clerical marriage. Luther does not simply argue that sexual urges are God's good creation and so marriage must be permitted. His consistent teaching on the creation of humankind as male and female and the divine institution of marriage as exclusively heterosexual are also keys to this argument. Now, if sexual desires as experienced after the fall are not good, then there can be no argument directly from sexual desires to permission to marry or to engage in sexual activity. For Luther, permission to marry and to engage in sex within marriage is based instead on the creation of heterosexual marriage at the beginning and on the nonbinding nature of man-made monastic vows. What role, then, do sexual desires play?

82 *Table Talk* no. 4153, November 25, 1538, recorded by Anton Lauterbach, AE 54:324; cf. WA TR 4:171–72.

83 WA TR 4:171, no. 4153, my translation.

They show that one was unable to take those man-made monastic vows. In this case, the divinely established remedy is heterosexual marriage. Marriage is there not to celebrate the sexual desires that people have but to channel those desires in a licit direction.

Is Chastity Impossible outside of Marriage?

In his effort to prove the permissibility of marriage for all men and women, Luther often stated that it is impossible for anyone without a special divine gift for celibacy to remain chaste. The desire for sexual release is present, burning, and even if it does not express itself outwardly, there will be a burning of sexual desire felt in the body and mind. From this Luther concludes that such people must be permitted to marry.

Yet for many reasons not all people are able to marry, even if they desire to do so. Perhaps they are too young. Perhaps they have not yet found suitable spouses. Perhaps their personal habits repel prospective spouses! Does Luther address these situations? Does he really say that a life of chastity is impossible for such people?

Kirsi Stjerna finds an argument from sexual desires to a right to marry in Luther's pamphlet *The Estate of Marriage* (1522).[84] Here Luther argues that the command to "be fruitful and multiply" is built into nature and cannot be resisted. Therefore each man must have a wife and each woman a husband, or else fornication and other unchastity will result.[85] Stjerna takes what Luther referred to heterosexual relations alone and applies this also to homosexual relations, contrary to Luther's intent. Yet Luther's categorical statement here is clear: chastity outside of marriage is impossible.

> It is certainly a fact that he who refuses to marry must fall into immorality. How could it be otherwise, since God has created man and woman to produce seed and to multiply? Why should one not forestall immorality by means of marriage? For if special grace does not exempt a person, his nature must and will compel him to produce seed and to multiply. If this does not occur within marriage, how else can it occur except in fornication or [worse][86] sins? But, they say, suppose I am neither married nor immoral, and force myself to remain continent?

84 Stjerna, "Luther on Marriage" (as in p. 184 n. 4), 137.

85 AE 45:18, WA 10/2:276.

86 *erger* (WA 10/2:300) instead of "secret" (AE 45:45).

> Do you not hear that restraint is impossible without the special grace? For God's word does not admit of restraint; neither does it lie when it says, "Be fruitful and multiply" [Gen. 1:28]. You can neither escape nor restrain yourself from being fruitful and multiplying; it is God's ordinance and takes its course.[87]

Stjerna also appreciates Luther's use of contemporary medical insights, that repressing sexual release would lead to poor health.[88] For Luther, however, this argument does not stand alone and is not used to justify any and all sexual expressions. Just the opposite! Since he thinks that biologically this is the case, and he is convinced that all sexual expressions are sinful except for that which occurs according to nature in heterosexual marriage, Luther concludes that men must be permitted to marry women. One cannot pluck this quote out of Luther's entire system of exegesis and argumentation without deforming the whole thing, claiming Luther's support for what he explicitly rejected. The main point for Luther is not that all manner of sexual release should be permitted since it is impossible to do otherwise, but precisely the opposite. None are permitted, except in heterosexual marriage. Yet the quotation does raise the issue of whether chastity outside of marriage is even possible.

Writing in 1525 to his former student Wolfgang Reissenbusch, Luther stated: "Now, chastity is not in our power. . . . Rather, all were created for marriage, as the body proves, and Scripture says (Genesis 2 [:18 Vg]): 'It is not good for the man to be alone. I will make for him a helper before him.'"[89] Again, in the *Large Catechism* (1529) Luther argued that it is not in our power to keep a vow of perpetual celibacy. Those who have tried to do so had hearts full of unchaste thoughts and evil lusts, with continual burning and secret suffering.[90]

This argument that chastity is impossible seems problematic. Traditional Christian morality, based on Holy Scripture, requires celibacy (chastity) of all nonmarried people, and some people cannot, for some reason, marry. Likewise, there are some married people who must remain in marriage without any hope for sex, such as a husband who must care for his invalid wife. In these cases Luther qualifies his statement that chastity is impossible. In *The Estate of Marriage* (1522), Luther deals specifically with such a case:

---

87 *The Estate of Marriage* (1522), AE 45:45, cf. WA 10/2:300–301.

88 Stjerna, "Luther on Marriage" (as in p. 184 n. 4), 139, referring to *The Estate of Marriage* (1522), AE 45:46–47, WA 10/2:301.

89 *Schrift an W. Reißenbusch* (1525), WA 18:275, my translation.

90 LC I 213–16, in Dau and Bente, *Triglot Concordia*, 641.

> What about a situation where one's wife is an invalid and has therefore become incapable of fulfilling the conjugal duty? May he not take another to wife? By no means. Let him serve the Lord in the person of the invalid and await His good pleasure. Consider that in this invalid God has provided your household with a healing balm by which you are to gain heaven. Blessed and twice blessed are you when you recognize such a gift of grace and therefore serve your invalid wife for God's sake.
>
> But you may say: I am unable to remain continent. That is a lie. If you will earnestly serve your invalid wife, recognize that God has placed this burden upon you, and give thanks to him, then you may leave matters in his care. He will surely grant you grace, that you will not have to bear more than you are able. He is far too faithful to deprive you of your wife through illness without at the same time subduing your carnal desire, if you will but faithfully serve your invalid wife.[91]

This is a clear limitation of the idea that chastity is impossible without sexual relations in marriage.

Likewise, in a sermon of January 8, 1531, Luther qualified his assertion that no one can live chastely without marriage. "It is certainly true that the young girls and guys feel passion, but a Christian heart can resist that and control it with prayer so that he can wait one, two, or three years until he reaches his twenties, and thus he ought to think: I will endure the passion a little for those three years."[92] In order to resist sexual temptation, he counsels: "In order to dispel this passion, I say that good hard work is appropriate along with putting food higher, that is appropriate. I say this so that each may prepare his heart for marriage and shun fornication, and God wants to give the means [for that] so that you can endure the passion, provided that you call on Him in faith."[93] So Luther's argument from the impossibility of chastity to the need to marry must be limited. He actually argues that no one can keep a *man-made* vow of *perpetual* chastity. In this sermon he preaches that young, unmarried people *can*, with God's help, remain chaste in body and wait for marriage. Rather than teaching the futility of trying to live a chaste life, he gives counsel that is still relevant to Christians today. Young people should not delay marriage, seeking casual sex or even

---

91 *Estate of Marriage* (1522), AE 45:35, cf. WA 10/2:291–92.

92 Sermon of January 8, 1531, WA 34/1:80 (AE 56, forthcoming), trans. James L. Langebartels.

93 Sermon of January 8, 1531, WA 34/1:81 (AE 56, forthcoming), trans. James L. Langebartels.

committed sexual relations (perhaps with cohabitation), but should instead focus on finding a marriage partner and being joined in matrimony.

Luther's arguments for the permissibility of marriage must be seen in the context of his teaching that heterosexual marriage is a God-given remedy against lust.[94] If, however, it is argued that the sexual urges which people feel are good and constitute a right to marry, then one might take the argument a step further to argue for promiscuity or homosexual marriage as well by simply expanding on this argumentation.[95] Not only do people feel heterosexual urges, but also some people feel homosexual urges. Of course, by this argumentation, nothing would rule out casual sex (fornication), polyamory, incest, or even bestiality, since some people have those urges too. When Luther argues for permission to marry, he does *not* argue that the sexual feelings people experience are good, but rather that heterosexual marriage is a *remedy* for lust.

Yet Luther's view of marriage as a remedy has also been attacked. Stjerna disparages Luther's doctrine that marriage is a remedy for lust (which is also St. Paul's doctrine in 1 Cor. 7:2), saying Luther taught that women are "lust control" for men. To prove this she cites AE 1:163–69, a passage from Luther's *Lectures on Genesis* (1535–45/1544–54), which says nothing of the sort. There, while discussing the addition of lust to sex because of the fall into sin, Luther describes marriage as something that benefits both husbands and wives in their godly duty of having control over their sexual urges.[96] The same theme runs throughout Luther's writings on marriage.

In 1521, Luther stated that a perpetual vow of celibacy is impossible for many (though not all) people to keep. He explains:

> I am discussing the case only of the man who wants to keep his vow of celibacy, but owing to infirmity of the flesh cannot, the man who has tried time and again and still cannot control the instincts of the flesh either by fasting or personal effort, the man who against his will is driven at one time or another to be overcome by burning lust, and experiences impure seminal emissions sleeping or waking, and yet who in all other respects lives a blameless life.[97]

94 Althaus, *Ethics of Martin Luther*, 85–86; Strohl, "Luther's New View" (as in p. 190 n. 25), 165; Cortright, "Luther, the Body, and Sexuality" (as in p. 184 n. 3), 8; Leppin, "Ehe bei Martin Luther" (as in p. 184 n. 3), 31.

95 See Stjerna, "Luther on Marriage" (as in p. 184 n. 4), 135.

96 AE 1:167–68, WA 42:125–26.

97 *The Judgment of Martin Luther on Monastic Vows* (1521), AE 44:338, cf. WA 8:630–31.

The sins that Luther wants people to reject and flee include sexual release outside of marital, heterosexual intercourse. "Marriage offers a middle course. Let him take a wife, and the law of chastity will be easier for him."[98] Lust is sinful. Those who have vowed perpetual celibacy but continue to suffer lust should be freed to marry. "If, then, God deals with us in this way, how much more ought we to have confidence in his goodness and believe that the vow of chastity will not be counted against us if it proves impossible to keep and if the danger of lust threatens. We need only abide within the limits of the humbler chastity of marriage and not walk according to the flesh."[99] So Luther's encouragement of chastity and his view of marriage as a remedy against unchastity are central to his argument for permitting marriage to those who have vowed celibacy.

The next year, in *The Estate of Marriage*, Luther did not argue directly from sexual desires to a right to marry, but from lust *regarded as sinful* to *heterosexual* marriage *regarded as a remedy* for lust. Luther's rejection of unchastity is central to this argument. If God's creation of heterosexual marriage is denied to people, then they will commit unchastity: fornication, adultery, and mute sins.[100]

In 1523, commenting on 1 Corinthians 7, the goal of chastity is again at the center of Luther's rejection of vows of celibacy. Those who defended vows of celibacy actually did not practice it. They advise people against marriage "although they themselves feel—and abundantly demonstrate by their actions—that they cannot do without women, these being created specifically for marriage; instead they run after and plague themselves with whores day and night."[101] Permanent vows of celibacy are invalid if one is inclined toward fornication.[102] Unlike other kinds of suffering, which can be borne with a good conscience, sexual temptation cannot. Sexual temptation is sinful in itself: "But this suffering is a sinful suffering that one cannot bear in good conscience, for in itself it is sin and wrong. Therefore there is no help or counsel for it except to escape it and get rid of it. This can be achieved through marriage and in no other way."[103] In fact, rather than arguing directly from sexual desire to permission to marry, Luther actually says this is a poor reason to marry. Among the poor reasons for marriage are to fulfill desires for money, property, *sensual pleasure*, and the desire to have

98 *The Judgment of Martin Luther on Monastic Vows* (1521), AE 44:341, cf. WA 8:632.

99 *The Judgment of Martin Luther on Monastic Vows* (1521), AE 44:375–76, cf. WA 8:653–54.

100 *The Estate of Marriage* (1522), AE 45:18–19, 43, WA 10/2:275–76, 299. See above, p. 193 at n. 44, where the passage is quoted.

101 *Commentary on 1 Corinthians 7* (1523), AE 28:5, cf. WA 12:93–94.

102 *Commentary on 1 Corinthians 7* (1523), AE 28:9–10, WA 12:98.

103 *Commentary on 1 Corinthians 7* (1523), AE 28:11, cf. WA 12:99.

an heir. The strongest and best reason to marry is "need." The body by nature will "express itself," and God does not want this to happen outside of marriage.[104] Here again is another testimony that Luther does not celebrate sexual desires as they are experienced after the fall into sin. The marriage of man to woman is the God-given remedy for those who "burn."[105]

The same year, in his sermons on Genesis 1 (at verse 28), Luther stated that the command to be fruitful and multiply is implanted in human nature, and this command gives all men and women permission to marry. Luther emphasizes that this inborn need to procreate necessitates heterosexual marriage not because a desire necessitates marriage but because God has created heterosexual marriage, and after the fall it serves as a remedy against unchastity. "Whether you want to or not, you must do as nature is, or else it will go in other directions, so that such misery follows from it, which must not be named."[106] Luther is basing his understanding of "nature" here not on the desires of fallen humans but on God's creation of male and female and His creation or implanting of sexual procreation within human nature.

Not just early on but throughout his career Luther emphasized marriage as a remedy against sinful lust. While other accents emerge, such as that marriage is an estate of obedience to God and neighbor,[107] in the *Large Catechism* (1529) he states that the main purpose of marriage (now after the fall into sin) is to avoid unchastity.[108] What makes vows of celibacy wrong is not that everyone *should* enjoy sex but that most people cannot actually keep those vows, and so they find sexual release outside of heterosexual marriage, which is horrible sin. Thus chastity (avoiding unchastity) is the main reason for marriage.[109]

The reason why Luther sometimes tells people to consult their feelings toward the opposite sex is because some people do not have this desire, and they are regarded as having a special divine gift for continence and celibacy. But the appeal to one's feelings is never separated from its biblical, creational, and natural law context. From Scripture and nature it is known that God has made man and woman for heterosexual marriage. If one feels this sort of desire, it is in accord with creation, and thus one should marry, not try to be perpetually

104 *Commentary on 1 Corinthians 7* (1523), WA 12:114, cf. AE 28:27; see also AE 28:26, WA 12:113.

105 *Commentary on 1 Corinthians 7* (1523), AE 28:27, WA 12:115.

106 *In Genesin Declamationes* (1523/1527), WA 24:53, my translation.

107 Cf. Strohl, "Luther's New View" (as in p. 190 n. 25), 160.

108 LC I 211–12, in Dau and Bente, *Triglot Concordia*, 641.

109 LC I 213–16, in Dau and Bente, *Triglot Concordia*, 641.

celibate. As we have seen, Luther did not argue directly from sexual urges to a right to marry. He instead argued from the binary creation of man and woman, and God's institution of heterosexual marriage, to permission to marry. And he acknowledged that there were exceptions, where those who might feel sexual passion would not be permitted to marry. From this it is clear that, for him, sexual urges do not of themselves entail a right to marry.

In all of this Luther appears not as a sexual liberator in the sense of the sexual revolution of Western societies in the twentieth century but rather as a champion of chastity, liberating consciences from man-made snares and leading them into pious self-control. Against an increasingly promiscuous culture, seeping into Germany from the south, Luther called people to live chaste lives.

> Both the pope and the Turk are so blind and senseless that they commit the [mute] sins shamelessly, as an honorable and praiseworthy thing. Since they think lightly of marriage, it serves them right that there are dog-marriages (and would to God they were dog-marriages), indeed, also "Italian marriages" and "Florentine brides" among them; and they think these things good. I hear one horrible thing after another about what an open and glorious Sodom Turkey is, and everybody who has looked around a little in Rome and Italy knows very well how God revenges and punishes the forbidden marriage [fn: i.e., homosexuality], so that Sodom and [Gomorrah], which God overwhelmed in days of old with fire and brimstone [Gen. 19:24], must seem a mere jest and prelude compared with these abominations.[110]

> This terrible and thoroughly papal, that is, epicurean and Italian, way of life is on the increase. Therefore let anyone help who is able to help. And pity the poor youth, those dear descendants of ours, as well as all the elect children of God still to be added, some of them yet unborn. . . . The prophecy I have cited will certainly be fulfilled. God grant that before it is fulfilled, we may prove to be men who have acted and taught against it, and that together with all those who are dear to us we may depart in a good hour and be rescued with Lot from condemned Sodom and Gomorrah (Gen. 19:16). Amen.[111]

Luther vigorously opposed the sexual revolution that he saw happening in Italy and did all he could to prevent it from taking hold in Germany.

---

110 *War against the Turk* (1529), AE 46:198.

111 *Commentary on Psalm 101* (1534), AE 13:192–93.

Conclusions

Luther, with Augustine, claims that sinful lust is now always experienced in sex, even within marriage. This is the so-called "negative" view of sex for which Luther and Augustine (and many of the church fathers) are sometimes criticized. Yet it must be remembered that Augustine's connection of lust with the fall into sin was explained especially amid the Pelagian controversy, in which Augustine argued for the pervasiveness of original sin and the necessity of grace. Augustine's best Pelagian opponent, Julian of Eclanum, opposed this teaching, claiming that if sexual desire was viewed as corrupted by sin, then marriage itself would be evil. In response, Augustine carefully distinguished between the ongoing goodness of marriage and sex within it from the addition of fleshly concupiscence.[112]

Luther believed, with Augustine, that the experience of sex before the fall would have lacked the erotic desire that is now always present in the conjugal act. In this these two great fathers of the church may have engaged in a little speculation, since Holy Scripture says nothing about the experience of sex before Adam and Eve fell into sin. Yet such an assertion may have been based on the basic conviction that erotic desire, that is, "lust" or "fleshly concupiscence," is sinful.[113] Paul Althaus rightly noted: "The demonic character of selfish desire is most clearly apparent in sexual love."[114]

Yet at the same time, Luther's concern and emphasis was to defend marriage and the practice of sex within marriage as good and right. There are even a few places (usually where he argues that perpetual celibacy is unnatural) where Luther says that the ardent or passionate desire for the opposite sex is God's work, even after the fall. Perhaps Luther's occasional statements on the goodness or naturalness of sexual desire in marriage can be reconciled with his many statements on the sinfulness of lust within marriage by noting a parallel in

112 Hunter, "Marriage" (as in p. 192 n. 37), 536–37. In response to Julian's criticisms, Augustine also in his later writings refined his argument. He allowed that even in Paradise before sin, Adam and Eve could have experienced a concupiscence of the flesh, though in an innocent form, completely subject to reason—an innocence that no longer exists.

113 Note that the New Testament Greek word for "lust" (ἐπιθυμία) is the same as "coveting," and thus is forbidden by the Decalogue (Exod. 20:17), which is quoted by St. Paul in Rom. 7:7 and 13:9 as οὐκ ἐπιθυμήσεις. See Friedrich Büchsel, "Ἐπιθυμία," *Theologisches Wörterbuch Zum Neuen Testament*, ed. Gerhard Kittel, vol. 3 (Stuttgart: W. Kohlhammer, 1938), 168–72.

114 Althaus, *Ethics of Martin Luther*, 85.

Augustine's *On the Good of Marriage*: "For what food is unto the conservation of the man, this sexual intercourse is unto the conservation of the race: and both are not without carnal delight: which yet being modified, and by restraint and temperance reduced unto the use after nature, cannot be lust."[115]

Therefore on the distinction of the goodness of marriage and the badness of fleshly concupiscence (or lust), Luther and Augustine are found to hold the same views. Perhaps this should not be surprising because of the connection between this teaching and that of original sin, which both theologians upheld. Scholars who find one of them objectionable will find the other one equally so. While not everyone who affirms the goodness of sexual desire after the fall is a Pelagian, a Pelagian denial of original sin can clearly be seen whenever our current sexual desires are claimed to be just as God created them.

Luther's reformation of marriage and sexuality raises the question of the relevance of Luther's views for people today. For those who are convinced that all kinds of sexual expressions are legitimate and good, Luther's authority will necessarily be limited if not rejected. Rather than taking Luther's theology of marriage as a whole, any argument for sexual permissiveness or homosexual marriage that draws from Luther will have to be selective and use some utterances of Luther against others.[116] For others, Luther will have to be set aside completely as irrelevant whenever he speaks on sex and marriage.[117] This is because Luther views the Bible as normative on sex, marriage, and gender relations, and many people simply reject what the Bible says here.[118]

Is Luther a teacher whose arguments should be heard? Those who count him as a father in the faith should say yes. Can the insights and feelings of human beings (after the fall) justify ignoring inconvenient parts of Scripture? Or is our own authority, by which we can determine whether Luther is right or wrong, the written text of Holy Scripture alone?

The issue of sexuality runs deeper than outward norms of behavior. How we regard sexuality and how we argue indicates what we think the sixteenth-century Reformation was about. For some today, echoing various Protestant

115 Augustine, *On the Good of Marriage* 18 (NPNF[1] 3:407).

116 Stjerna does this explicitly. "We know better than Luther in this regard. . . . Luther advanced his times' conceptions of these things; in his footsteps, so can we" ("Luther on Marriage" [as in p. 184 n. 4], 136).

117 Gerle, "Luther and the Erotic" (as in p. 184 n. 3), 198–208; Leppin, "Ehe bei Martin Luther" (as in p. 184 n. 3), 32.

118 Christoph Bultmann makes explicit the connection between the Bible and Luther's view of marriage and sex: Christoph Bultmann, "Luther on Gender Relations: Just One Reading of Genesis?" *Currents in Theology and Mission* 29, no. 6 (2002): 424–28.

radicals in Luther's day who rejected Luther's Reformation, the Reformation was about people's well-being and status in the world, interpreting the "liberating power of the Gospel" as a call to free people from oppression.[119] For Luther and for those who grasped his central insight that the Gospel is God's action to justify sinners, liberating them specifically from sin, death, and the power of the devil, the Reformation was a return to and renewal of the ancient, catholic, apostolic, and evangelical faith proclaimed in the New Testament.

Luther's theology of marriage and sex teaches that there was a real fall into sin, which really corrupted and vitiated human nature. Modern theologians, if they deny the historicity of the first few chapters of Genesis or fail to grasp the theological and anthropological truths of the narrative, may find it difficult to understand Luther's theology on this point. Without a real fall into sin, one may be tempted to view the current situation of humanity as the way God created it, or to posit an evolutionary scheme which has no room for a fall from initial created goodness.

More than that, how we regard sexuality shows what we think the Gospel is. Some view it as simply emancipation. Those who are heirs to Luther's Reformation see the Gospel as the forgiveness of sins through faith in Christ, who died and rose to put us back into God's family and who gave us the Holy Spirit to re-form the lost image of God within us and conform us to God's eternal, immutable righteousness. If the Gospel does not give a Holy Spirit who leads sinful mankind to holiness and conformity with the unchangeable and holy triune God, then it is not St. Paul's Gospel, nor that of the Lord Jesus Christ. The Gospel is not simply freedom from laws. It does not cancel the Commandments of God. Christ came not to destroy the Law but to fulfill it (Matt. 5:17). "The freedom of the gospel is valid only in matters relating to the relationship between you and God, and not in matters between you and your neighbors. . . . God does not want his law thrust aside to enable you to serve him."[120] The specifics of Luther's exposition of the Law, creation, and human nature really matter and cannot be divorced from the basic structure of his evangelical way of thought (sin and justification).[121] Rejecting Luther's view of marriage and sexuality requires either misunderstanding him or rejecting the connection of sexual morality with creation and with the immutability of God and

119 Stjerna supports a "radically emancipatory 'Lutheran liberation theology'" ("Luther on Marriage" [as in p. 184 n. 4], 128).

120 *On Monastic Vows* (1521), AE 44:313–14.

121 Cf. Leppin, "Ehe bei Martin Luther" (as in p. 184 n. 3), 33.

of the moral Law.[122] Why is it important that the Law is immutable and rooted in creation? It is important because God is truthful, reliable, and certain. If He and His will were mutable, there would be no foundation of reality, no absolute truth. But in fact the faith which His Spirit creates in people is sure and certain because it rests on an unchanging God who has spoken to His people in human language through the apostles and prophets.

Moreover, the life of chastity is one of spiritual safety and peace of conscience. It is in agreement with natural law and with our creation as either male or female. And it is a way to obtain freedom from servitude to one's own fallen, corrupt desires.

> Marital chastity is very highly spoken of in Scripture, as, for example, in Heb. 13:4. Marriage has a great blessing also in the matter of chastity, for he who has the gift of marriage does not go insane with lust. Those who are devoted to their own wives do not lust for others. In those who are worthy of the blessing with which God blesses marriage, the madness of lust is extinguished. That is, they are content with their marriage and have the blessing of marriage, so that they do not grow tired of their own spouses and lose their desire for them. I have seen many who became disgusted with marital relations. Where this is not the case, there will be moderation in intercourse, to resist Satan.[123]

> For that reason each one should guard against adultery and whoredom, which sins must not be borne by us in Christendom; we want to prevent them with the preaching of the Word. For if we learn that someone is an adulterer, we will not give them the Sacrament nor ought they share in our spiritual treasure nor can they be sponsors, etc. If anyone wants to be a Christian, let him be satisfied with his wife.[124]

Luther called his generation, five hundred years ago, to a life of chastity. Churches and individual Christians should do the same today.

---

122 See FC SD II 50; V 17; VI 15; VIII 49; XI 75, 95; *Lectures on Genesis* (1535–45/1544–54), AE 5:43.

123 *Lectures on Titus* (1527), AE 29:55–56.

124 Sermon of January 8, 1531, WA 34/1:79 (AE 56, forthcoming), trans. James L. Langebartels.

Luther and the Sacramentarians: A Necessary Division?

Roland Ziegler

WRITING ABOUT LUTHER AND THE SACRAMENTARIANS means first to acknowledge that "Sacramentarians" is a polemical term used by Luther and the Lutherans for their opponents who certainly did not use the term themselves. It is thus not a neutral term, but one that neatly divides the reformers of the sixteenth century into two camps: On one side are Luther and his followers, affirming the substantial presence of the body and blood of Christ with bread and wine in the Lord's Supper; on the other side are those who deny this presence. Such a binary division can be helpful to get a grip on certain facts, but it can also be blinding to other differences. To illustrate the point: authors from the time of the Reformation to modern times sometimes put Lutherans and Roman Catholics together on the doctrine of the Lord's Supper as "Sacramentalists," a categorization that obscures more than it clarifies. Following the Golden Rule, Lutherans should be careful not to do to others what they do not want to be done to themselves. Thus a discussion of "Luther and the Sacramentarians" can either disavow the use of this term as unhelpful for grasping the rich reality of the debate on the Lord's Supper in the sixteenth century, or it has to make a point defending the continued use of this category or term for understanding the past.

Let us first say in what sense the term is not helpful. Although there was a unity among those who fall under that rubric—namely, that they rejected the substantial presence and oral eating of the body and blood of Christ in the Lord's Supper—there were also differences among these theologians, and even different stages in the development of their thought and teaching on the sacraments. The Zurich reformer Huldrych Zwingli was, so to speak, on the one extreme, since he saw the Lord's Supper in the decisive years purely as a memorial and eucharist—that is, the Lord's Supper is the remembering of and thanksgiving for Christ's atoning death on the cross. The Basel reformer Johannes Oecolampadius and later the Geneva reformer John Calvin, on the other hand, saw a divine action in the Lord's Supper and could talk about the Christian eating and drinking Christ's body and blood in the Lord's Supper.[1]

The term is not arbitrary, however. There is, after all, agreement among those who are called Sacramentarians in their rejection of the statement that the Christians eat and drink Christ's body and blood with their mouth. After all, even Zwingli would claim that despite some divergences in exegetical questions, there was a unity among those attacked by Luther.[2]

In this essay, I will first sketch the controversy on the Lord's Supper between those who advocated evangelical reform and the traditionalists (Roman Catholics). This initial discussion set up a common front among evangelical reformers, which then in the second act would be disrupted and has caused ever since the question of whether the unity of the first act could not have been retained. Second, I will retell the story of the controversy between Luther and his opponents on the Lord's Supper concerning the real (or substantial) presence of Christ's body and blood under bread and wine.[3] Third, I will look at the theological issues involved in the discussion.

We look at the history of the controversy not only out of historical interest. The divisions of the time of the Reformation continue today, obviously between Roman Catholics and those churches that in the sixteenth century ended up

---

1 The Formula of Concord does acknowledge this difference, see, e.g., VII 4–7. Citations from the Lutheran Confessions are taken from *The Book of Concord: The Confessions of the Evangelical Lutheran Church*, ed. Robert Kolb and Timothy J. Wengert (Minneapolis: Fortress, 2000). This difference also accounts for the fact that hymns by Reformed authors sound somewhat Lutheran and can even make it into Lutheran hymnals, for example, the hymn "Here, O My Lord, I See Thee Face to Face" (*LSB* 631).

2 Not discussed here and not perceived as being in the same camp, even though there was agreement on rejecting the real presence, is Caspar von Schwenkfeld and the so-called radical reformers who rejected infant Baptism.

3 I will use the term "real presence" to denote the Lutheran position, despite its historical problems. See Albert B. Collver, "'Real Presence': An Overview and History of the Term," *Concordia Journal* 28, no. 2 (2002): 142–59.

separating from the papal church over the issues of reform, but also between Reformed, Lutheran, and Anabaptist churches. There is also the contemporary question of whether it is still justified to uphold these divisions; or if the theological issues of the sixteenth century have been either resolved or can be considered to have been a misunderstanding; or whether new insights have been found that enable us to go beyond the discussions of the sixteenth century, or even if there was a degree of consensus in the sixteenth century that is more important than the differences. Berthold von Schenk, a leader in the liturgical renewal movement in The Lutheran Church—Missouri Synod in the mid-twentieth century and a proponent of sacramental piety, dismissed the sacramental controversy of the sixteenth century as something that does not concern the essence of the Sacrament. Von Schenk wrote: "The Great Concurrence of the Church is the Real Presence, a truth that is deeply imbedded in the consciousness of Christians, evangelical and catholic. There have been controversies as to the exact nature of the Presence of our Lord and of His Body and Blood, but the fact which matters most is that He comes, not the way in which He comes."[4] A close look at the history will enable us to see what the theologians of the Reformation thought was "the fact which matters most."

The First Controversy on the Sacraments: The Sacrifice of the Mass

Before one can go into the debate on the Lord's Supper between Luther and his Protestant opponents, one has to realize that this was the second phase of a struggle about the Lord's Supper in the time of the Reformation. The first phase was the struggle against the Roman Catholic teachings on the sacrifice of the Mass, transubstantiation, and Communion under one kind. In this first phase there was unity among the different reforming movements and their leaders that made the later break among them quite painful.

The Reformation started with a debate on indulgences, not on the Lord's Supper. But the principle behind the debate on indulgences—namely, what takes care of sin and its consequences—soon also bore on the view of the Lord's Supper. It was Roman Catholic dogma that the Lord's Supper was a sacrifice for sin, offered by the priest for the living and the dead. As an act of the Church

4 Berthold von Schenk, *The Presence: An Approach to Holy Communion* (New York: Ernst Kaufmann, 1945), 30–31. This quote also shows that "real presence" can be used in a different meaning than "real presence of the body and blood of Christ."

through its priesthood, it was one way that God's grace was obtained. Luther soon attacked this understanding of the Mass because he saw here the same kind of works-righteousness as in indulgences. As indulgences dishonored Christ as the one who had accomplished everything for the salvation of sinners, so also Luther and other reformers viewed the sacrifice of the Mass as an insult to Christ because it added onto Christ's work a human work.

Luther's critique was fully articulated in 1520 in his treatise *On the Babylonian Captivity of the Church: Prelude*. Luther begins his discussion of the Lord's Supper by addressing the Catholic practice of withholding the cup (wine) from the laity, with the statement that John 6 is not to be used at all in the discussion on the Lord's Supper since the passage deals not with the Sacrament but with faith in the incarnate Word.[5] The basis for any discussion of the Lord's Supper are the Words of Institution as recorded in the Gospels according to Matthew, Mark, and Luke, and in Paul's testimony in 1 Corinthians 11. Luther then summarizes his critique of the sacramental practice of the Roman Church in three points, which he calls a threefold captivity of the Sacrament. First, from the Words of Institution it follows that both priests and laity should receive Communion under both kinds.[6] Luther also argues that the laity receive the reality which the Sacrament gives, to which the elements point as signs. Since this real gift is more important than the signs pointing to it, it makes no sense to refuse to laity both signs. Here Luther uses a long-standing distinction in the Western Church that defines sacraments as visible signs of an invisible grace. The "thing" or reality (Latin: *res*) of the Sacrament is neither bread and wine nor the body and blood of Christ, but that which is given through them, namely, incorporation in the mystical Body of Christ (i.e., the Church), or grace, or, as Luther now emphasizes, the forgiveness of sins. The problem with this schema of sign and thing signified is that the real presence of Christ's body and blood in the Sacrament is somewhat gratuitous, a point that will become important later in the discussion. For if the thing signified is grace, what purpose does the bodily presence of Christ have? To come back to the point of Communion

---

5 WA 6:502.7–10; AE 36:19. It is therefore not correct to view Luther's rejection of understanding John 6 as referring to the Lord's Supper as a reaction to Zwingli's use of the passage for his symbolic understanding of the Lord's Supper. From the beginning in his dispute with the Roman Church, Luther affirms that John 6 does not talk about the sacramental eating of Christ's body and blood. His patristic witness for this is Augustine, who wrote in his sermons on John: "Believe and you have eaten" (*Tract. In Ioan.* 25.12). Cf. also Luther's remark that John 6 has nothing to do with the Lord's Supper in his *On the Lord's Supper: Confession* of 1528, at the end of part 2 (WA 26:498.12–15; AE 37:360).

6 WA 6:503.20–23; AE 36:21.

under both kinds: Luther concludes that it is unchristian and tyrannical to refuse Communion under both kinds to the laity.[7]

The second captivity concerns transubstantiation.[8] This is a point that is not as dangerous to consciences as the first one, Luther states. Nevertheless, since transubstantiation is proclaimed as a dogma (official Church teaching) without scriptural proof, Luther rejects its binding nature. He is still willing to tolerate it as an opinion or hypothesis, though he regards as the simpler view the hypothesis of the fifteenth-century theologian Pierre d'Ailly that both substances, the earthly elements and Christ's body and blood, coexist in the Lord's Supper. Luther's preference for the continued existence of the substance of bread and wine is also grounded in his view of how the Scripture must be interpreted. The default attitude in reading Scripture should be to understand the words according to their proper grammatical sense, not in a figurative sense, unless the latter is proven by the words themselves.[9] This hermeneutical rule will be important in the later debates on the Lord's Supper: A nonliteral understanding of Scripture has to be proven, since the literal understanding, that which takes into account the most common use of words and sentences, is the default position. Thus, against the Roman understanding of transubstantiation, in which "bread" in 1 Cor. 10:17 is interpreted as "accidents of bread," Luther holds that "bread" must be understood as "the substance of bread" since this is the common meaning of the word.[10] Thus Luther wants to avoid departing from the literal understanding because of the difficulties encountered when one applies the categories of Aristotelian ontology, which distinguishes between the

7 WA 6:506.5–507.33; AE 36:25–27.

8 WA 6:508.1–512.6; AE 36:28–35.

9 WA 6:509.8–12: "Est autem meae sententiae ratio magna, imprimis illa quod verbis divinis non est ulla facienda vis, neque per hominem, neque per angelum, sed quantum fieri potest, in simplicissima significatione servanda sunt, et nisi manifesta circumstantia cogat, extra grammaticam et propriam accipienda non sunt, ne detur adversariis occasio, universam scripturam eludendi." AE 36:30: "But there are good grounds for my view, and this above all—no violence is to be done to the words of God, whether by man or angel. They are to be retained in their simplest meaning as far as possible. Unless the context manifestly compels it, they are not to be understood apart from their grammatical and proper sense, lest we give our adversaries occasion to make a mockery of all the Scriptures."

10 Luther is not exalting a slavish literalism. Of course he is aware of the manifold use of metaphors and similes in Scripture and everyday speech. Context leads us to understand a word metaphorically. But if the context does not give a clear indication that the word (or a phrase) is to be understood metaphorically, the literal sense has to be assumed, since otherwise all communication collapses.

"substance" and the "accidents" of any given thing. He rather forsakes these categories and instead uses analogies to be able to conceive the presence of two substances at the same place: fire and iron, the birth of Christ keeping Mary's virginity inviolate (as one believes), the risen Christ passing through the locked doors.[11] Luther does not avoid following the Anselmian maxim "faith seeking understanding" (*fides quarens intellectum*), but in the end he does not believe that the body and blood of Christ are received because he has solved the metaphysical questions, but because he believes the words of Christ.[12]

The third captivity of the Sacrament is the "most impious abuse," namely, that the Mass is a good work and a sacrifice. This view was deeply ingrained in the life of the Church and had produced Masses for the dead and its consequences, such as fraternities and anniversary Masses. Because there was a stipend for Masses, this doctrine was also closely connected with the economic base of the Church and the clergy.

Since this was a very sensitive issue, Luther again starts with the institution. What actually did Christ institute? Luther directs the attention of the reader away from the historically accrued liturgical forms back to the words of Christ. Christ institutes a testament at the eve of His death. He is the testator, the disciples and all believers are the heirs, the inheritance is the promise of forgiveness.[13] From the character of the Mass as a promise or testament, the right use of the Mass can only be receiving the gift in faith. The Mass, Luther says, really is essentially nothing but "take, eat," "take, drink." The body and blood of Christ are signs and memorial of the promise.[14]

From this follows that the Mass can only benefit those who believe these words and receive the Sacrament. Second, the Mass is in no way either a work or a sacrifice by man. Luther emphasizes here the preeminence of the word over

---

11 WA 6:510.4–8; AE 36:32. The analogies of fire and iron and Christ's appearing in the locked room after His resurrection are standard arguments used by Luther in his later controversies.

12 WA 6:511.18–21: "Ego, sane, si non posse consequi, quo modo panis sit corpus Christi, captivabo tamen intellectum meum in obsequium Christi, et verbis eius simpliciter inhaerens, credo firmiter, non modo corpus Christi esse in pane, sed panem esse corpus Christi." AE 36:34: "For my part, if I cannot fathom how the bread is the body of Christ, yet I will take my reason captive to the obedience of Christ [2 Cor. 10:5], and clinging simply to his words, firmly believe not only that the body of Christ is in the bread, but that the bread is the body of Christ."

13 WA 6:513.15; AE 36:37. A testament is a promise that includes the death of the one who promises.

14 WA 6:515.17–24; AE 36:40.

the sign. Man can have the testament without the sign or sacrament.[15] Luther's fight against the sacrifice of the Mass, his emphasis on the word as the center of the Mass and on faith as the means by which the gift of Communion is received, leaves the body and blood of Christ, though strongly affirmed as really present, somewhat at the sidelines. As the later controversies would reveal, here was some need for further theological reflection.

The three points Luther articulates in his critique of the Roman Mass—Communion under one kind only for the laity, the doctrine of transubstantiation, and especially the sacrifice of the Mass—were shared by those he later called Sacramentarians. In their fight against Rome, they saw themselves as allies of Luther. They saw themselves as even more consistent fighters against Rome than Luther, drawing out the consequences of his insistence that man is saved by faith alone, not by works, and stating that the "work" of eating and drinking cannot convey the forgiveness of sins.

Main Actors in the Sacramentarian Controversy

In hindsight, Zwingli's name overshadows the names of Karlstadt and Oecolampadius, and both are relegated to the second row of reformation theologians. For Luther, however, the battle for the Sacrament did not start with Zwingli but with his colleague Andreas Karlstadt. Luther's view of Zwingli and Oecolampadius was influenced by his previous experience with Karlstadt.[16] And even though Luther then simply put Karlstadt, Oecolampadius, and Zwingli in one sack, so to speak, there were differences among them. To understand the later controversy, it is important to understand what made each of these three take the approach he took.[17]

Andreas Karlstadt

Andreas Rudolf Bodenstein von Karlstadt (1486–1541), Luther's colleague at the University of Wittenberg, became the first to oppose Luther on the

15 WA 6:518.18–20; AE 36:44. Luther quotes again Augustine's statement "believe and you have eaten."

16 For the historical background, see Martin Brecht, *Martin Luther: Shaping and Defining the Reformation 1521–1532* (Minneapolis: Fortress, 1990), 157–72.

17 For there were others, e.g., Schwenkfeld and especially the Strassburg reformer Martin Bucer could be mentioned. The selection of names is admittedly shaped by the writings of Luther and whom he chose to address.

Sacrament, and thereafter Luther viewed all the others as followers or tropes, if one wants to use a pun, of Karlstadt. In 1524, Karlstadt published *On the Anti-Christian Abuse of the Lord's Bread and Cup.*[18] Karlstadt understood the Words of Institution in such a way that Christ said: "Take and eat. This (referring to this body sitting at the table) is My body, given for you. Take and drink. This (referring to His blood in His body) is the new testament in My blood." His argument was grammatical, since the pronoun "this" is neuter and could not refer to bread, which is masculine.[19] But behind Karlstadt's interpretation was a denigration of the idea that something external could justify or have any spiritual impact or significance. Rather, faith comes through hearing and reflecting upon the Word of God. To know Christ means to know the death of Christ and its cause, namely man's sin, and its effect, namely salvation. Out of this knowledge of Christ grows the remembrance, which is not a mere mental act but is an affective remembrance, a joyous remembrance, which leads to thanksgiving, which transforms man into Christ's likeness and leads him to shun sin. The Lord's Supper is not given to forgive sins. For Christ gave His body and shed His blood not in the Lord's Supper as a sacrifice for sin, but on the cross. To ascribe forgiveness of sins to the bread and wine, or to the body and blood of Christ present in the bread and wine, is ascribing to creatures what should be ascribed to Christ alone. The meaning of the Lord's Supper is thus to look back to the cross and be transformed by the remembrance of it. Karlstadt's objections to the doctrine of the real presence of Christ's body and blood in the Lord's Supper were deeply influential, but after he was exiled from Saxony by order of Elector Frederick on account of his views and especially his attacks on Luther, Karlstadt spent the crucial decade of the controversy without a firm base, and his influence faded into the background.[20]

---

18 *Von dem widerchristlichen mißbrauch des hern brodt und kelch.* It is reprinted, in a modernized version, in Martin Luther, *Sämmtliche Schriften* (St. Louis: Concordia: n.d.), 20:92–109. This and other treatises by Karlstadt are now available in English translation: *The Eucharistic Pamphlets of Andreas Bodenstein von Karlstadt*, trans. and ed. Amy Nelson Burnett, Early Modern Studies 6 (Kirkwood, MO: Truman State University Press, 2011).

19 This question Luther had already addressed in *On the Babylonian Captivity of the Church*, WA 6:511.13–17; AE 36:34–35.

20 On Karlstadt's importance nonetheless, see Amy Nelson Burnett, *Karlstadt and the Origins of the Eucharistic Controversy: A Study of the Circulation of Ideas* (New York: Oxford University Press, 2011). On Karlstadt's influence on the Anabaptist movement, see Calvin Augustine Pater, *Karlstadt as the Father of the Baptist Movements: The Emergence of Lay Protestantism* (Toronto: University of Toronto Press, 1984).

Huldrych Zwingli

Huldrych Zwingli (1484–1531), the reformer of Zurich, emerged as the main opponent of Luther in the second half of the 1520s. He died early, fighting for his state, and his teaching on the Lord's Supper was later overshadowed by the teaching of John Calvin, though even today we find views similar to Zwingli's in Protestant churches.

Unlike Luther, Zwingli was neither a monk nor an academician. He was a secular priest, that is, a regular priest serving a congregation and under the authority of a bishop. Zwingli was well educated, having earned the master of arts degree in Basel. He, like Luther, learned Greek on his own in order to read the New Testament in its original language. He was connected with the humanist circles in Switzerland and with Erasmus of Rotterdam. Although the sources are scarce in the early years, we know enough to say that Zwingli did not have anything like the interior struggles that Luther had. Zwingli later on was also intent on denying any dependence on Luther in his theological development, emphasizing that he came to his positions by studying Scripture.[21]

Like Luther, Zwingli criticized the sacrifice of the Mass and the practice of Communion under one kind.[22] He explained his position at length in the eighteenth of the *67 Theses* he wrote for the first disputation in Zurich, called by the Great Council of Zurich on January 3, 1523, to meet on January 29, 1523. All pastors in the town and surrounding territory of Zurich were invited to discuss and resolve the religious divisions.[23] After the disputation, he commented on the *67 Theses* and published them on July 14, 1523, as "Interpreting and Foundation of the Theses" (*Auslegen und Gründe der Schlußreden*). The topic of the eighteenth article is the sacrifice of the Mass, not the real presence.[24] In the thesis itself, the Mass is called a memorial (*Wiedergedächtnis*) and a seal. But Zwingli has already a spiritualized understanding of the Lord's Supper, for he states that

21 See Zwingli's lengthy disquisition on his relationship to Luther, in Huldreich Zwingli, *Sämtliche Werke* (Leipzig: Verlag von M. Heinsius Nachfolger, 1908), 2:144.17–150.25 (hereafter cited as Zwingli, *Sämtliche Werke*); and W. P. Stephens, *The Theology of Huldrych Zwingli* (Oxford: Oxford University Press, 1986), 45–49.

22 Zwingli, letter to Wyttenbach, June 15, 1523 (Zwingli, *Sämtliche Werke*, 8:84–89). On Zwingli's doctrine of the Lord's Supper in general, see Stephens, *Theology of Huldrych Zwingli*, 218–59; and W. P. Stephens, *Zwingli: An Introduction to His Thought* (Oxford: Oxford University Press, 1992), 94–110.

23 Zwingli, *Sämtliche Werke*, 1:466–68.

24 Text in Zwingli, *Sämtliche Werke*, 2:111–57; an English translation can be found in Huldrych Zwingli, *Writings*, vol. 1: *The Defense of the Reformed Faith* (Allison Park, PA: Pickwick Publications, 1984), 92–127.

only true believers eat the body of Christ.[25] Of equal importance is the overall theological framework of Zwingli's thought.[26] There is stark opposition between God and creature, between spiritual and material realities. From this follows that spirit and creature are opposed and that practices such as the sacrifice of the Mass, sacramental absolution, invocation of the saints, and veneration of images are a divinization of the creaturely and thus idolatrous. Since Christ has freed mankind from sin through His death, there is no place for sacramental forgiveness of sins, only for the proclamation of the forgiveness of sins. Zwingli uses here already John 6:63 as a proof-text for his spiritual view of the Lord's Supper.[27] But Zwingli is not yet aware that he differs from Luther in any way. As much as he asserts that he came to his views through his own study of Scripture and not through reading Luther (though his opponents called him a Lutheran), he praises Luther highly and sees the agreement between himself and Luther as a sign that the Spirit is working through both of them.[28]

In the second Zurich disputation, October 26–28, 1523, Zwingli also attacks only the sacrifice of the Mass, not the real presence. Even in April 1524, Zwingli uses the language of eating the body and blood of Christ in the bread and wine.[29] It is only later in 1524 and in his letter to Matthew Alber, pastor in Reutlingen, that Zwingli rejects any notion of eating and drinking the body and blood of Christ. He was influenced in this by the letter of the Dutch theologian Cornelius van Hoen, from whom he took the understanding that "is" means "signifies." But the question is still, why was he susceptible to such an interpretation? After all, Luther had read the letter too, and had confessed that he was tempted to adopt such an understanding.

One theory is that Zwingli was far more deeply influenced by the reformist thought of Erasmus of Rotterdam. Erasmus, the prince of the humanists, was

---

25 Walther Köhler, *Zwingli und Luther: Der Streit über das Abendmahl nach seinen politischen und religiösen Beziehungen. I. Band: Die religiöse und politische Entwicklung bis zum Marburger Religionsgespräch 1529* (Leipzig: Verein für Reformationsgeschichte/Vermittlungsverlag von M. Heinsius Nachfolger Eger & Sievers, 1924), 24.

26 On the following, see Ulrich Gäbler, *Huldrych Zwingli: Leben und Werk* (Munich: C. H. Beck, 1983), 69–70.

27 Gäbler (*Huldrych Zwingli*, 70) mentions among Zwingli's fundamental principles also his ecclesiology, in which Zwingli distinguishes between the universal, invisible Church, which cannot be represented by the pope or councils or any human institution, and the assembly of Christians at a certain locality, as well as the distinction between divine and human righteousness as a core principle of ethics.

28 Zwingli, *Sämtliche Werke*, 2:150.5–21.

29 Köhler, *Zwingli und Luther*, 44.

interested not only in the reform of studies but in an overall reform of church and society. As the editor of the Greek New Testament and of numerous editions of the church fathers, he did his share to enact the humanist motto *Ad fontes* ("To the sources!"). Although he remained a Roman Catholic, Erasmus, too, had a spiritualizing view of the Lord's Supper, as it is expressed, for example, in his *Handbook for the Christian Soldier*. Not that Erasmus denied the real presence, but rather that he, in his fight against an externalized piety, stressed the spiritual apprehension and spiritual effects of the Lord's Supper.[30] The true use of the Lord's Supper consists in the Christian's life in the *synaxis*, the community of Christians, especially through love for the neighbor. This is one instance where we encounter the overarching view that the Christian needs to progress from the visible to the invisible, from the material to the spiritual.[31] While Erasmus never denied or fought against the real presence, his emphasis on the Lord's Supper's spiritual use and ethical consequences made the real presence in a way a doctrine without function. The teaching remains, but it is of no great use. Thus the teaching of the real presence becomes systematically vulnerable.

Going back to Zwingli's letter to Matthew Alber, Zwingli first explains his position in regard to Karlstadt.[32] He had read Karlstadt's *On the Anti-Christian Abuse of the Lord's Bread and Cup* and approves of the content, even though he criticizes Karlstadt for his offensive tone. For the matter at hand, Zwingli starts with John 6, even though he admits that the chapter does not deal with the Lord's Supper. Nevertheless, Zwingli develops from his exegesis of John 6 that the flesh of Christ that is eaten for salvation is not simply the substance of Christ's body but rather Christ's flesh that is given in His death. Zwingli sees here a dialectic of spirit and flesh expressed: the spiritual eating is salvific; no fleshly eating can have spiritual effects, for the spiritual affects the spiritual, but the bodily or physical can only affect the physical. Additionally, it is faith that

30 Ernst Wilhelm Kohls, *Die Theologie des Erasmus* (Basel: F. Reinhardt, 1966), 1:121. See also Stefan Niklaus Bosshard, *Zwingli–Erasmus–Cajetan: Die Eucharistie als Zeichen der Einheit* (Wiesbaden: Franz Steiner Verlag GmbH, 1978), 47–52.

31 Kohls, *Theologie des Erasmus*, 1:119: "Wie schon von seiner Christologie her, so besteht für Erasmus gleichfalls auf Grund seiner Pneumatologie der von heir ausgehende Impuls für die wahre Frömmigkeit darin, 'von den sichtbaren Dingen, die teils nahezu unvollkommen und teils neutral sind, zu den unsichtbaren Dingen vorzuschreiten.'"

32 The letter, "Ad Matthaeum Alberum, Rutlingensium ecclesiasten, de coena dominica Huldrychi Zuinglii epistola," is printed in Zwingli, *Sämtliche Werke*, 3:325–54. An English translation can be found in Huldrych Zwingli, *Writings*, vol. 2: *In Search of True Religion: Reformation, Pastoral and Eucharistic Writings* (Allison Park, PA: Pickwick Publications, 1984), 127–45.

apprehends Christ's benefits, as John 6:29 states, which rules out that physical eating apprehends Christ's benefits. Zwingli also mentions in this context that a physical body is a body that is perceived by the senses. A body not perceivable by the senses is a contradiction in itself.[33] Zwingli cites John 6:63 as proof that bodily eating does not profit. Only then does Zwingli engage the Words of Institution. But though he praises Karlstadt for his insistence that salvation comes by faith in Christ, not by eating, he rejects Karlstadt's interpretation of the Words of Institution and proposes instead that there is a figure of speech in the copula "is."[34] Zwingli sees here the same way of speaking as in Gen. 41:26 (the seven fat cows are seven fruitful years), John 15:1 (I am the vine), Luke 8:11 (the seed is the Word of God). Thus the Words of Institution are to be understood as "take, eat, this signifies My body." The purpose of the Lord's Supper is commemoration.[35] Zwingli quotes Tertullian and Augustine as patristic witnesses. First Corinthians 10:16–17 is to be understood from verse 17: those who are members of the Body of Christ through faith. The communication of the body and blood is a sharing not through eating but through the gathering of the Church. Thus the Lord's Supper is a sign of church membership, and so Zwingli comes to his concept that the Sacrament is an oath of allegiance, which is one of the meanings of the Latin word *sacramentum*.[36]

---

33 "An ne corpus aliud est, quam quod sentitur? Quod autem sentitur, organorum est obiectum. Organa igitur, qum hic nihil aliud sentiant, sed intus fit, quicquid agitur: quid opus est de corpore, quatenus corpus est, loqui?" (Zwingli, *Sämtliche Werke*, 3:12–14). "Is there any other physical body than that which is perceived? Yet what is perceived is an object of the senses. Since the senses perceive nothing here, and whatever is done takes place inwardly, what need is there of talking of the body insofar as it is body . . ." (Zwingli, *Writings*, 2:134).

34 As might be remembered, Karlstadt does not say that there is a figure of speech in the Words of Institution. They are to be understood literally, though the word "this" does not refer to the bread but to the body of Christ.

35 "Fitque horum verborum Christi sensus ad hunc modum apertissimus: Hoc convivium significat aut symbolum est, quo refricabitis meum ipsius corpus dei filii, domini vestri et magistri, pro vobis esse traditum" (Zwingli, *Sämtliche Werke*, 3:345.39–346.2). "The meaning of Christ's words becomes perfectly plain to this effect: 'This feast signifies or is the symbol by which you will recall that my body, mine, the Son of God, your Lord and Master, was given for you'" (Zwingli, *Writings*, 2:139).

36 ". . . communicationem non pro esu accipi, pro quo hactenus acceperunt theologi, sed pro communicatione ecclesiae, hoc est, quod quisque hoc pacto se ecclesiae probat et inserit tanquam praestito sacramento" (Zwingli, *Sämtliche Werke*, 3:349.5–8). ". . . sharing is not used for the eating—as the theologians have thus far taken it to be—but for the sharing of the Church, that is, to show that everyone in this way recommends himself

Zwingli's *Commentary on the True and False Religion* of March 1525 contains a significant chapter on the Lord's Supper, in which he attacked Luther, Karlstadt, and Johann Eck. Zwingli again starts with John 6:63 but excludes the misunderstanding that he views the flesh of Christ per se as useless. It is of course of great benefit for us as the flesh on the cross, but not as something eaten by us.[37] As a foreshadowing of things to come, Zwingli also starts discussing the relationship between the divine and human natures in Christ in the context of the Lord's Supper, though not yet as an argument against the real presence. Christ is salvific according to His divine nature; He dies according to His human nature. When salvation is attributed to the flesh, then this should be attributed to the person, not to the human nature.[38] Besides the arguments already mentioned, Zwingli denies that the Lord's Supper forgives sins in any way.[39] Since the argument is made in the section against Luther and Eck, Zwingli seems to conflate here the question whether the Sacrament forgives sins by delivering forgiveness or by propitiating sins.[40] A new argument is that an eating of the body of Christ must mean that the body of Christ is present to the senses. This would not be an article of faith, however, since belief is in that which is not seen. A spiritual eating of the literal body of Christ would be a mixing of categories. Thus one ends up talking either nonsense or about some form of cannibalism.[41]

What, then, is the Lord's Supper for Zwingli? It is eucharist and memorial. "The Greeks, who, I say without envy, are more diligent and learned than the Latins, as their writings witness clearer than the sun, have called the Lord's Supper *eucharistia*. Without doubt they gave it that name, because they understood by faith and the words of Christ and the apostle, that Christ wants this meal to be a joyous commemoration of him, to be held publicly as a thanksgiving for the gift which he has generously given to us. For the *eucharistia* is a thanksgiving."[42] "The 'eucharist' or 'synaxis' or 'Lord's Supper' is nothing other than that: a commemoration, through which those who firmly believe that they

---

to the Church and associates himself with it just as with an oath of allegiance" (Zwingli, *Writings*, 2:141–42).

37 Zwingli, *Sämtliche Werke*, 3:792.30–33.

38 Zwingli, *Sämtliche Werke*, 3:780.3–7.

39 Zwingli, *Sämtliche Werke*, 3:803.28–29.

40 Zwingli, *Sämtliche Werke*, 3:807.33, where he denies that the Sacrament expiates.

41 Zwingli, *Sämtliche Werke*, 3:789.3–4.

42 Zwingli, *Sämtliche Werke*, 3:775.20–26.

are reconciled to the Father by the death and blood of Christ, show forth this life-giving death, that is: praise, give thanks, and proclaim."[43]

Johannes Oecolampadius

Johannes Oecolampadius (1482–1531) lived since 1522 in Basel, in relatively close proximity to Zwingli in Zurich, not only geographically but also theologically. His contribution to the debate on the Lord's Supper, besides his exegetical argument that "body" means "sign of body," was the patristic argument. For he stated that the early church had a symbolic understanding of the Lord's Supper, and he therefore published extensively on the church fathers.[44] Oecolampadius rejects a substantial presence of the body and blood in the Lord's Supper. Although Christ's body is absent, Christians receive the benefits of His body in the Lord's Supper, just as somebody can receive the fruit of a field that is far away. Oecolampadius rejects, however, the accusation that Christians have only common bread and wine in the Lord's Supper. Just as the shewbread in the Old Testament was not common bread, neither is the bread in the Lord's Supper common bread. As the Holy Scriptures, through which the Christians are enlightened, are honored also as physical objects, so also bread and wine are honored as sacrament, that is, as signs. Since the most holy thing is the memory of the death of Christ, therefore the celebration of the memory of the death of Christ is most holy. Oecolampadius will even say that the remembrance of the body of Christ is more than the presence of the body of Christ, since the remembrance includes the use of the body, meaning its salvific application.[45] The Sacrament is a visible word: as the word communicates audibly, the Sacrament portrays visibly that the death of Christ is

---

43 "Est ergo 'eucharistia' sive 'synaxis' sive 'caena dominica' nihil aliud quam: commemoratio, qua ii, qui se *Christi* morte et sanguine firmiter credunt patri reconicilatos esse, hanc vitalem mortem annunciant, hoc est: laudant, gratulantur et praedicant" (Zwingli, *Sämtliche Werke*, 807.11–14).

44 On the use of the patristic argument in the Sacramentarian Controversy, see Amy Nelson Burnett, "'According to the Oldest Authorities': The Use of the Church Fathers in the Early Eucharistic Controversy," in *The Reformation as Christianization: Essays on Scott Hendrix's Christianization Thesis*, ed. Anna Marie Johnson and John A. Maxfield (Tübingen: Mohr Siebeck, 2012), 373–95.

45 See the first of two "Sermons on the Dignity of the Sacrament" (1525) in Johann Oecolampadius, *Apologetica Ioann. Oecolampadii. De dignitate Evcharistiae Sermones duo* (n.p., 1526), Aijr–Bijr. A German translation is available in Luther, *Sämmtliche Schriften*, 20:709–34.

the salvation of man and thus the promise of the forgiveness of sins is communicated in this act.[46]

Discussions Before the Great Controversy

The "Syngramma Suevicum"

We have seen how Zwingli was in correspondence with pastors in south Germany. There were not only those who sympathized with him but also a sizable opposition who sided with Luther. To combat the spread of Zwingli's doctrine, these preachers, fourteen all together, assembled in 1525 under the leadership of Johannes Brenz (1499–1570), then serving in Schwäbisch Hall. Brenz drafted a document, the *Syngramma Suevicum*, answering Oecolampadius's *De genuina verborum Domini.*[47] Luther was so impressed by the document that he wanted to translate it, but when Johann Agricola finished his translation before Luther got to it, Luther wrote a preface to the German edition.[48] The *Syngramma Suevicum* stresses that the word of Christ brings the body and blood to bread and wine, just as in Mark 2:5 and Luke 7:47 the word of Christ brings the thing.[49] Thus a purely significative understanding of language is rejected. The suspicion is articulated: "And unless our assumption is incorrect, this sacramentarian spirit breathes this, contrives this, with the result that it deprives us of the external Christ, the external word."[50]

Oecolampadius answered Luther's preface and the *Syngramma.* He is willing to praise Luther as a faithful preacher and co-worker, except on the matter of the Lord's Supper. Against the complaint that the Lutherans are maligned as eating a bread-God and a baked-God, and as devourers of God's flesh and drinkers of God's blood, Oecolampadius defends such language as a true description of the necessary consequence of Luther's doctrine.[51] He counters the accusation

---

46 Johannes Oecolampadius, *Billiche Antwurt Joan. Oecolampadii auff D. Martin Luthers bericht . . .* (Basel: Thomas Wolff, 1526), Lr–Lv.

47 The Latin text can be found in Johannes Brenz, *Frühschriften: Teil 1* (Tübingen: J. C. B. Mohr [Paul Siebeck], 1970), (222), 234–78.

48 For English translations of Luther's prefaces to the two translations of the *Syngramma*, see AE 59:150–62.

49 Brenz, *Frühschriften*, 241.28–33.

50 "Et nisi vana sit coniectura nostra, spiritus ille sacramentarius hoc spirat, hoc machinatur, ut nobis Christum externum, verbum externum subripiat" (Brenz, *Frühschriften*, 254.3–6).

51 Oecolampadius, *Billiche Antwurt*, Bv.

that Karlstadt, Zwingli, and Oecolampadius do not agree on the interpretation of the Words of Institution with the argument that Luther and the Roman Catholics, though asserting the real presence, do not agree on the meaning of the text either (transubstantiation or supposition). Oecolampadius does not believe that the discussion is about an essential point of the Christian faith and accuses Luther of lacking love, comparing his opponents with the dragon of Rev. 12:3. Oecolampadius urges again the question of the proper use of the body and blood of Christ in the Lord's Supper, for God does not teach useless things.

In his answer to the *Syngramma*, Oecolampadius uses the christological argument: a body that is invisible and omnipresent is not a true body, for the nature of a body is to be local and visible. He attacks the theology of the word in the *Syngramma*. There is no promise of Christ that the words will make the body and blood present, and thus the Words of Institution are not miracle-working words but common words that signify, admonish, and remind. Similarly, also the Gospel is not salvific as the external Word; rather, it saves by pointing to the events of Jesus' life and death and by the internal operation of the Spirit. Word and Spirit are not inextricably united, because otherwise there would be no fruitless hearing of the Word. Words are external signs, and as such they teach and admonish through what is signified.

Johannes Bugenhagen's Letter to Breslau

The debate with Zwingli moved closer to Wittenberg when Johannes Bugenhagen wrote a letter to Johann Hess, a pastor in Breslau, in September 1525, warning him against the "new error concerning the sacrament of the body and blood of our Lord Jesus Christ," naming Zwingli as the one bringing up the interpretation of "is" as "signifies."[52] Bugenhagen attacks the use of John 6:63 as hermeneutical key to the Lord's Supper and asserts that Christ's flesh is not useless, for it is the flesh in which God has come among us. He also rejects the denunciations that the Lutherans are Christ-eaters and flesh-eaters, tearing into the flesh of Christ with their teeth. Zwingli responded quickly, claiming that his doctrine was not new, as Bugenhagen had claimed, but rather was the patristic doctrine.

The Great Controversy

In this section I will narrate the progression of the discussion between Luther and his Sacramentarian opponents, focusing on the main writings of Luther up

52 See Köhler, *Zwingli und Luther*, 196–97.

to the first and only personal conversation between Luther and Zwingli, at the Marburg Colloquy in 1529.

Against the Heavenly Prophets

Luther published his treatise *Against the Heavenly Prophets: On the Images and the Sacrament*, in two parts, in December 1524 and January 1525, as an extensive critique of Karlstadt's positions on reform. Luther distinguishes between an internal and external operation of God. God uses the external operation of the Word and the Sacraments to give internally the Spirit and faith. Thus Karlstadt's rejection of the external in the name of the spiritual severs what God has joined together. This spiritualization of the faith destroys God's order and leaves people without the connection to God established by God Himself. Luther attacks Karlstadt's exegesis on grammatical grounds and from the common way of speaking. If there is a break between "take, eat" and "this is My body," with a change of reference, then one would expect some kind of indication of such a break. Otherwise, it would be like somebody who wears a fur-lined overcoat giving a grey coat to another person and saying, take and wear, this is a fur-lined overcoat (referring to the coat of the owner). Nobody talks like that.[53] Such a way of speaking would be downright deceptive.

Since Karlstadt had used John 6:63 in his *Dialogus*, Luther engages the meaning of this passage.[54] Luther distinguishes between "flesh" in general and "Christ's flesh," objecting to the interpretation that the passage means "Christ's flesh profits nothing." Since Karlstadt believes that bread and wine profit if eaten with heartfelt knowledge, why should the body of Christ not profit if eaten in faith? Christ's body does indeed bring spiritual benefits, even though it only profits the person with faith. Luther also discusses the question of what "remembrance" means. He accuses Karlstadt of having, like the scholastic theologians, a purely mental understanding of remembrance. For Luther, remembrance means an external remembrance, a preaching of Christ's death.[55] Therefore the remembrance of Christ is a fruit of justification, not the means of justification.

Karlstadt rejected the teaching that communicants receive forgiveness of sins.[56] How can bread forgive sins? Luther answers that of course bread does not forgive sins. Rather, one has to distinguish how forgiveness of sins has been

53 WA 18:159.26–30; AE 40:169.

54 WA 18:192.1–195.8; AE 40:202–5. Cf. Karlstadt, *Dialogus*, C4b.

55 WA 18:197.8–32; AE 40:207.

56 WA 18:200.20–204.30; AE 40:210–14.

gained from how it is distributed. Forgiveness of sins has been gained on the cross by Christ, but it is distributed by the word of the Gospel. The sinner is comforted "not by bread and wine, not by body and blood, but by the word, that offers, donates and gives to me in the sacrament the body and blood as given and shed for me."[57] Against Karlstadt's scorn that the Lutherans believe the stinking breath of the priest makes Christ come down from heaven when he says the Words of Institution, Luther affirms that Christ now fills everything (Eph. 1:23), just as Christ never left heaven when He became incarnate. But Luther rejects here all further discussions of this sort as not worthy of an answer.[58]

Friendly Exegesis

Zwingli entered the debate with Luther directly in his *Friendly Exegesis*, written from mid-December 1526 to the end of February 1527.[59] This was in answer to Luther's *Sermon on the Sacrament of the Body and Blood of Christ, Against the Fanatics*.[60] Zwingli starts out with the impression that Luther seems to put the emphasis on the physical eating of Christ's body rather than on faith. Against this, Zwingli states that salvation is in the cross of Christ, not in the eating of man. If one sees the eating of man as salvific, then one falls back into a form of works-righteousness. He derides the *Syngramma Suevicum* as the work of some insignificant little bishops and rejects the thesis that the Word makes anything present. Rather, since justification comes by faith, and faith is not a bodily work, the application of the physical body cannot help to justification. Zwingli also attacks Luther's explanation concerning the possibility of the bodily presence of Christ. He accuses Luther of arguing from the possibility of something to its actuality, a logical error that Luther himself had attacked when he had discussed transubstantiation. Regarding the presence of Christ, Zwingli states that there is no other mode of presence than divine omnipresence. Of course Christ is omnipresent; of course He reigns everywhere. But that does not prove the presence of His human nature. The properties of both natures are not identical. The human nature does not know the date of the second coming; the divine nature does. The human nature leaves this earth and goes to heaven, to return at the second coming. Thus the presence of Christ between ascension and the second coming is one of the person in the divine nature alone.

57 WA 18:204.6–9; AE 40:214.

58 WA 18:206.10–23; AE 40:216.

59 Latin text in Zwingli, *Sämtliche Werke*, 5:562–758; English translation in Zwingli, *Writings*, 2:233–383.

60 WA 19:482–523; AE 36:335–61.

Here Zwingli introduces *alloiosis*, a figure of speech in which the members of a category are used for each other. In the New Testament, sometimes there is an exchange between the two natures. Thus the human nature is mentioned, but what is meant is the divine nature. For example, in Matt. 21:33, the son of the householder (God) is Christ. Since He is son by virtue of the divine nature, one would assume that this parable refers to His divine nature. But the son is slain. Since the divine nature is not slain, it refers to the human nature. Thus also what is said of the person really pertains only to the divine nature. The statement of Jesus that He will go away (John 16:28) means His human nature will go away. Jesus promises that the disciples will be where He is (John 12:26), that is, where His human nature is. He does not promise them divine omnipresence. But couldn't it be said that it is simply a miracle, beyond our ken? Miracles, according to Zwingli, are visible manifestations of God's power to incite faith. An invisible miracle would be useless.

Zwingli repeats his view of the Words of Institution. "This do" means to celebrate the Lord's Supper as an act of thanksgiving (eucharist) and as a memorial. He rejects Luther's point that the fact that Zwingli and Oecolampadius see different tropes in the Words of Institution shows that there is no unity between them. One can analyze language in different ways; the question is if one agrees on what the text says. On this, they do: Jesus institutes a memorial meal, using bread and wine as signs of His body and blood.

In the exegetical section of his treatise, Zwingli does include some hermeneutical reflections on the right interpretation of Scripture. One needs to know the different figures of speech; one needs to compare Scripture with Scripture; one needs to apply the rule of faith, that is, the summary of the Christian faith. Although a deep understanding of the Scripture is impossible without the Holy Spirit, exegetical questions cannot be resolved by invoking the Spirit, nor another opinion rejected by claiming that the opposing teacher does not have the Spirit. Rather, interpretations must be tested by the wording of Scripture.

That These Words of Christ "This Is My Body" Still Stand Firm, Against the Enthusiastic Spirits

Until 1526, Luther had not written a detailed rebuttal of the symbolic understanding of the Lord's Supper as it was being defended by the Swiss. He had only written the *Letter to the Christians in Reutlingen;* two prefaces to the *Syngramma Suevicum*; and the *Sermon on the Sacrament of the Body and Blood of Christ, Against the Fanatics.*[61] This relative silence was unusual for Luther,

61 WA 19:118–25, 457–61, 529–30, 482–523; AE 59:150–62 (prefaces), 36:335–61 (sermon).

and Oecolampadius thought that this was a sign that the Holy Spirit had left Luther and made him speechless.[62] Philip of Hesse urged him, sending him the writings of Zwingli and Oecolampadius and saying that if Luther would not write against them, he would not read anything Luther would publish in the future. Even mild Melanchthon wanted Luther to respond. He finally did and wrote *That These Words of Christ "This Is My Body" Still Stand Firm, Against the Enthusiastic Spirits*.[63] This book and Zwingli's *Friendly Exegesis* were published almost at the same time.

Luther has low expectations concerning the effect of his arguments on the leaders of the other side. Their hearts are hardened. But he hopes that at least some of their students and the simple folk who follow them will see the truth. Luther cannot see anything but the devil's work in the symbolic understanding of the Lord's Supper. He also uses language that is polemical, as had Zwingli and Oecolampadius. If one reads only Luther's treatise, one might be repelled by the invective he uses, but one has to remember that this was the style of the time, not only Luther's style. Luther sees in the other side a certain hypocrisy. They claim to want peace, and that the matter in dispute is not of great importance, yet they publish continuously and vigorously attack the Lutheran position. So, what is it? Why aren't they quiet for peace's sake? The question at issue is an important one, Luther argues, and one side must be wrong in their understanding of Christ's words and thus preaching falsely.[64] Neither can one claim that this is only a small part of God's Word, of no importance for unity if one agrees in other matters.[65]

Luther addresses three points in this writing. First, he asserts that the Words of Institution have to be understood literally.[66] Zwingli and Oecolampadius have not shown that the Words of Institution have to be understood figuratively. Their parallels of metaphorical speech in the Bible do not establish their point, since the question is not if the Words of Institution *can* be understood metaphorically, but if they *have to* be understood metaphorically. Second, Luther discusses the question of whether the session of Christ at the right hand of

62 WA 19:452.

63 WA 23:(38) 64–320; AE 37:13–150. Luther's manuscript survived, so that the Weimar edition reproduces both the manuscript and the first printed edition. Since it seems that Luther made some last-minute changes to his manuscript, all references are to the first printed edition.

64 WA 23:83.10–30; AE 37:25–26.

65 WA 23:85.1–12; AE 37:26.

66 WA 23:83.10–131.6; AE 37:26–54.

God contradicts His bodily presence in the Lord's Supper.[67] Luther first rejects a local understanding of the right hand of God. It is not a place; it refers to the omnipotence of God and the active, personal presence of God (Ps. 139:7ff.). The session at the right hand of God means that Christ is omnipresent. Luther does not develop this thought in regard to the humanity of Christ in this writing, though he clearly teaches the omnipresence not only of the divine but also of the human nature. But if Christ's flesh is present everywhere, does this not mean that one eats it in every meal? No, since there is a difference between the presence simply and the presence *for you*.[68] But does it not dishonor Christ to be so objectified that His body and blood can be manhandled by impious priests? No, because Christ's honor does not consist in being worshiped and adored, but in serving sinners. Third, the interpretation of John 6:63 is at issue.[69] Luther argues, first, that John 6:63 does not refer to *Christ's* flesh, since the possessive pronoun "my" is lacking; second, that "flesh" in this passage does not mean material flesh but "coming from the old Adam" as opposed to "coming from the Holy Spirit." Otherwise, one could even think that the incarnation ("en-fleshment") was of no use. Against the spiritualizing tendencies of his opponents, Luther maintains that not all objects of faith are spiritual, but their use has to be spiritual. Spiritual in this sense means: the Word of God is added to something and it is used in faith. But what about John 3:6, "That which is born of the flesh, is flesh"? Luther's opponents hold that this verse proves that to hope to gain spiritual benefits from eating the body of Christ goes against Christ's word. Here again Luther discusses the semantic range of "flesh" and asserts that Christ's flesh is not what is meant in John 3:6, which speaks rather of "sinful flesh," but that Christ's flesh came into existence through the Holy Spirit and can give the Holy Spirit.[70]

---

67 WA 23:131.7–167.27; AE 37:54–78.

68 All too often in modernity the emphasis is on God's presence absolutely rather than on God's gracious, communicative presence. I suppose that is because modern man is affected by the process of secularization, which gives him the fundamental feeling that he lives in a universe without God or that God is absent, even if the person consciously believes differently. Luther is eminently biblical: God is everywhere, in everything; He is an inescapable presence. The important question is how God relates to man. Thus the question of God's gracious presence (His presence in the Gospel) is the all-decisive question. This harmonizes with the language of the Old Testament, where the absence of God does not mean that God has vacated space but that God has withdrawn His *gracious* presence.

69 WA 23:167.27–209.27; AE 37:78–104.

70 Luther also discusses extensively the patristic argument and contradicts Oecolampadius and Zwingli's view that the early church fathers are on their side. But because for Luther the position of the early church fathers is not decisive in deciding the question under

Finally, Luther addresses the dogmatic question about the benefit of the oral eating of Christ's body and blood in the Sacrament. Since Luther and the Sacramentarians agree on the necessity of the spiritual eating and also that John 6 talks about spiritual eating, what need is there further for a substantial presence and for a sacramental eating of Christ's body and blood?[71] For Luther, this is an illegitimate question. Christians should simply do what Christ has commanded and be content with it. But he is willing nevertheless to address this question. First, the bodily presence humbles reason. Second, it is an indication that the body, too, shall live. Third, it is God's order to work through created means. God connects His Word of promise with earthly creatures, and they are thus communications of His grace.

That These Words "This Is My Body" Will Retain Their Old Sense Forever

After Zwingli received Luther's book, he set himself immediately to answer and wrote *That These Words "This Is My Body" Will Retain Their Old Sense Forever* in about one-and-a-half months.[72] It was published in June 1527. This time, Zwingli used German, as Luther had done, even though Zwingli thought that Latin would be more appropriate because the scholars should hash out their differences before they involved the laity. Many arguments are repeated from his previous writings, something almost inevitable at this stage of the debate. What was new was the detailed christological argument. Zwingli rejected the presence of Christ because it was unscriptural, since he did not believe that the Words of Institution were to be understood literally, and as contradicting established articles of the faith, namely, Christ's ascension and session at the right hand of God, and thus the absence of Christ's human nature from earth until the second coming. Luther's teaching of the omnipresence of the human nature is according to Zwingli a form of Docetism. From the Greek word *dokéō*, meaning "to seem, to have the appearance of," Docetism refers to a range of heresies in the early church that held that the divine Logos, or Son of God, did not assume a true human nature but only appeared to have a human nature. Divinizing the human nature in this way denies the reality of the incarnation. In Zwingli's view, since the divine nature is immutable, it cannot be changed into the human nature, nor can the human nature become divine. Zwingli introduces a rhetorical figure to explain how certain statements in the Gospels have to be

---

discussion, even though their opinion should not be despised, for the sake of space this is not further explicated in this chapter.

71 WA 23:247.26–269.18; AE 37:127–41.

72 Zwingli, *Sämtliche Werke*, 5:795–977.

interpreted, namely, those that suggest either a change in Christ's divine nature or a sharing of the human nature in divine attributes. The person of Christ can stand for one nature, as can one nature for the other. For this exchange in terms he uses the word *alloiosis*. Thus when, in John 12:32, Christ says that He will be lifted up, He is speaking solely about His human nature; the eternal Logos cannot be lifted up, for the eternal nature of Christ is immutable. In this passage the personal pronoun "I" as grammatical subject does not mean the person of Christ but only His human nature. Similarly, when Jesus says that His flesh is life-giving (John 6:53), this does not refer to His human nature (despite the word "flesh"), for Christ's human nature is by its nature not life-giving; here the subject must be His divine nature, which is by nature life-giving. At the end of this writing Zwingli summarizes his objections to six points in Luther's teaching that he finds false: (1) the omnipresence of the body of Christ; (2) Christ shows Himself in the Sacrament so that we know where to find Him; (3) the bodily eating of Christ takes away sin; (4) the flesh of Christ is spiritual; (5) the bodily eating of Christ's flesh keeps our body unto the resurrection; (6) Christ's body, eaten bodily, gives or increases faith.[73]

On the Lord's Supper: Confession

This is Luther's last word in the great exchange. Luther had received Zwingli's *Friendly Exegesis* with a letter by Zwingli[74] after he had already finished *That These Words etc.* Thus in *On the Lord's Supper* Luther responded to both major treatises Zwingli had published in this literary debate. It is Luther's final word. Commonly the title in English is *Confession Concerning Christ's Supper*, sometimes also called the "great confession" since Luther later published a shorter treatise (the "brief confession") with the same title in 1544.

The major new points (for there is much repetition also on Luther's side at this stage of the controversy) are in Luther's answer to Zwingli's accusation of Docetism. Luther stresses that the personal union of the two natures in Christ means that there cannot be a presence of Christ that does not include

73 Zwingli, *Sämtliche Werke*, 5:976.11–977.6. Zwingli also has in this writing a lengthy discussion of the Passover and its parallels to the Lord's Supper. For him, the Passover is a memorial of redemption, in which the meal itself is called the "pass-over," i.e., the passing over of God. He holds that this commemoration of the passing over of God supports his view of the Lord's Supper as strictly a commemoration of the salvific event of the crucifixion.

74 Zwingli, *Sämtliche Werke*, 9:78–81. Zwingli also sent along a short writing in German, the *Friendly Defense and Refutation on the Sermon of the Excellent Martin Luther against the Enthusiasts* (Zwingli, *Sämtliche Werke*, 5:763–94).

His human nature. Wherever Christ is, He is present as the God-man. Luther rejects Zwingli's use of *alloiosis* as a reading of Scripture that separates the two natures, with the result that Christ's person is so distanced from His humanity that one could no longer say, for example, that the person of Christ suffered and died, but only that His human nature suffered and died. Nevertheless, Luther answers the question of how it is possible that the body of Christ is present at all places.[75] He uses the model of three modes of presence: local, definitive, and repletive.[76] Local presence is the presence of a body in a circumscribed way, as we ordinarily understand presence. Definitive presence means that something is present at a place without being circumscribed, as, for example, in regard to the body of Christ when He leaves the closed tomb and goes through the stone. This is the mode of presence in the Lord's Supper. Repletive presence, finally, means omnipresence. This does not mean that the body of Christ is infinitely extended, as little as one should think of God's presence as the infinitely extended presence of something. Rather, Christ, true God and true man, is wholly present at any point in the universe as true God and true man.[77] Thus Luther answers in detail Zwingli's objections concerning Christology, and in addition to the difference in the doctrine on the Lord's Supper, a difference in Christology opened up between the two reformers, a difference that continued between Lutherans and the Reformed.[78]

Luther then explicates his understanding of the Words of Institution. Against Zwingli, for whom sentences can only report and command (indicative and imperative verbs), Luther states that the Words of Institution actually do

---

75 WA 26:324.1–17; AE 37:212–13.

76 WA 26:326.12–330.11; AE 37:214–17. This statement is later quoted in the Formula of Concord, SD VII 99–103.

77 For Luther, the three forms of presence are used to speak about the christological implications and to show that the Scriptures do talk about more than one mode of the presence of Christ. They are not the foundation of the doctrine of the real presence of Christ's body and blood in the Lord's Supper, but they prove false the accusation that the presence of Christ's body and blood in the Sacrament is incompatible with the ascension of Christ. Rather, the discussion shows that Zwingli's understanding of the ascension as a local movement to a different locality in the universe, in which the human nature of Christ is now fixed, is false.

78 The teaching that Christ's body is omnipresent because it participates in certain properties of the divine nature was later called *genus maiestaticum* or "principle of majesty." It was rejected not only by Reformed theologians but also by Roman Catholic theologians as a form of monophysitism, an early church teaching that Christ's divine nature has so overpowered the human nature that the human nature is divinized and no longer is truly a human nature.

more: Christ's words do not state simply what is there without these words, but rather the words are performative, and through them, enclosed in the command of Christ, the bread is the body and the wine is the blood of Christ.[79]

What about the *use* of the real presence? Luther first rejects that he had ever taught that the mere eating, without faith and the Word of God, is of any benefit. Rather, eating the body of Christ without faith is poison to the recipient. Outside of faith there is no reception of forgiveness of sins.[80] He then emphasizes that forgiveness of sins, the Words of Institution, and the body and blood of Christ form a unity that is received by the Christian as one salvific reality.[81]

The Marburg Colloquy

For the first and the only time Luther and Zwingli met at Marburg, at a colloquy organized by Landgrave Philip of Hesse.[82] Philip was seeking a Protestant union in the face of growing Catholic power. Luther was at first not inclined to come, as he freely states in his opening remarks, but he agreed to it since Philip had asked him. The two sides were the Swiss and Strassburg delegation: Zwingli, Oecolampadius, Caspar Hedio, Jacob Sturm, and Martin Bucer; on the Lutheran side were Luther, Melanchthon, Justus Jonas, Andreas Osiander, Stephan Agricola, and Johannes Brenz. The negotiations were not public and were held, for the most part, in a rather friendly atmosphere, especially considering the previous polemical exchanges in writing. It is not surprising that no new arguments were brought up in the colloquy. In the first round, Luther and Oecolampadius discussed the relevance of John 6:63 and whether the Words of Institution must be understood figuratively. Oecolampadius also argued that the spiritual eating makes the oral eating superfluous. Zwingli offered his view that since all parties agree on the spiritual eating, one should not call the other a heretic. Zwingli attacked the understanding of the Words of Institution as consecratory. Luther emphasized that the Words of Institution are not mere human words but the words of Christ. The difference in the understanding of God's Word is obvious. Zwingli

79 WA 26:285.13–24; AE 37:184–85.

80 WA 26:353.10–354.4; AE 37:238.

81 WA 26:478.37–478.9; AE 37:338, quoted below, pp. 246–47 at n. 90.

82 The Marburg Colloquy has been reconstructed in Walter Köhler, *Das Marburger Religionsgespräch: Versuch einer Rekonstruktion* (Leipzig: M. Heinsius Nachfolger Eger & Sievers, 1929); and in Hermann Sasse, *This Is My Body: Luther's Contention for the Real Presence in the Sacrament of the Altar*, rev. ed. (Adelaide: Lutheran Publishing House, 1977), 180–220.

claimed that Melanchthon agrees with a purely significative understanding of language.[83] Luther distinguished between language used by humans, which is mere sound, and language used by God, which not only signifies but brings about that which is signified. For Zwingli, it is absurd to maintain that the impious can produce the body of Christ in the Lord's Supper. This is for him the reestablishment of popery.[84] As before, Zwingli and Oecolampadius argued that the church fathers, especially Augustine and Fulgentius, support their position. Luther rejected the force of the patristic argument by pointing to other church fathers, but he was quite unconcerned with the patristic argument since, as he continued to affirm, his position is based on the Words of Institution. He also rejected the argument from the nature of a body. True, everything that is in space is a body, but Luther rejected the inverse syllogism that therefore every body is in space. The whole question of the philosophical impossibility of a body that is not local, even though Luther had discussed it extensively in *On the Lord's Supper: Confession*, he does not deem worthy of discussion and refers to it as a "mathematical" question. Zwingli admitted that God can make a body present at several places at the same time, but still wants proof that it is this way in the Lord's Supper. It was in this context that Luther, when again urged to prove his point, folded back the velvet tablecloth and showed what he had written with chalk on the table: *Hoc est corpus meum*—"This is my body." Later, when urged by Oecolampadius that he should raise his mind to the divine instead of being obsessed with the humanity and the flesh of Christ, Luther answered: "I do not know of any God than the one who became man; thus, I do not want to have another one."[85]

Unity was not achieved. But Luther drew up fifteen articles (the Marburg Articles), which articulated a consensus in fourteen points and also where they were agreed in regard to the Sacrament of the Altar. This fifteenth article went on to note the difference on the Lord's Supper: "And although at present we are not agreed as to whether the true body and blood are bodily present in the bread and wine, nevertheless each party should show Christian love to the other, so far as conscience can permit, and both should fervently pray Almighty God that He, by His Spirit, would confirm us in the right understanding."[86] But that there

83 Köhler, *Das Marburger Religionsgespräch*, 21; Sasse, *This Is My Body*, 198.

84 Köhler, *Das Marburger Religionsgespräch*, 22–23; Sasse, *This Is My Body*, 199.

85 Köhler, *Das Marburger Religionsgespräch*, 27; Sasse, *This Is My Body*, 203.

86 Sasse, *This Is My Body*, 219–20.

was a true agreement in the other articles is questioned by Hermann Sasse.[87] The Marburg Articles played no role in later negotiations.

The Aftermath

Despite the signing of the Marburg Articles, the disunity among those who advocated reform and had rejected papal jurisdiction led to the submission of several documents at the Diet of Augsburg in 1530. While the Lutherans submitted their Augsburg Confession, four south German cities presented to the diet their own confession, the *Confessio Tetrapolitana* (*Confession of the Four Cities*). Zwingli, even though neither he nor Zurich had any standing at the diet, submitted his *Exposition of the Christian Faith* (*Fidei Ratio*). When in 1536 Luther and the Wittenbergers again negotiated with the preachers of Strassburg on unity on the Lord's Supper, a new document was drafted, often called the "Wittenberg Concord." This document affirmed the presence of a heavenly and earthly thing in the Lord's Supper, as well as the oral eating (*manducatio oralis*) of Christ's body, also by the unworthy (*manducatio indignorum*). Although unity between the Lutherans in Saxony with some of the south Germans was later achieved through the Wittenberg Concord in 1536, the Swiss churches rejected the Concord.

The Wittenberg Concord was hardly the end of the debate though. True, Zwingli had died in 1531 in the Battle of Kappel, fighting for his canton. But the Zurich reformation continued to teach a symbolic understanding under Zwingli's successor, Heinrich Bullinger. A new star rose on the theological sky: John Calvin, the reformer of Geneva, who had yet another view of the Lord's Supper, though his rejection of the real presence of Christ's body and blood led eventually to a union with Zurich. Luther himself did not engage Calvin. He thought it necessary, though, to make a final confession in *On the Lord's Supper: Confession* of 1544, in which he reaffirmed his rejection of all deviations from the literal understanding of the Words of Institution.

A second controversy on the Sacrament started long after Luther's death, when Joachim Westphal attacked John Calvin. Calvin had become the most influential theologian of the part of the Reformation that rejected the real presence, commonly called the Reformed churches. Attempts to heal the divisions of the time of the Reformation have been made more recently by various union movements and ecumenical agreements, but these have led not to reconciliation and a unanimous confession, but either to a declaration that the differences are not church dividing (and thus each party can hold on to its own view and yet

87 Sasse, *This Is My Body*, 225–26.

share in church fellowship) or to the creation of a new doctrine of the Lord's Supper based on what were viewed as new insights, a doctrine that was neither Lutheran nor Reformed.[88]

Dogmatic Issues

Exegesis

The debate on the Lord's Supper was a debate on how to interpret certain biblical texts, especially, of course, the Words of Institution. On an elementary level, it was the question when to interpret a passage literally and when to interpret a passage in a nonliteral, "figurative" sense. All parties agreed that this was a valid distinction, and all parties also agreed that one criterion for a legitimate nonliteral interpretation was nonsense resulting from a literal understanding or when a literal interpretation conflicts with an article of faith. Thus, in one sense, the dividing point is not the question of hermeneutical principles or, as Lutherans have tended to phrase it, that the other side was "rationalistic." If anything, the debate was over what constitutes nonsense and what constitutes a contradiction to an article of faith. For this reason, Luther made painstakingly elaborate arguments regarding how the presence of Christ can be understood, and what the nature of the body of Christ is like, in order to show that the literal understanding does not result in nonsense or in heresy.

Exegesis, however, is never done by interpreting passages in isolation. The nearer and wider contexts are essential for the understanding of a passage. Thus defining what this nearer or wider context is becomes an important task. For Zwingli, a decisive passage that bears on the understanding of the Lord's Supper is John 6:63: "The flesh profiteth nothing."

Luther denied that John 6 deals with the oral or sacramental eating of the body and blood of Christ. He had developed this position long before the controversy on the Lord's Supper.[89] For Luther, the words had to be taken by their common meaning, for he denied Zwingli's claim that a literal reading would

88 The first way was the way of the Prussian Union after 1854; the other, the way of other Union churches and numerous dialogues and agreements between churches, e.g., in Europe the so-called Leuenberg Concord (1973) and in North America the Formula of Agreement (1997) between the Evangelical Lutheran Church in America, the Presbyterian Church (U.S.A.), the Reformed Church in America, and the United Church of Christ.

89 The thesis that Luther was pushed toward a "nonsacramental" reading of John 6 by his opponents in the Sacramentarian Controversy has no support in the evidence. Neither is Luther's position historically an idiosyncratic oddity, as the history of exegesis shows. On this, see the overview that Rudolf Schnackenburg, a Roman Catholic biblical scholar,

result in a contradiction in Scripture. He extensively discussed Zwingli's contention that a literal reading would result in a docetic view of Christ and would effectively deny the ascension. More on this below. But for Zwingli one would also encounter a contradiction soteriologically if one assumes the real presence. For Zwingli, faith is created and sustained by the Spirit of God. Grace can only be mediated spiritually, and the idea that grace can be mediated through eating and drinking, a physical activity, would be a denial of justification by faith alone and grace alone. For Luther, this misses the point that the Spirit is mediated through creaturely means. Even the Word of God as language, or as preaching, as "external word," is something creaturely. Of course it is not merely physical; it is not the human act of eating and drinking but the reception in faith that is spiritual and that justifies. Against Zwingli's spiritualizing Christianity, Luther put forth faith that clings to whatever means God has established. Spiritual and material are not opposed but come together in God's institution, in Baptism (water, Word, and Spirit) as well as in the Lord's Supper (bread and wine, Christ's body and blood, Word, and Spirit).

The Nature of "Body"

A major point of contention was the nature of a body. Zwingli and Oecolampadius adhered to a commonsense view of "body": a body is a circumscribed object. Thus an uncircumscribed body is self-contradictory, something akin to a square circle. To speak of Christ's body as being omnipresent destroys it as a true, natural body. Luther, on the other hand, though seeing of course the difficulties of an uncircumscribed body, defended his view with biblical evidence. The body of Christ is, even besides the question of the Lord's Supper, not simply a circumscribed material object. Thus the commonsense definition of body must be enlarged.

The Nature of the Words of Institution

We see in Zwingli and Oecolampadius an understanding of the Words of Institution according to the Augustinian understanding of language as significative: sentences and words are signs pointing to the things they signify. Against this view as the sole understanding of language, Luther emphasizes that God's Word is active and not only denotes but also does. Thus the Words of Institution do not simply describe what is there, but rather they *cause* the

---

gives in his commentary: *The Gospel according to St. John*, vol. 2: *Commentary on Chapters 5–12* (New York: Seabury Press, 1980), 65–67.

presence of Christ's body and blood to be under (or in, or with) the bread and wine in the Lord's Supper. To put it differently, the words do not simply point to the thing outside of them, but the words bring about and give what they say. For Zwingli and Oecolampadius, such an understanding was a regression into Roman Catholicism with its teaching that an ordained priest can work the "magic" of consecrating bread and wine so they are changed into the body and blood of the Lord. For them, words were informative only. For Luther, this question pertains not only to the Words of Institution but to the Word of God generally. If the Word of God does not bring about what it says, one falls either into an intellectual-moralistic understanding of the Word of God, or one has to assume the work of the Holy Spirit without the Word of God.

The Use of the Real Presence

Luther's opponents consistently argued against the real presence in the Lord's Supper from the point of view that such a bodily presence would be useless. If salvation is given through the Word of God and received in faith, what good can be a bodily eating? Not only that, does such an eating, a mere bodily activity, then not destroy the strict correlation between faith and salvation, namely, that salvation can never be achieved by human work or effort?

Luther on principle rejects this argumentation. The question of whether the body and blood of Christ are received in the Lord's Supper cannot be decided on the question of its usefulness. Rather, the question can be answered only by the words Christ Himself spoke at the institution of the Supper. The question of its usefulness is a question that comes later. In regard to the accusation that Luther's view destroys salvation through faith alone and introduces salvation through a work anybody can do (eating the consecrated bread and drinking the consecrated wine), Luther consistently rejects any view that the mere eating communicates any benefits. Rather, only the believer receives the benefits of the Supper. Luther responded to this point already in 1527:

> When have you ever heard from us that we eat or teach to eat Christ's Supper in such a manner, that there is only an external bodily eating of the body of Christ? Have we not taught in such a way, through many books, that one has to be aware of two things in the Supper? One is the highest and most necessary, that is the words "Take, eat, this is My body" etc. The second is the sacrament or bodily eating of the body of Christ. Now, nobody can chase the words through the throat into the stomach, but he has to grasp them through his ears into his heart. What does he grasp into his heart through the words? Nothing but as they read, namely, "the body given for us," which is the spiritual

> eating. And we said additionally that who eats the sacrament bodily without such words or without such spiritual eating, he does not only not profit, but it harms him, as Paul says . . .[90]

But what is the purpose of the real presence? In the early writings, Luther emphasizes the character of the Supper as a seal and pledge that is attached to the testament. The discussion with Zwingli led him to emphasize that the word of forgiveness and the body and blood of Christ belong together—as the Words of Institution themselves state. This is best expressed in a passage from his *Confession concerning Christ's Supper* of 1528:

> See, then, what a beautiful, great, marvelous thing this is, how everything meshes together in one sacramental reality. The words are the first thing, for without the words the cup and the bread would be nothing. Further, without bread and cup, the body and blood of Christ would not be there. Without the body and blood of Christ, the new testament would not be there. Without the new testament, forgiveness of sins would not be there. Without forgiveness of sins, life and salvation would not be there. Thus the words first connect the bread and cup to the sacrament; bread and cup embrace the body and blood of Christ; body and blood of Christ embrace the new testament; the new testament embraces the forgiveness of sins; forgiveness of sins embraces eternal life and salvation. See, all this the words of the Supper offer and give us, and we embrace it by faith. Ought not the devil, then, hate such a Supper and rouse fanatics against it?[91]

Christology

Luther did not include the debate on Christology in the discussion on the Lord's Supper by his own volition. He responded to Zwingli's accusation. Neither was his view of the Lord's Supper derived from his Christology; it was based on the words of Christ. But the occasion to articulate the christological implications of the bodily presence of Christ in the Lord's Supper led Luther to some of his finest christological reflections. Luther asserted the consequences of the personal union of God and man in Christ against all tendencies to reduce the humanity of Christ as a mere tool that does not affect the identity of Christ. The person of Christ is constituted as the God-man, and thus Christ is never simply present or active as the eternal Son of God, only according to His divine nature, but always as the incarnate Son who has assumed a true human nature. This

90 WA 23:178.21–33; cf. AE 37:86.

91 AE 37:338; WA 26:478.37–478.9.

means that because of the personal union the human nature shares in certain properties of the divine nature. The communication of attributes is thus central for Christology. The human nature of Christ not only is important for salvation through the sacrifice on the cross but also for the mediation or distribution of salvation, whereas in Zwingli's understanding, after His atoning death Christ's human nature is without function.

The Debate on the Lord's Supper—Not a One-Point Issue

In retrospect, we see therefore that the debate on the Sacrament in the sixteenth century was not simply the issue of the bodily presence of Christ in the Lord's Supper. Rather, in this debate a multitude of issues came up, revealing that there were fundamental differences in the understanding of Christianity among the reformers. It is therefore not hyperbole when Luther attests that his opponents on the Sacrament were of "another Spirit." Far from being a debate on one detail of Christian doctrine, it revealed that there were deep-seated differences in the understanding of Christ and the mediation of salvation.

Looking back at the controversy on the Lord's Supper at the time of the Reformation, we can deplore the disunity. However, we also have to be honest that a close look at the history shows that this was no inane discussion, but that central issues of the Christian faith were at stake. Thus the contention of Berthold von Schenk quoted at the beginning of the essay, that there was really a basic unity in the view of the Lord's Supper, betrays an elementary lack of understanding of what the debate was about during the Reformation.

Is the debate still relevant today? It is, since the Words of Institution—"This is My body, given for you; this cup is the new testament in My blood"—still stand, and we are asked to confess what these words mean. During the past nearly five hundred years, the options for interpreting Christ's words in non-literal ways have increased beyond the theories of Karlstadt, Oecolampadius, Zwingli, and Calvin. But the basic question is still this: are we to take these words in some symbolic way or in a literal way? Is the meal that Christ instituted primarily a meal in which we remember and symbolically enact our fellowship? Or is it primarily a meal in which Christ as the host gives with His words His true body and blood to eat and to drink for the forgiveness of sins? In this debate, Luther's arguments are still relevant. The history of the debate in the Reformation makes us also aware that christological and soteriological questions are at stake here. Far from a purely antiquarian interest or out of mere traditionalism, the Lutheran Church upholds the confession of the true body and blood of Christ in the Lord's Supper because it is convinced that this is the only faithful response to the clear words of Christ.

Contributors

Timothy P. Dost is Associate Professor of Historical Theology at Concordia Seminary, St. Louis, Missouri

Jason D. Lane is Assistant Professor of Theology at Concordia University Wisconsin, in Mequon, Wisconsin

Cameron A. MacKenzie is the Forest E. and Frances H. Ellis Professor of Historical Theology and Chairman of the Department of Historical Theology at Concordia Theological Seminary, Fort Wayne, Indiana

John A. Maxfield is Associate Professor of Religious Studies at Concordia University of Edmonton, in Alberta, Canada

Benjamin T. G. Mayes is Assistant Professor of Historical Theology at Concordia Theological Seminary, Fort Wayne, Indiana

Jonathan Mumme is Assistant Professor of Theology at Concordia University Wisconsin, in Mequon, Wisconsin

Roland Ziegler is the Robert D. Preus Associate Professor of Systematic Theology and Confessional Lutheran Studies at Concordia Theological Seminary, Fort Wayne, Indiana

Person Index

Works of Martin Luther

Scripture Index